A STRATEGIC APPROACH TO CORPORATE GOVERNANCE

A STRATEGIC APPROACH TO CORPORATE GOVERNANCE

Adrian Davies

Gower

Published by
Gower Publishing Limited
Gower House
Croft Road
Aldershot
Hampshire GU11 3HR
England

Gower
Old Post Road
Brookfield
Vermont 05036
USA

British Library Cataloguing in Publication Data
Davies, Adrian H.T.
   A strategic approach to corporate governance
   1. Corporate governance 2. Corporate governance – Case
   studies
   I.Title
   658.4

ISBN 0 566 08074 5

Library of Congress Cataloging-in-Publication Data
Davies, Adrian
      A strategic approach to corporate governance / Adrian Davies.
         p.   cm.
      Includes index.
      ISBN 0-566-08074-5
      1. Corporate governance.   I. Title.
   HD2741.D38   1999
   658.4--dc21   98–47107
                                                                                CIP

Typeset by Saxon Graphics Ltd, Derby and printed in Great Britain at the University Press, Cambridge

CONTENTS

❖

FOREWORD

❖

What impressed me about *A Strategic Approach to Corporate Governance* was the breadth of Adrian Davies' thinking on thinking on the subject. My work has been in the narrower field of the governance of business enterprises and our Committee defined corporate governance, in that context, as '*the system by which companies are directed and controlled*'. As Adrian Davies makes clear these questions of direction and control apply to organizations of every kind.

The issues which arise in the governance of voluntary agencies, public sector bodies and professional organizations are broadly similar to those that arise in the governance of companies. In some ways governance structures are even more important outside the corporate sector than within it. Clear statements of purpose and clear processes for turning purpose into action are simpler to draft and put in place for a company than they are for a voluntary agency, or for any organization which has a balance of aims, rather than a single overriding goal. Yet the disciplines of governance are at least as necessary in a not-for-profit organization, as they are in a publicly-quoted company.

The essential point is that good governance is an aid to effectiveness. It is not there to shackle enterprise, but to harness it in the achievement of its goals. The interest which investors have taken in the governance of publicly-quoted companies originated in their concern about the performance, or lack of it, of the businesses in which they held shares. The governance movement, which started in the United States and Britain, has now spread worldwide and it is instructive to pick out the common threads which run through the codes of good governance that have been published internationally.

The foundation of all these codes is disclosure. Transparency is the key to the governance of any organization. Openness about the way institutions are run enables all those with an interest in their activities to influence their direction positively and constructively. Openness is also the basis of public confidence in institutions.

A second common thread is the impotance of the presence of indepen-dent outsiders on any governing body. Those in executive charge of an enterprise have, quite properly, their own aims and priorities. They look inwards at the body for whose activities they are responsible and judge issues primarily by their impact on the enterprise itself. Their expertise as insiders needs to be complemented by a leavening of independent-minded outsiders, who can look outwards and take an objective view of how the bal-ance of internal and external interests should be struck. This is as true of a public body, or of a professional organization, as it is of a business. Conflicts between the interests of those running an organization and those whom they are there to serve need to be mediated by colleagues who share the commitment of the executives to the organization's aims, but whose inter-ests in the outcome are less directly at stake.

This leads on to the final point common to all codes, which is that there have to be checks and balances within any system of governance to ensure that too much power is not concentrated in one pair of hands.

Openness and accountability are the governance watchwords and ethical standards are the basis on which lasting governance systems are built. These are the lessons we have all learnt from the work which has been done worldwide on the governance of companies. Adrian Davies' book will, with advantage, help to spread corporate experience in this field to a wider range of organizations.

September 1998

PREFACE

Governance, like 'the poor', has always been with us. It may be submerged for long periods, where regimes exert dictatorial powers or when survival is more pressing than fairness, but it surfaces at times of revolution and, in modern times, when individual human beings are empowered.

All institutions require a framework of governance, comprising a mission to be accomplished with clear rules and recognized conventions to guide its accomplishment. The governance of companies, or corporate governance as it is now known, is seen today as a distinctive brand of governance. In fact the challenge of reconciling the ambitions of individuals with the interests of the institution which they serve is similar for nations, for companies and for sports clubs. The struggle to balance personal freedom and collective responsibility is at the heart of corporate governance. Institutions have no souls and can only be animated by human beings and by their interaction in pursuit of a common goal. I have therefore resisted the temptation to treat corporate governance otherwise than within a framework of wider principles and practices.

The emergence of a series of frauds and scandals in the corporate sector, allied to a growing culture of greed and aggressive takeovers and restructuring from the late 1980s onwards, has stimulated interest in corporate governance. Initially this phenomenon was seen as the working of Anglo-Saxon liberalism, but it was accompanied by a steady trend towards deregulation which has more recently produced an unprecedented growth in productivity and profits. This success has challenged the comfort of the internal concordats which support the industrial models of countries outside the USA and UK.

In the recent past I was invited to make a presentation on corporate governance to the European Commission. This arose from earlier work in this area for my book *Strategic Leadership* and other research, including work on directors' competences with Henley Management College. It was interesting to note that corporate governance was initially seen as a possible mechanism for reducing redundancies rather than as a process for improving effectiveness in the interest of all stakeholders. The potential power of effective governance is, I believe, now part of the Commission's forward thinking.

The failures of corporate governance in the USA and UK stemmed largely from lack of leadership from company boards and indifference from institutional investors. Market pressures have subsequently forced both parties to improve their performance through greater commitment. In parallel with failures of corporate governance there were increasing failures in performance and of accountability in the UK public sector, which caused John Major to launch the Nolan Committee Enquiry into Standards in Public Life. The scandals in the private sector had earlier led to the establishment of the Cadbury Committee to investigate the financial aspects of corporate governance, followed by the Greenbury Committee's urgent review of remuneration policies and practices and culminating in the consolidating review by the Hampel Committee. The non-financial issues of corporate governance were subsumed in a separate inquiry sponsored by the Royal Society of Arts into 'Tomorrow's Company'. This inquiry and subsequent work by the Centre for Tomorrow's Company has shifted the focus of company accountability from the traditional exclusive concern to satisfy shareholders to a wider mandate including customers, employees, suppliers and other stakeholders in the company's success.

Today there is an intensive debate over the purpose of corporate governance. Traditionalists see the need to build long-term shareholder value (some still hanker after short-term shareholder value!) while the socially-conscious see the need to share wealth in order to stop anybody from strangling the Golden Goose. This debate will continue for several years but as it rumbles on the world is changing fast and globalization is forcing everyone to cooperate in order to be able to compete. Individuals and groups have greater choice than ever before in the Western World; greater openness and diminishing deference make it increasingly hard to force 'win: lose' situations onto those who may once never have known that they had lost. In a world of free traders only 'win: win' deals will be acceptable, although the incompetent and criminal will have to continue to lose so that standards do not fall.

I believe that we shall see a convergence between the public and private sectors in the next millennium. The work of Nolan/Neill has established principles which are needed to underpin the work of Cadbury, Greenbury and Hampel. As Sir Adrian Cadbury said in his 1998 Gresham Lecture in the Mansion House, personal morality is the driver of business morality. It is the interaction of the professionalism of individuals in a company which produces the quality of corporate governance which can achieve sustainable competitive advantage for their enterprise and just rewards for all who have contributed to that success.

Adrian Davies

ACKNOWLEDGEMENTS

Corporate governance is all about open and selfless cooperation. In writing this book I have been helped by a considerable number of people who have contributed their ideas with generosity and imagination.

I am grateful to Gower for allowing me to develop this book on a broad and philosophical canvas in order to advance the debate on corporate governance beyond the boardroom and its relationship with shareholders, into a framework which includes a wider society and a more complex set of relationships and values. A considerable debt of gratitude is due to all who have contributed through the case studies which constitute Part II of the book. Their quality is due to the professionalism of those whom I interviewed, and I am sure that these case studies bring a whole new dimension to the basic argument of the book.

A number of other people have contributed advice and refinements to the book. Notable among these are Sir Adrian Cadbury, and Professor Bernard Taylor of Henley Management College. Valuable thoughts have been contributed by Dr Bruce Lloyd of the Strategic Planning Society. I am grateful to these and to many others who are too numerous to name individually.

Adrian Davies

INTRODUCTION

For company directors preoccupied with meeting the profits expectations of shareholders a book on corporate governance must seem as irrelevant as a course on umpiring for a world-class batsman. Yet, in the same way that cricket has lost its innocence to expensive and demanding sponsorship, forcing a stricter and camera-supported umpiring regime, business has been forced by scandal and increasing consumer power to make itself more accountable to the society in which it operates.

Corporate governance is no longer optional for businessmen – it is a vital issue. In the same way that the public is demanding accountability in war, with the Bosnian trials, and politicians are forced to answer accusations of 'sleaze', there is growing criticism of greed and abuse in business, fed by the media and reflected in popular distrust. Pop stars and sports personalities are seen to justify their high salaries and outlandish lifestyles, but business has failed to perform and win the hearts of ordinary British voters, putting at risk the support of politicians.

The crisis of corporate governance developed out of the secretive, clublike relationships which characterized the City and Whitehall in the years following the last war. These relationships could be manipulated by determined outsiders such as Robert Maxwell and Asil Nadir, as well as by insiders as in the Guinness takeover of Distillers. The crisis came with the end of the 1980s bull market and its extent may be gauged from a few examples:

O   Polly Peck (Asil Nadir) went from a market value of £1.75 billion to a deficit of nearly £400 million within one month.
O   British and Commonwealth (John Gunn) had a market value of nearly £2 billion in 1987 and went into administration in 1989.
O   Robert Maxwell transferred some £450 million from a quoted company (Mirror Group) to support his private companies.
O   Bank of Credit and Commerce International (BCCI) was destroyed by internal fraud totalling several billion pounds.

The crisis involved fraud in the most extreme examples, including, in the case of the de Lorean car plant in Northern Ireland, defrauding the Government. British and Commonwealth failed due to poor due diligence in acquiring Atlantic Computers; the Blue Arrow scandal was caused by manipulating DTI regulations; TSB managed to destroy shareholder value on an unprecedented scale by unwise acquisitions; Barings was destroyed through the failure of internal controls; and the list continues. Only recently fraud struck again at Cendant, where the profits of one of the merger partners, CUC, had been egregiously overstated. The challenge to corporate governance seems to be reviving as, at the time of writing, the 1990s bull market rushes to its peak!

Corporate governance is at the core of the process of directing a company. It provides the leadership which gives it purpose and the strategy and processes to achieve this. It provides the values to enable it to work well with others and the checks and balances needed to ensure survival. Where corporate governance is harnessed to optimize working relationships with customers, employees, suppliers, local communities and other stakeholders, it can be used to create competitive advantage through maximizing the effectiveness of the operating system of which the company is the centre. Such a company moves off the back foot onto the front foot like our winning, world-class batsman!

HOW TO USE THIS BOOK

I have attempted to set corporate governance in a wider framework of governance both historically and geographically so that it can be appreciated as part of a long tradition and of a system that affects our lives at all levels and in most places.

The structure of the book is made up of the following main chapters:

1   sets the scene and defines the overall scope of governance;
2   raises the key issues of the governance of organizations;
3   identifies the wide range of stakeholders in corporate governance;
4   traces the historical development of corporate governance, illustrating why it has become such a major issue of concern;
5   examines other models of corporate governance, both in other countries and in organizations other than joint stock companies;
6   reviews different approaches to governance and the board's role in effecting it, emphasising the role of non-executive directors;
7   shows the interaction between governance and strategy in creating competitive advantage, showing two practical approaches to making governance more effective;

8   suggests ways of sustaining the positive impact of corporate gover-
      nance over time;

9   explores the potential impact of corporate governance in the global
      economy of the 21st Century.

For those who have limited time and seek the core of the book Chapters 6,
7 and 8 are essential reading, while Chapters 2, 3 and 4 provide useful background. For readers wanting to find a practical approach to implementing
an effective corporate governance system the end of Chapter 7 offers two
options in detail. For those who wish to understand governance 'in the
round' there is no alternative to reading the whole book with considerable
care.

PART 1

❖

1

WHAT IS GOVERNANCE? WHY DOES IT MATTER AND WHOM DOES IT AFFECT?

❖

One of the towering figures of the 20th Century, Mao Zedung, was idolized by the Chinese people as 'The Great Helmsman'. His charisma and leadership came not only from a powerful vision, but also from the ability to steer China towards realizing that vision. The Greek work for 'steer' is *kubernaein*, which provides the root for 'governance'.

The *Oxford English Dictionary* defines 'governance' as 'the act, manner, fact or function of governing, sway, control'. 'To govern' is 'to rule with authority', 'to exercise the function of government', 'to sway, rule, influence, regulate, determine', 'to conduct oneself in some way; curb, bridle (one's passions, oneself)', or 'to constitute a law for'. Governing is, therefore, a whole range of actions, in a spectrum from rule through influence to self-control. By inference it includes 'driving' as well as 'steering' – might Mao have been the 'Great Driver' as much as the 'Great Helmsman'?

It is important to address the issue of governance with a clear recognition that there is no single definition or model of it which is universally recognized or applicable. In seeking to define governance it is helpful also to consider its antitheses – freedom, licence, individualism, and so on. These are all concepts rooted in the interests of the individual person; freedom implies choice, licence implies unlimited choice and individualism places the interests of the person above those of all others. There is, therefore, a fundamental tension between freedom and governance, which has existed ever since individuals found the need to relate to others, and recognized that workable relationships require ground rules to be successful.

The primitive ground rules which evolved to shape early tribal relationships seem to have moved with the passage of time into two main categories

3

– *customs* (which are a means of working together effectively), and *moral codes* (which are ends in their own right). Over time increasing tensions have developed between these categories – for example, there is a moral imperative not to kill, yet custom supports killing in war. Time has also brought different moral codes, within a wide range of religions, and customs have increasingly diverged between different societies.

Governance may be seen as a process for reconciling the ambitions of the individual with the need to preserve and develop the 'common weal' which binds individuals through shared interests. It may be useful to explore the reasons why governance may be important for each and all of us.

WHY DOES GOVERNANCE MATTER?

There are a surprising number of issues which surround us which may be called 'hygiene factors'. These are matters which we expect to take for granted, such as that lights will switch on, newspapers will be delivered and the sun will rise each day. These factors are only remarkable when they fail. Governance has been largely taken for granted in the past, both because most people were not aware of alternatives and because its failure was only apparent in infrequent crises, such as revolutions, or major systemic failures such as that caused by the Black Death. For most of human existence governance has been imposed on the majority by a small elite, whose power has been legitimized by a priesthood which had a virtual monopoly of knowledge. This form of governance depended on curtailing the freedom of the ruled in order to maximize the power of their rulers. In the words of Geoff Mulgan, the founder of Demos:

> The final dimension of freedom is power. To be free means to be powerful. The word freedom came originally from the barbarian conquerors of Rome, for whom it was one of the virtues of the warrior, and certainly not something to be widely shared. Freedom was a privilege of elites, nobles and later of the bourgeois in the self-governing towns of medieval Europe (*Connexity*, Chatto & Windus, 1997).

The monopolizing of power by rulers made it virtually impossible for defects in governance either to be recognized by the ruled or to be challenged by them. Sometimes secret groups formed in self-protection; some examples survive today – the Mafia and the Freemasons. For much of history governance has gone by default since regimes did not share decisions with their subjects but left them to suffer the consequences of failure. The Medes, Persians, Trojans, Carthaginians, Egyptians and others were early victims of this myopic process.

A narrow focus of power has almost invariably led to failure in history. The conquests of Alexander the Great exhausted Greece and opened the door for Rome to take over supreme power. In turn the corruption of Rome led to its downfall. Even with a wider dissemination of learning and wealth it proved impossible to stop adventurers like Napoleon and Hitler from seizing power and bringing catastrophe upon their people.

In more recent times the growth of democracy together with the waning of communism and other extreme regimes has led to increasing concern at undue concentrations of power. Geoff Mulgan sees it thus: 'Power has lost its equation with respect, and today, amidst a marketplace of facts and interpretations, presidents, kings and chairmen of companies can no longer count on any automatic respect.' The loss or depreciation of long-accepted models has created intellectual turmoil (as evidenced in Will Hutton's *The State We're In*, Vintage, 1995) and a search for better processes of governance.

One of the new models of civilized society is developed in a book by Jane Jacobs (*Systems of Survival: a Dialogue on the Moral Foundations of Commerce and Politics*, Vintage, 1994). Society is seen as having two sets of values, those of the 'guardian', bent on plunder and control, and those of the merchant, based on relationships and deals. She sees a symbiosis of these two groups in any society, with the balance of power shifting over time. Civilization depends on the relationship between both groups being mutually supportive rather than openly antagonistic.

In earlier times governance was a process that most people suffered and could not influence. Democratization and education, coupled with better communication of facts and opinions, has revealed how inadequate are many of the established procedures we have inherited. The spread of wealth in the past 50 years has given a growing number of ordinary people a stake in the success of capitalism (not least through their share of the burgeoning pension funds which depend on effective corporate governance to meet their obligations). Where governance fails the results can be catastrophic; in the words of Will Hutton:

> Insurance company salesmen have wrongly advised as many as 400 000 members of occupational pension funds, who bought individual pension schemes which were no good to them at all. As many as 2 million more were persuaded to cash in their rights to the state earnings related pension scheme (SERPS) and to buy personal pensions – again to their disadvantage. Insurance companies sell policies they know are unsuitable and calculate their profits on the certainty that buyers will cash in their inappropriate policies early, for a fraction of their proper value.

Failures such as the collapse of BCCI, the demise of the Maxwell empire and the Barlow Clowes fraud are no longer remote from ordinary people but are increasingly damaging to their wealth. Governance is no longer a matter for others to worry about – now it affects us all.

HOW DOES GOVERNANCE RELATE TO THE INDIVIDUAL AND TO SOCIETY?

In his book *The Hungry Spirit* (Hutchinson, 1997) Charles Handy seeks for purpose in the modern world. He attempts to harness selfishness to more altruistic goals and develops the concept of 'proper selfishness' as a motive power for progress – 'to be ourselves we need other people'. This idea of self-fulfilment through working through other people is not new; 'no man is an island' said John Donne and society has always depended on the creative tension between individual ambitions and communal progress.

The interaction between individuals and working groups has increasingly been examined by psychoanalysts such as Kets de Vries, but results to date are far from conclusive. Observations have been careful and some under-standing of the process obtained, but there remains some concern that work to date has ignored 'a central tenet of psychoanalytic thought, namely uncon-scious motivation' (McKiernan and Urquhart, 1997). Writers such as Erikson have tried to explore the relationships between individuals and groups by relating them back to childhood development, with the tension between per-sonal identity and a sense of belonging which reemerges in Charles Handy's 'proper selfishness'. It would seem that there are some insights into an indi-vidual's relationship with external groups (and thus to the need for gover-nance), but that the deepest understanding of individual motivation towards groups, which include other people, remains tantalizingly elusive.

Throughout history individuals have been subjected to the tyranny of their environment. Freedom for most individuals was not an issue until Thomas Paine wrote on 'The Rights of Man' and found an echo in the American and French Revolutions. Geoff Mulgan quotes Duke Ellington's funeral oration for Louis Armstrong: '[he] was born poor, died rich, begat a great new form of art and hurt no one along the way'. Freedom allows indi-viduals to develop their potential and offers them choice in the key deci-sions of their lives. John Locke saw freedom as power unfettered. Such power does not have to be harmful to others: in the words of Geoff Mulgan:

> free men or women are those who have learned sufficient control over their psychic energies to be able to direct them to goals, and above all per-haps to goals that are cumulative and longterm in nature, that deliver fulfil-ment, leading the self to greater awareness, complexity and integration. Bringing up a child, creating a garden, supporting a group of friends or learning to write poetry would all be examples.

Personal freedom has, therefore, only recently become more generalized and most people still struggle to cope with it. The growth of personal freedom has also been constrained by a growth in interdependence, caused by the increas-ing complexity of society and the need to contain the excesses of personal freedom. These issues were, of course, grappled with in shaping Athenian democracy in the fifth century BC, but failure to protect freedom of speech, not least by Socrates, led to a progressive extinction of political freedom. The early ideals, however, were built into the foundations of Greek philosophy and have survived 25 centuries to help shape the modern world. It is this long tradition of democracy, filtered through centuries of abuse and exploitation, which has given such resilience to the concept of personal freedom.

It is clear that untrammelled personal freedom is akin to lawlessness. It is significant that, where new frontiers are opened up, as in the Wild West or in Russia today, excessive personal freedom needs to be curtailed by the rule of law. In an ideal world personal freedom would be used, as Louis Armstrong used it, as an instrument of self-fulfilment without hurt to others. Such an employment of personal freedom requires a strict internal discipline or self-governance that is rare. Rousseau's 'noble savage' was untainted by moral doubt and would not have needed any conscious process of self-governance. If we admit the concept of original sin, however, we are faced with the need for a code of morality and a process of self-governance.

As Geoff Mulgan suggests 'morality is a word that can be notoriously abused'. He sees morality as being derived from customs (hence the Latin root *mos*) but now overlaid by a system of rationally deduced ethical principles, much as organized religion has subsumed pagan customs into its rituals. At its crudest, morality is the basis for judging between 'right' and 'wrong'. Such judgements are rarely clear-cut and may vary over time or between tribes: for a long time slavery was seen as 'right' by developed nations and is still acceptable to many Arabs. Geoff Mulgan sees three distinct sources of moral behaviour – the dispositions embedded in our genes, the influence of tradition, and our ability to deduce moral choices from abstract principles. When each source is pointing in the same direction, moral issues are simple, but where they point in different directions we enter a 'moral maze' from which it may be impossible to escape.

The dispositions embedded in the genes of an individual are the most fundamental yet the least easy to understand of the sources of individual behaviour. We have seen how Louis Armstrong maximized his potential, but it is doubtful if even he fully understood the role of his genes in that achievement. There is considerable controversy about the balance of nature and nurture in shaping adult behaviour. Was Adolf Hitler inherently wicked or was his adult behaviour a product of his experience? Was St Francis largely untouched by original sin or did he master his genes in pursuit of a loftier cause? How far can we be in control of our genes? Are they able to ambush us unexpectedly (like the plea of the lady caught shoplifting from the smoked salmon counter!). Experience seems to suggest that the role of human genes in behaviour is problematical and largely unpredictable and that this makes self-governance an imperfect art and a shaky foundation for the governance of groups.

HOW FAR DOES GOVERNANCE EXTEND?

The ideal of a world government has intrigued human kind for centuries and has consistently eluded its grasp. Attempts to integrate the known world by Alexander, the Romans, the Chinese and other conquerors have consistently failed; the first wave of religious conquest by Islam also failed and we await the possibility of another Islamist surge with trepidation. If Nostradamus was right, even this wave will do nothing to create a world government but only unleash untold misery and destruction.

The first serious attempt to create a world government was the founding of the League of Nations in 1919. This was the dream of Woodrow Wilson, intended to ensure that nations would work together and, where necessary, pool their sovereignty. Many of Germany's former colonies were placed under League of Nations trusteeship, administered on its behalf by Britain, France and others. 'The world must be made safe for democracy' was Wilson's cry in 1917 but, when his presidency terminated, America drew back into itself and never joined the League of Nations, whose feeble performance in seeking to contain the ambitions of Adolf Hitler destroyed completely the first attempt to create a forum for world government.

Following the Second World War greater care was taken to establish international institutions to provide a global framework for peaceful development. The Bretton Woods agreement established the World Bank and International Monetary Fund (IMF) and governance was focused through the United Nations Organisation (UN) and its supporting agencies. In order to encourage trade liberalization a General Agreement on Tariffs and Trade (GATT) was concluded, which served as the vehicle for reducing tariffs and solving trade disputes. The success of GATT has led to its expansion into a new World Trade Organization (WTO) which has a wider remit and stronger powers.

The institutions established by the victorious Allies after the Second World War have had mixed success. The UN has emerged as a large 'talking shop' in which nations of all sizes simply talk at each other and often hamper the moves for action urged by others. Ideals of the UN as an instrument of world government remain frustrated, yet the UN may well have helped to defuse many incipient crises and has provided the means for bringing support to struggling countries through its many agencies. Arguably the largest successes for world agencies have been those of GATT in liberalizing trade and of the IMF in macroeconomic regulation. Most of the success of agencies has been achieved in spite of a vacuum in world leadership. The current drive towards globalization is being spearheaded by the WTO, which continues to extend regulation into new areas, such as telecommunications. In an article in *Financial Times* (2 March 1998) Guy de Jonquieres sees future dangers for the WTO in being forced to challenge imperfect regulation in most countries and the effects of corruption, abuse of human rights and defective health and safety standards on world trade. Such a challenge could trigger a return to protectionism but it must be made if the benefits of globalization are to be enjoyed by consumers in most countries rather than merely by self-chosen elites.

The role of international law in effecting governance across boundaries has grown steadily, in line with the increasing globalization of trade in goods and services. The legal structure pivots on The International Court in The Hague for disputes between states, with criminal cases being brought to special tribunals such as that established for war crimes in Bosnia. Following the Nuremberg and Tokyo war crimes trials it had been intended to create an international criminal court, but this has never been achieved despite continuing efforts. There is a body of international law covering most activities which cross boundaries or have effects outside the country of origin. The limits of international law are increasingly being tested – for example, in respect of human rights within China, Myanmar or elsewhere, and in settling issues of conflict of laws in civil cases. It has been noticeable that contracts are increasingly being written with arbitration clauses in order to avoid the cost and uncertainty of international litigation.

It may be argued that the vision of a United Europe which shaped the Treaty of Rome was a projection of the idealism which created the UN and the new world order after the Second World War. Some forty years later the drive for political integration seems to have slowed worldwide, apart from conquests such as that of Tibet by China, and a trend to political devolution seems to be gaining ground. Post-Franco Spain has been forced into devolution to survive as an entity; the archetypal 'nation state', France, has devolved increasing powers to its regions. The United Kingdom is now embarking on a process of devolution whose outcome is impossible to predict.

A different pattern for Europe was proposed some years ago by Freddie Heineken, the Dutch brewery owner. He believed that human organizations need to be of a manageable size in order to work successfully. Heineken's Europe would have 75 countries each with a population of between five and ten million and each based on a shared ethnicity, culture and language. At the level of individual companies this approach of devolution into business units on a human scale has been powerful at ABB, Proctor and Gamble and elsewhere.

There is a very important paradox in this struggle between integration and devolution. Larger units are expected to be more economic and more homogeneous. Much of the reality of larger units is that they become more bureaucratic and internecine. The United Nations is an excellent example of this phenomenon; the World Bank has degraded in a similar fashion. To an increasing degree the world's largest companies have restructured themselves to achieve internal devolution. ABB now has numerous small companies in 128 countries and a headquarters staff of less than 200. Its former CEO, Percy Barnevik, states: 'We are not a global business. We are a collection of local businesses with intense global coordination.' Increasing complexity makes the running of large organizations increasingly difficult. It is nearly forty years since President de Gaulle complained 'how can one run a country with over 500 different cheeses' and since then the challenge has intensified. Is it now becoming impossible to achieve effective governance in organizations which are beyond a certain size?

John Naisbitt highlights the paradox between the globalization of the world economy and the devolution of businesses into smaller and stronger units. He quotes Jack Welch of GE: 'What we are trying relentlessly to do is to get that small company soul – and small company speed – inside a big company body'. We have moved far from the 1960s model of a small number of monolithic global corporations. Large businesses today have downsized and refocused their structures and are often more open to alliances than to megamergers. In the same way that countries can only survive by increasing devolution of power, companies are being forced to recognize and respond to pressures from a growing range of 'stakeholders' who can 'make or break' their business. These 'stakeholders' are increasingly demanding and most of them are local in their impact on the company's operations. Shell has suffered in its global business from a failure of local governance in Nigeria; with global communications media 'little local difficulties' become instant issues across the world.

THE HIERARCHY OF GOVERNANCE SCOPE

As we have seen, the principles of governance are applicable to organizations of all sizes and in all parts of society. In considering world government we have tested the governance model to its global limit and have found a dichotomy between global scope and the human dimension. In a free society only the human dimension can deliver effective governance and there may be constraints caused by size and diversity which have to be overcome in seeking effective governance.

In organizations of all sizes governance has a core purpose although it may be delivered in different ways. Müller (1981) defines governance thus:

> Governance is concerned with the intrinsic nature, purpose, integrity and identity of an institution with a primary focus on the entity's relevance, continuity and fiduciary aspects. Governance involves monitoring and overseeing strategic direction, socioeconomic and cultural context, externalities and constituencies of the institution.

Governance is usually delivered through an agreed constitution, through a complex web of customs and practices, underpinned by a shared system of ethics, to a range of stakeholders in that institution. There is a hierarchy of institutions which require effective governance, starting with supranational organizations, for example the European Union, and moving down through national, regional and local government, with similar hierarchies for defence and public services, business organizations, special interest groups, churches, clubs, and so on. The issue of ethics in a business context is examined in Case Study 1.1 in Part II of this book.

STYLES OF GOVERNANCE

Styles of governance vary depending on the nature and size of the body concerned. At one extreme is the rule-based style adopted by public sector bodies which may be concerned with conformity rather than performance. At the other extreme are the churches and clubs where governance is based on trust. Most bodies have an amalgam of both trust and rules in appropriate proportions. Trust can only work with open governance; in bodies which are opaque in their governance rules become an essential sheet anchor.

ELEMENTS OF GOVERNANCE

All bodies need to establish certain criteria for their governance. As a minimum these are likely to be:

1   the identity of the body;
2   definition of its purpose;
3   how the purpose is to be achieved;
4   membership criteria (both explicit, such as shared interests, and implicit for example shared values);
5   how the body is to be administered;
6   how the body relates externally;
7   how success is measured;
8   termination arrangements.

It may be helpful to relate these elements to a specific body – a medium-sized 'learning' society, incorporated with limited liability under guarantee and having charitable status.

1   The Strategic Planning Society.
2   To help members to understand and influence an increasingly complex and uncertain future.
3   Through dissemination of a learned journal ('Long Range Planning') and a management magazine ('Strategy'), organizing special interest group meetings in London and in the regions, operating an Internet website, organizing technical workshops and

strategy-focused conferences, managing the Public Management Forum and facilitating networking between members.

4   Membership is open to all persons interested in strategic management.

5   The Society is administered through an Executive Committee, supported by a group of Vice-Presidents, with teams organizing special interest and regional groups, with a General Manager and team to operate in detail. The Society is run in accordance with its Memorandum and Articles, together with Standing Orders.

6   External links including USA and Europe are promoted by the Chairman, with support from the General Manager.

7   The key performance measures are (a) membership growth and (b) membership participation.

8   The Society is not time-limited but has plans for orderly liquidation if necessary.

In practice the constitutional details of most organizations will be more complex than the example given, even at top level, but the basic elements need to be present in order that the body can function. In most organizations the strength of the different elements is likely to vary; it is noticeable that few bodies have performance criteria which really drive achievement of their purpose.

KEY ISSUES

1   Is our organization clear about the importance of corporate governance?

2   Do we have an agreed set of values by which we manage ourselves?

3   Have we addressed all the criteria for effective governance?

What action am I committing myself to take? _____

2

GOVERNANCE OF THE ENTERPRISE – KEY ISSUES

❖

At the heart of the issue of governance is the tension between achieving the objectives of the organization and the fulfilment of the personal objectives of its members and other stakeholders. Every relationship between individuals requires some trade-off of their separate interests. In healthy relationships these trade-offs are negotiated openly, explicitly or tacitly, and the bargain is kept. Where the trade-offs are not recognized, or the bargain is imposed from one side or is undermined unilaterally by stealth, there can be no healthy relationship. When the relationship is multilateral, the challenge is much greater and the process of achieving a workable balance much harder. This process is at the heart of governance.

The breakdown of bilateral contracts is evident in divorce statistics and in the growth in civil suits. This change is not driven by an increase in original sin as much as by a shift in power. Women are now freer to run their own lives and not share them with bullies; the average citizen is now more aware of their rights and more confident in standing up for them. Under the harsh scrutiny of the media governments today are being forced to be more accountable to their electors. Deference to those in office is fading as their stewardship is increasingly called into question and found to be unsatisfactory.

This shift in power is a key driver of the growing interest in corporate governance. It is supported by greater public awareness of the results of poor corporate governance, most dramatically in the plight of the 'Maxwell pensioners', but more pervasively in the sustained decline in the relative strength of British companies in world markets. A series of well-publicised scandals, beginning in the 1950s with Rolls Razor and continuing unabated to this day with the Regan raid on the Cooperative Wholesale Society, has made the public increasingly cynical about business. These scandals are seen as the tip of a very unpleasant iceberg in which is hidden a mass of

13

corruption. Examination of the different scandals reveals not only a common corruption but also a skilled manipulation of the legal system. The weakness of English trust law opened the gates to the manipulation of the Maxwell pension fund. British traditions of self-regulation have made it easier for manipulative operators such as Roger Levitt to escape detection for long periods of time; the supervision of the Bank of England has been called into question in respect of BCCI. The report on the Guinness bid for Distillers reveals a whole series of market manipulations which were illegal but supported by prominent parties in the City. If English law has been so regularly manipulated for personal gain, where are its weaknesses and how can they be remedied?

The basis of the limited liability system in the UK is a series of Companies Acts, beginning in 1862 and consolidated through to 1985. The concept of limited liability for shareholders was driven by a need to attract massive risk capital to develop Victorian businesses. Shareholders could only be at risk to the extent of the full value of their shares; creditors were at risk for any shortfall. The Companies Acts place the ownership of the company solely in the hands of equity shareholders. Holders of preference shares have no rights of intervention unless their dividends are unpaid, investors of loan capital also have limited rights and the directors have unlimited liability and are appointed by the equity shareholders. No other parties have rights under the Companies Acts; employees are subject to employment legislation, customers and suppliers are subject to commercial contracts and the government exerts its rights through the appropriate regulations.

Other corporate bodies were established under partnership law or special regimes (friendly societies, building societies, cooperatives, and so on). Ownership was limited to partners or members as appropriate. Partners owned a share of the accumulated profits of their firm. Until the recent spate of demutualizations members of mutual societies owned their investment but not the accumulated reserves built up by different generations. Many thinking people are uncomfortable that these reserves have now been released from trust status and appropriated by transient investors. That such events occur is as much a result of trying to use outmoded legal structures as of human greed.

Another key issue of governance is that of family ownership. Many businesses are started in order to provide employment for family members and a number of major companies such as Sainsbury's and Cadbury retain close family connections. Some families, such as the Agnellis and the Wallenbergs remain in control of substantial business empires.

Governance of family-controlled businesses presents special challenges. First, there is the danger of bringing family issues into consideration of the issues faced by the business, as happened dramatically at Christian Salvelsen two years ago. Personal rivalries and jealousies are difficult enough to cope with, and too often the business becomes the battlefield on which to fight them out. The impact of this in battling for succession is well illustrated in a case study in *Harvard Business Review* (January/February 1998). Second, families have to recognize when to sit back and allow professional managers to direct their company. Sometimes a key family member dies, as happened with the Agnellis, or the talent runs out, as with Ford, or needs support, as with Rothschild. Occasionally there is too much family involvement, as in the case of Ahlström of Finland, where Krister Ahlström had to battle with older family directors to make strategic changes to the business (*Harvard Business Review*, January/February 1998). The Wallenberg family has recently appointed Percy Barnevik to revitalize the range of businesses in which it has a controlling interest. It seems that mixing family concerns with business is rarely a formula for sustained success.

None of these models reflects the reality and complexity of modern life. They were created when capital was scarce, labour was cheap and markets were closed. Today's open markets are driven by knowledge, innovation and relationships – there is plenty of capital to support winning companies. The success of companies depends increasingly on the quality of employees and their relationship with customers and other outside parties, including suppliers and distributors. New structures are needed to reflect new and more complex relationships.

If Victorian structures have failed the test of modern life, are there earlier models which may be more all-encompassing and effective? Before joint stock companies corporations were formed by royal decree or by Act of Parliament in order to have legitimacy. Such bodies included craft guilds, trading enterprises (such as the East India Company), banks and insurance companies (such as Equitable Life) and utilities (roads, canals, ports and so on). There is little evidence that many of these enterprises were better run than those incorporated under Victorian models. The South Sea Bubble which failed in 1720 was only an extreme example of fraudulent manipulation, and most of the guilds and others who sought charters were concerned to limit access to their trade and control markets rather than to bring benefit to all parts of society. The activities of the trading enterprises were characterized by exploitation and even fraud; the impeachment of Warren Hastings was not the only stain on the record of the East India Company.

Another group of organizations developed partly in the ambit of the church. These include schools, universities and hospitals. Kings School Canterbury claims to be 1400 years of age; St Bartholomew's Hospital was founded in 1100. Corporate governance for such bodies has tended to be focused on lofty aims such as learning or healing, so that the means become justified by the ends. It is not obvious that such organizations offer a persuasive model for corporate governance, although the collegiate style of governance seen in some of these organizations is interesting. Some of the issues of governance in the voluntary sector are examined in Case Study 2.1 in Part II of this book.

What form does collegiate governance take? The concept of collegiate governance is one of a group of individuals working together for a common purpose with equally shared authority. As such a pure model invariably lacks direction, most collegiate structures allow for a source of leadership within the group, a *primus inter pares*, or first among equals, both to give focus to the group's activities and to provide a figurehead for external contacts. Most voluntary groups adopt a collegiate form of governance.

Collegiate governance is closest to commercial activity in the form of partnerships. These are most often a vehicle for running small businesses of all sorts (plumbers, builders, shops and so on) or for organizing the provision of professional services. Partnerships are usually registered and administered under the current partnership legislation. One characteristic of smaller partnerships is that the partners are involved both in managing the business and in delivering its services. This makes them sensitive to customers' needs but often less skilful at analysing the strategic needs of their businesses and ensuring their long-term survival. An article by Ashley Pinnington and Timothy Morris ('Long Range Planning', December 1996) comments on a model of strategic decision-making in professional firms (Greenwood *et al.*) which shows how a small group of partners will typically be delegated to 'manage' the firm on behalf of the whole partnership: 'Professionals' disinterest in managing the firm as opposed to executing client assignments means the management of the firm is a necessary burden but one wherein peer consensus, or at least extensive consultation, is required'. It should, however, be recognized that not all partnerships are democratic and that founder partners and powerful individuals hold sway in many partnerships as do their equivalents in other organizations.

TRUST

The foundation of all governance is trust, which is defined in the Oxford English Dictionary as 'firm belief in the honesty, veracity, justice, strength and so on of a person or thing'. Trust is also 'responsibility arising from confidence reposed in one', hence the position of holding property in trust for another party. Those who hold office usually do so in trust for others and may be held accountable for their actions. Trust is implicit in every relationship on which effective governance is built.

Trust law, which derives from the second definition above, underpins much of the structure of governance. Wherever people act for others and not for themselves they become trustees in fact, if not always in law. Trust law has grown to support relationships where the interested party is disadvantaged (a minor, absent overseas or, for executors, dead). It has been built on the basis of a disinterested willingness to act without payment on behalf of another person. Such altruism is not in unlimited supply and the history of fiduciary trusts is scarred with abuse and even scandal.

In addition to the obligations of trust written into the laws which govern companies and other associations, there is a body of law which relates to financial trusts. This has grown up over centuries to meet the need to protect the assets of those who are unable to act effectively for themselves. From a body of law to administer small values it has grown to accommodate the management of large pension funds and other major assets held in trust, such as charitable foundations. The law has been developed on the assumption that trustees will be honourable and efficient in their stewardship. As a result trust law is not tightly drawn and leaves considerable space for discretion, or for abuse. The scandal of the Maxwell Group pension funds is an extreme example of the manipulation of trust law and underlines the urgent need for new legislation for the administration of trusts which matches the less honourable and more complex times in which we live.

A change in law needs to be matched by a change in human behaviour. In the words of Robert Puttnam (*Making Democracy Work*, Princeton UP, 1993): 'the greater the level of trust within a community the greater the likelihood of cooperation. And cooperation itself breeds trust'. There is the possibility of a virtuous circle to drive social and economic progress which can be facilitated by trust, provided that that trust is supported by workable laws and directed to lawful ends. Geoff Mulgan warns against the dangerous manifestations of trust; cartels, secret societies and crime syndicates. 'Healthy societies depend on mistrust as well as trust, and one of the virtues of connexity is that it tends to weaken the power of closed cells that are always resistant to transparency and accountability'. Trust laws need to accommodate awareness of mistrust and to focus on clarity and honest stewardship.

Trust in the sense of 'responsibility arising from confidence reposed in one' is wider than the areas covered by trust law. The trust of children in their parents is one of the largest fields of responsibility and is often not well repaid. Such trusts are, however, not totally one-sided, since there is an implied contract to help the parents when they are too old to care for themselves. More important, the nurture given to the children becomes their pledge to do the same down the generations. Trust is the force that sustains every human relationship; sceptical mistrust is essential to keep that force in balance and to prevent abuse.

One instrument of sceptical mistrust which has been developed with considerable success in the USA is 'whistleblowing'. US courts have been very supportive of genuine whistle-blowers who have uncovered abuse in their companies, such as GE and SmithKline Beecham. For the purpose of protecting the public Andrew Millar of British Biotech has recently revealed problems with a major product. British attitudes to 'whistle-blowing' are negative and most whistle-blowers lose their jobs. There is a strong case for a review of English law and attitudes on this issue. The possibility of a Public Interest Disclosure Act is a first harbinger of change towards openness. Another instrument of sceptical mistrust which is well established is regulation.

REGULATION

Better building regulations might have prevented the construction of the Tower of Babel, but there is evidence of regulation in human activities since records began. The Babylonian, Persian and Egyptian civilizations were characterized by strong central control and regulation, usually carried out by priesthoods who did so in the name of the ruler and of a higher order of deities. Regulation by priesthood has continued through to the present day, most evidently in Iran where the radical model of Ayatollah Khomeini is imposed on citizens who find Islamic ideals to be incompatible with the daily task of making money.

Regulation was increasingly challenged, in particular from the Reformation through to the 18th Century. The search for freedom led to the liberal ideal and the growth of individualistic societies in the West. Regulation has been reduced to the minimum needed to prevent the collapse of society and where possible, has been replaced by self-regulation. Geoff Mulgan sees a need to redress the balance:

> We have grown so used to struggling against authority that it is not easy to acknowledge that any institutions, whether they are firms or families, sports teams or nations, need some basis of authority if they are not always to take the line of least resistance, but rather to act for the long term.

Self-regulation also has a long history. Monasteries were regulated by their founding order, guilds regulated themselves under their charter, and educational establishments were mainly self-regulating. Sir Geoffrey Vickers (*Freedom in a Rocking Boat*, Penguin, 1972) identifies two sorts of institution, *general* and *functional*. General institutions are those of government, both central and local. Functional institutions are those, both public and private, which provide goods and services, oversee the employed or self-employed or provide education. He sought the expansion of the functional institutions in order to limit the growing power of the state (in the 1970s). Since Sir Geoffrey wrote, we have seen the devolution of state power to Brussels and to the regions and a growing number of failures of self-regulation by financial institutions. The power of the trades unions has been diminished, yet the professions remain unchallenged. A view about the regulation of the professions may be found in Case Study 2.2 in Part II of this book.

New models of regulation are emerging. The privatization of utilities has led to the appointment of regulators to constrain their monopoly powers. Will Hutton sees this as a failure:

> One regulator may interpret the competitive model as an excuse for breaking up the industry into smaller competing parts; another for setting minimum rates of return; another for regarding pressure from the capital markets as a surrogate for competition and allowing the monopoly to remain intact. None of them have any clear idea of the national or common interest; some may feel that it is naturally achieved by competition, others that it has to be asserted.

Is this regime too personal and arbitrary to serve as a long-term model? The failure of Peter Davis as regulator of the National Lottery has fuelled the debate about the personal power given to British regulators. Another model to emerge is the new Financial Services Authority which integrates the regulatory role of the Bank of England with that of the Securities and Investment Board. It is expected that the new Authority will have powers which resemble those of the Securities and Exchange Commission in the USA rather than the self-regulatory powers of some of its predecessors. Another move towards new regulation is evident in the appointment of a 'Better Regulation Task Force' led by Sir Christopher Haskins of Northern Foods. This will focus on the quality and quantity of state regulation, seeking to strike a balance between over-regulation and the excessive deregulation pursued by the Tory Government. It will use the principles of transparency, accountability, targeting, consistency and proportionality in evaluating regulations which it will review.

In considering regulation, are we constrained by systems thinking so that our models are all discrete and integral? In a world where boundaries are porous and sovereignty diluted do we need more flexible and chaotic modes of regulation? Are we committed to the idea that there is a 'right and wrong' approach to regulation rather than finding one which produces workable arrangements most of the time? In a world of relativity there are unlikely to be absolute solutions. A view of regulation by a practitioner may be found in Case Study 2.1 and by the head of a trade association in Case Study 2.3.

CORPORATE GOVERNANCE

The growing interest in corporate governance was stimulated by the startling evidence of its failure, both in the collapse of major British businesses, such as Rolls Royce, and in the series of scandals which punctuated these collapses. The historical details are explored in Chapter 4, but their impact forced a radical reassessment of how companies are directed.

Out of this process there have emerged two major approaches to improving corporate governance, which we may characterize as (a) traditional corporate governance and (b) inclusive corporate governance. These may be compared and contrasted as follows:

TRADITIONAL CORPORATE GOVERNANCE

This approach follows the established philosophy underlying the Companies Acts and complementary legislation. It underlies the findings of the Cadbury, Greenbury and Hampel Reports and focuses on the work of the Board and its relationship to shareholders. The basic concern is to improve current practice and avoid further embarrassing scandals. Shareholders are to be encouraged to be more active. The focus is on process rather than philosophy.

INCLUSIVE CORPORATE GOVERNANCE

The Hampel Report states (1.3): 'Good governance ensures that constituencies (stakeholders) with a relevant interest in the company's business are fully taken into account' and does not elaborate. The wider approach to corporate governance has been pioneered by the RSA enquiry into 'Tomorrow's Company' and subsequent work which is featured in Case Study 5.1. This book will attempt to develop a broad strategic approach to corporate governance, involving stakeholders other than shareholders and the Board, which may be called 'inclusive corporate governance'.

The work done by the Committee on Standards in Public Life, the Nolan (now Neill) Committee, has focused on principles as well as processes. The 'Seven Principles of Public Life' distilled by the review process have resonance beyond the public sector. These are selflessness, integrity, objectivity, accountability, openness, honesty and leadership. We shall explore the implications for societies of the process of globalization, not least in the convergence of the principles of governance in the public and private sectors.

KEY ISSUES

1   Do we understand the implications of changes in society on the power of our stakeholders?
2   How do we develop an ethic of cooperation rather than confrontation?
3   What do we have to do to make the Nolan principles work for our organization?

What action am I committing myself to take? _____

3

THE STAKEHOLDERS IN CORPORATE GOVERNANCE

At one time a stakeholder was the person who held wagers for others pending the outcome of the event on which bets had been placed. Those who placed the wagers were fortunate if the stakeholder did not elope before the payout! Today the term 'stakeholder' is used for all parties who have an interest in a particular enterprise whether that interest is legitimate or not; formerly the term 'constituency' was used but this has been seen as less proprietorial than 'stakeholder' in a world where shouting is possessing.

Stakeholding is, then, basically about ownership. In company law ownership belongs exclusively to ordinary shareholders; other classes of shareholder have lesser rights to reflect the lower risk attaching to their investment. Lenders have the right to interest, to repayment in due time or to a prior claim on assets in liquidation. Ownership is, however, not simply about a claim on nett assets. For the directors it can be the right to secure tenure and to deploy the company's assets as they see fit. For employees it can be about having a safe job and prospects of advancement which they may wish to protect by membership of a trades union. For customers it can be about the right to demand outstanding service for an economic price; for suppliers and distributors it can be about a stable and profitable trading relationship. For government it is about providing sufficient jobs and paying all dues and taxes without problems or delay. For competitors it is about sharing a marketplace and protecting it from new entrants. In addition to these and other 'involved' stakeholders there are other parties who make claims upon the company, such as local schools, charities, the media, pressure groups, churches, hospitals, and providers of amenities. As government funding fails to meet the needs of public services and demands on charities increase as a consequence, the number of claimants on companies and the pressure of their demands

23

rises inexorably. How are companies to evaluate the competing claims of their stakeholders? How many of these claims are legitimate and how many are an unwarranted burden on the true stakeholders?

At one extreme of the spectrum lie the exploiters. Many Italian companies are obliged to pay 'protection money' to the Mafia and few multinational companies have avoided the attention of kidnappers. This cannot be seen as stakeholding, but is pure criminality. The involved stakeholders may also indulge in criminality, through fraud or theft. If detected they forfeit their status as stakeholders and may be liable to criminal prosecution.

Companies can still be exploited by stakeholders without criminal intent. Contributions to political parties were for many years seen to be a legitimate claim on companies. Recent concerns about 'sleaze' and about secret contributions, mainly from overseas, have made companies less willing to support political parties. Contributions to registered charities remain an acceptable charge on profits and enjoy a large measure of support from other stakeholders. There is, however, some concern that not all charities are charitable; charitable status can be secured by fringe churches and other bodies whose activities do not match their declared aims. Many lobbyists are registered as charities and this status helps them to legitimize their myopic drive on a single issue. Animal rights groups have been among the most fanatical and have imposed their view of the world on any companies which cross their path.

How can the legitimacy of stakeholder claims be tested? In a democracy power is legitimized by elections. Elected governments at all levels are therefore legitimate, even though many Scots never accepted Tory government. Directors are elected by shareholders. Union leaders are elected by their members. It is reasonable to suppose that a relationship entered into freely by two parties is legitimate. Employees and their employer have a contractual relationship which is supposedly even-handed. Customers choose their suppliers and contract with them without undue constraint. In reverse the same may be said of suppliers. Shareholders contract with the company by buying its shares, lenders contract by making loans.

There is a third category of stakeholder which is distinct from company suppliers in that their relationship with the company is to some extent mandatory. Companies are required by the Companies Act to appoint an auditor and are obliged by custom and practical need to nominate bankers and solicitors. Companies may appoint several bankers in order to have some control over the banking relationship and they may choose to use different firms of solicitors for distinct purposes (mergers, international work, secretarial work, and so on). A company's auditors are unique and the relationship should be close and detailed but not over-intimate, as it too often becomes.

Many of the scandals which have caused the recent growing interest in corporate governance have raised questions about the role of the auditor. A number of these cases remain *sub judice*, but there has been a growing number of law suits involving audit firms. Since accountancy firms have traditionally been established as partnerships with unlimited liability, the growing burden of claims for damages has been driving them to incorporate in order to limit their liability or to register their partnership offshore. There is little evidence that this self-preservation is being matched by any new initiatives to make auditing more effective. On the contrary, many firms have been relying on their audit relationship to increase their consultancy work for clients, raising issues of conflict of interest.

There is talk of requiring companies to change auditor at frequent intervals in order to bring fresh eyes to the audit process. The use of audit firms both for the audit and for consultancy work is beginning to be queried, but in any case the rapid concentration of audit firms worldwide is seriously limiting the choice of auditor for most companies. It may be time for a wider range of contractors to be licensed to audit company accounts much as solicitors have lost their monopoly of conveyancing. The market for professional services needs to be opened up to competition if those who provide such services are ever to be seen as legitimate stakeholders in the companies with which they deal.

Employees have been identified as legitimate stakeholders and their importance for the success of the company is growing relative to that of shareholders. When employees had less power they often sought to increase their bargaining weight through membership of a trades union. Where companies recognized trades unions, the role of the unions was to act as the agent of the employees. At a later stage after the Second World War the unions virtually became a power in their own right and were able to impose themselves as stakeholders on the companies in which their members worked. Union power has diminished in recent years, but their role as agents for employees remains where they exercise bargaining rights. There are some signs of an increase in union membership in the USA which may in time be reflected in the UK.

The role of trades unions as agents for employees opens the door to other agency stakeholders. There is an obvious need for small shareholders to escape from their individual weakness by having a mechanism for concentrating voting power. The vehicle for exercising proxy voting power would itself become an agency stakeholder, whether it was a friendly institutional shareholder or a shareholders' club.

A fifth category of stakeholder which is growing significantly and is likely to become increasingly important as business globalizes is that of alliance partners. These may be separate companies with a minority shareholding in the company, in effect trading shareholders. LVMH is a minority shareholder in Diageo and has trading agreements with the group in some overseas markets. At the other extreme companies may make a joint venture to develop a new market or product, as W H Smith and Virgin did with music shops. Another growing form of alliance is outsourcing. This usually differs from a normal supplier relationship in that the trained and experienced staff of, for instance, the IT department are transferred *en bloc* with their equipment to the new supplier. This makes the relationship more intimate and potentially more effective than that with a new supplier.

Many alliances lead to mergers; if the relationship does not become more intimate it may atrophy, as have some of those between banks and insurers. Other alliances are destroyed by third parties, such as that between Honda and Rover and, more recently, the alliance between BT and MCI. Alliance partners are members of the family until they are divorced.

There is a sixth category of stakeholder whose relationship with the company may be mutually beneficial. Such groups might include local schools which may educate future employees, local amenities which attract and retain employees and local charities which employees may wish to support. While both parties combine to find benefit in some sort of relationship, such stakeholders must be seen as legitimate. British Telecom takes great care to develop helpful relationships with disabled people who have special communication needs. Centrica finds business benefits from close involvement in community work. The activities of 'Business in the Community' are referred to in Chapter 4, and these activities are supported by various social entrepreneurial initiatives which are beginning to reclaim lost communities. These are integrated into '2000 by 2000' led by Rev. Andrew Mawson, and these initiatives are receiving substantial financial support from local and national companies.

Government at all levels is a seventh category of stakeholder. In some countries companies are subject to considerable administrative guidance but, except in wartime, Anglo-Saxon companies may expect to operate freely within a supportive framework of laws. It is therefore disturbing when politicians seek to steer company policy as John Prescott is doing by pressurizing Railtrack to rescue the Channel link project.

The legitimacy of unilateral relationships must be open to doubt. Where it is exploitative, as in the onslaught of hackers on computer systems or the abuse of the natural environment by the company, it cannot be legitimate. Where the motivation of the relationship is not open and consistent, as with the media and pressure groups, it cannot be seen as a stakeholder relationship. Intermittent events, like hiring a taxi or booking an hotel, are contracts not relationships; they are to be picked up and dropped at will. Any attempt by media or pressure groups to force themselves on a company is as illegitimate as importuning by a taxidriver. Such a relationship can only be legitimized by the acquiescence of the company, and too many give in to pressure. The media and pressure groups are not elected bodies; their agenda is not the public good but their own profits and their own narrow causes respectively.

In recognizing that the media and pressure groups are not stakeholders in a company, it is prudent to deal with them with care. The media may raise issues which are in tune with government policy or for which there is a demonstrable level of public support and it would be unwise to dismiss these out of hand. Wise companies engage the media only on the basis of facts, not of opinions, and seek to defuse confrontation rather than intensify it. In dealing with the media and pressure groups it is often prudent to understand the position of the company's legitimate stakeholders on the issue in hand and to shape the company's stance accordingly.

CONFLICTING CLAIMS

Often the position of stakeholders will not be shared and different stakeholders will make conflicting claims on the company. The expectations of shareholders may clash with those of employees; in recent times the need for companies to lower costs in order to compete and pay competitive dividends, has led to severe 'downsizing' and loss of jobs. Often a predator will appeal to shareholders over the heads of the company's directors and sweep them out of office, as happened with the Granada bid for Forte. Sometimes a customer will severely damage his supplier to gain a lower cost source of supply; for example the switch from coal to gas by electricity generators. Sometimes employees with skills in short supply can force settlements which damage their company and the interests of shareholders and other stakeholders – for example, the dealers in investment banks. The greedy deals made by directors of many large US companies are now being replicated in some British companies, not least in some of the privatized businesses where huge productivity bonuses can be earned by removing generations of accumulated overstaffing. Such bonuses are windfalls and often penalize other stakeholders, not least the staff who remain and must carry the weight of change.

These and other conflicting claims demonstrate that not all stakeholders are equal and that their relative power may change with events. Stakeholders interact within a system (the company and its environment) which has ever-widening boundaries, due both to complexity and to globalization. Change drives the system and alters the balance of power in ways difficult to predict. Automation and new delivery systems have loosened the grip which joint stock banks once had on their customers. The increase in the role of financing has weakened the hold of car manufacturers over the business of providing personal transportation. Not only is the relative balance of power variable with events, but the commitment of each stakeholder to the company itself becomes variable. Openness is the key to dealing with stakeholders. Companies like Ben and Jerry's and The Body

Shop publicize mission statements which tell investors clearly that they have to share the fruits of success with employees, society and other stakeholders. Those that share the values of such companies rarely hesitate to invest in their shares.

When joint stock companies were established, shareholders would typically pass their shares down the generations. Today most shares are owned by institutions and bought and sold opportunistically. A few shares are seen as a key part of the portfolio, for example Marks and Spencer, but most are held only as long as they meet the obligations of the institution. In earlier days the directors were often the nominees of specific shareholders and were given unlimited liability in order to protect their principals. Later the greater complexity of business made it necessary to bring specific skills to the board table and executive directors had to be given wider discretion in order to direct the company. This enabled many boards to concentrate control in their hands, leaving shareholders to act as rentiers. After the Second World War the rapid expansion and progressive integration of businesses into larger groups led to a diminution in the power of the holding company boards, who were forced to give greater discretion to the managers of business units in order to maintain the impetus of growth. This extension of power to match the increasing dispersal of operating units also opened the door for trades unions to extend their influence and membership. In the resulting confrontations involved stakeholders fought for power, largely ignoring shareholders and holding company boards, so that relationships with customers and suppliers also became more confrontational and operations were increasingly bedevilled by strikes, quality failures and inefficiencies.

By the end of the 1970s the postwar experiment with social policies and Keynesian economics gave way to a new wave of individualism and monetarism. For some twenty years business flourished as a result, initially, of large increases in defence expenditure which broke the back of communism, and latterly of a dramatic growth in world markets. According to the Joseph Rowntree Foundation, between 1979 and 1994 the incomes of the poorest 10 per cent of Britons, adjusted for housing costs, fell 13 per cent, while those of the top 10 per cent rose 60 per cent. In this period power moved back to the centre, to Whitehall and to corporate HQ, as information technology facilitated control and large operational units were 'downsized' or sold off. Holding company boards were able to reward themselves with ever-increasing bonuses based on the profits derived from restructuring. The fear of unemployment made it harder for most employees to improve their lot, with the exception of those with special skills in high demand. At this time the concept of shareholder value won increasing support, encouraged by investment houses competing for business and by pension funds which found themselves increasingly in competition with each other.

Today there is growing talk about social inclusivity and of the need to recognize and balance the claims of different stakeholders. New stakeholders are emerging, notably the natural environment and future generations. Long-forgotten ethnic groups are staking claims, Aboriginees in Australia, Inuits in Canada and North American Indians. Groups without votes, such as other species, are having their claims advanced by human beings with the right to vote. Shall we eventually have lobbyists claiming stakes for the dead? Might that not prove enormously expensive in some cases?

SHAREHOLDER VALUE

Francis Gouillart and James Kelly (*Transforming the Organization*, McGraw-Hill, 1995) see the origins of the concept of shareholder value in the activities of corporate raiders, such as Carl Icahn, T. Boone Pickens and Lord Hanson. These were the first people to dissect living companies and find 'breakup value' within them. They developed techniques such as 'Shareholder Value Analysis' (SVA) which later evolved into 'Economic Value Added Analysis', known as EVA.

After the corporate raiders had taken over and dismantled some one-third of the world's most powerful corporations in the 1980s, company directors began to look at their own companies through the eyes of a raider. GEC began to break up only when threatened with takeover; ICI also reacted to the same pressure and split into two businesses. In the USA Sears restructured its whole business in 1993 and increased its market value from $8 billion to $25 billion. To do so it had to shut its catalogue business and sell off strategic stakes in its financial services businesses. During the past fifteen years there has been a growing volume of buyouts and buy-ins of business units which did not meet the criteria of creating shareholder value or of sustaining the core focus of the group.

The use of SVA and EVA techniques has not only helped to restructure businesses but has enabled clear profit and investment targets to be driven down to the lowest operating levels. This strengthens the hand of group directors in the strategic management process and makes it easier to manage reward systems throughout the group.

The issue of shareholder value has been focused primarily on serving the interests of shareholders. A significant part of the growth in stock market indices has been driven by shareholder value, even where buyouts and buy-ins have enriched their new owners handsomely. The search for shareholder value has also increased directors' bonuses and the rewards of those who manage key parts of the group business portfolio. In achieving shareholder value most companies have also outsourced many services which were previously managed in-house. This has enriched service providers, such as Andersen, EDS, Manpower, Compass and a host of small businesses offering sporadic support.

Shareholder value began as an instrument of 'financial engineering', aimed at enriching corporate raiders over the short-term. With EVA there is now growing emphasis on long-term shareholder value, which allows for higher levels of targeted investment and focused expenditure on research and development. The decline of conglomerates such as BTR and Hanson, contrasted with the sustained growth of strategically-managed businesses such as Shell, Unilever and Marks and Spencer, has made thoughtful investors aware of 'the long game', developed and played so successfully by groups such as Berkshire Hathaway.

There remains the question of how the benefits of shareholder value should be distributed among stakeholders. Will Hutton (*The State to Come*, Vintage, 1997) sees a significant shift coming, driven by the New Labour programme:

> In the labour market, for example, trade unions will be strengthened in their capacity to represent workers and there will be a minimum wage. Even if there is nothing more than a change to the capital gains tax regime and the launch of closer links between institutional shareholders and British companies, that will trigger important 'reflexive' changes in a stakeholding direction and encourage more initiatives thereafter.

In an article in *Harvard Business Review* (November/December 1997) entitled 'What's Wrong with Strategy?' Andrew Campbell and Marcus Alexander examine the issue of 'stakeholder value'. They see it not as an objective but as an economic constraint. They define competitive advantage as 'a requirement for retaining stakeholders' support over the long term'. Their way of achieving this is by engaging stakeholders in order to develop superior insights into what they value and turning these insights into effective strategies. VW achieved this by focusing on the average family. As Campbell and Alexander say 'developing a winning strategy is messier than most textbooks suggest'. However, if the strategies are successful, they will not only bring stakeholder value but will also build long-term shareholder value.

Given the pressures of global competition there would seem to be a firm case for continuing to maximize long-term shareholder value. In order to do so, it seems likely that the long-term benefits will need to be shared more equitably with the stakeholders who can demonstrate that they are contributing to their achievement. Others who claim to be stakeholders but who do not contribute to a company's long-term success, or who are seeking to tax that success for their own purposes, will have to be managed firmly and contained.

KEY ISSUES

1   Do I have a clear idea of the range of contacts which may be considered to be stakeholders?
2   Can I distinguish between real stakeholders and those who wish only to exploit our company?
3   Can I identify the trade-offs we should make with each stakeholder?

What action am I committing myself to take? _____

4

THE HISTORY OF CORPORATE GOVERNANCE

The developed world has moved from the Agricultural Age, through the Industrial Age and now stands at the threshold of the Information Age. We have moved from feudalism, through industrialization towards globalization. In this journey governance has evolved to match new needs and increasing accountabilities. In extreme circumstances governance is an instrument of survival, as with the focus of early Egyptian governance on placating the gods and ensuring the annual flooding of the Nile. Here there can be no tolerance of dissent or of change (the reforms of Akhnaton were annihilated on his death).

We have seen the development of governance through the years of ruler/priesthood dominance, through feudalism (which lost its effective power when the Black Death raised the value of labour), to the exploitation of the Industrial Revolution and the rise of capitalism in the last century. J.K. Galbraith (*Money*, Penguin 1975) sees capitalism as having been driven by high prices and low wages, generating 'high savings and a strong incentive to their investment'. The initial impetus came from the wealth looted from the Americas and was sustained by closed systems of trading with the colonies.

The gradual growth of trades unions in the first half of this century began to offset the power of companies which had been able to force down wages to maintain profits even as trading became more competitive. This phenomenon made governance more complex, adding a new dimension to the shareholder/board of directors axis. This situation was consolidated by the need to work together through the war and the unions entered the second half of the century with enhanced and growing power. The war also strengthened the impact of government on businesses, bringing in a mass of new regulations many of which survive their usefulness.

By the third quarter of this century corporate governance had evolved into a process in which the main protagonists were managers of operating units and the shop stewards of the trades unions. National wage agreements, negotiated by company representatives and trades unions, provided a framework within which local deals were fought out and used to escalate wages through arguments of 'comparability'. Often the unions were able to negotiate deals over the heads of local managers with the group managing director or chairman. For a number of years until the early 1980s company directors seemed to be preoccupied with avoiding strikes rather than making profits. Over this period a number of major industries were damaged beyond redemption, including the motor industry, shipbuilding and motorcycles. The aircraft industry was only rescued by government intervention. The trades unions also gained the initiative in the governance of most public sector activities, notably in coal mining, local government and the health service.

As the shortages created by the war disappeared and companies found themselves increasingly obliged to compete for customers, the power of customers as stakeholders grew steadily. Driven by the expanding influence of advertising, in particular on television, a consumer revolution took place in the 1960s which stimulated consumption and encouraged greed. Consumerism further weakened producer power and was supported by politicians who sought consumer votes. Government had to cope with a series of 'stop-go' cycles, caused by consumer booms and macroeconomic busts. Attitudes to borrowing changed as consumers sought out new sources of credit to feed their desire for durable goods. Consumer greed and gullibility helped to create the climate in which corporate governance met a new series of challenges.

One of the earlier challenges was the Rolls Razor scandal. John Bloom bought Rolls Razor and used it to manufacture and market cheap washing machines with tempting hire purchase terms. The result was an uncontrollable bubble in which large numbers of consumers lost their deposits and suppliers became unsecured creditors. In the mid-1970s a cut-price retailer, Brentford Nylons, went into receivership having recently reported profits of £130 000. About the same time scandal hit Lloyd's, the London insurance house, when a star underwriter, Ian Posgate, was accused of writing business for his own account. The growing volume of takeovers in the mid-late 1970s also produced a number of accusations of 'insider trading' but few convictions.

A decade later the scandals were on a larger scale and involved 'bigger fish'. The cult of greed had developed further and the beginning of the privatization programme in the UK took greed potentially into every household, particularly as many had become capitalists by buying council property at subsidized prices. In a climate where personal gain was the key motivating force it was not surprising that impatient people at all levels sought quick returns. Companies were built by takeovers, funded often by debt, so that their directors could earn ever larger bonuses. The Bank of Credit and Commerce International grew like a mushroom from a small Pakistani bank into an international giant with a significant presence in most key markets. In 1980 Polly Peck had been a small UK textiles company until it became the vehicle for Asil Nadir's ambitions. In 1986 John Gunn became chairman of British and Commonwealth, having made a reputation for creating wealth at Exco, a money broker. In three years he had borrowed nearly £2 billion and had created an opportunistic collection of disparate companies. Robert Maxwell, an adventurer who had earlier been blacklisted as a company director, built an empire comprising a number of private companies and two quoted companies, Maxwell Communications Corporation and Mirror Group Newspapers. This empire enabled him to indulge in a high-profile lifestyle appropriate for a successful man at that time.

The recession of the late 1980s, combined with special circumstances in each case, caused the collapse of all these groups in the early 1990s. Hubris was a common factor, fraud was a key element in most of them and damage was done not only to shareholders, but to employees, suppliers and, in the case of Maxwell, pensioners. Questions about the effectiveness of banking supervision at BCCI and of DTI supervision in the other cases, remain unanswered. Other corporate failures at the time and subsequently, Coloroll, Brent Walker, Barlow Clowes, Barings and many more, have only increased the sense of betrayal on all sides. In addition to these dramatic failures we have seen the progressive destruction of wealth in many businesses, such as TSB, and the painful decline of companies built on individual power, including Lonrho and Hanson. This nemesis has caused the beginning of a reappraisal of the whole purpose and process of business enterprise which will probably continue well into the next century.

CAUSES OF GOVERNANCE PROBLEMS

From the history of corporate governance can we identify the key causes of failure so that they can be addressed and, hopefully, remedied? It would seem that these key causes probably fall under the following headings:

O   A culture of secrecy
O   Tribal loyalties
O   Legislative weaknesses
O   Lack of commitment.

It may be useful to explore these causes in more detail:

A CULTURE OF SECRECY

Secrecy has been endemic in British society for many years. Britons tend to be private individuals and slow to share confidences. Salaries are hidden from wives and information given on a 'need to know' basis. When many Britons die, the extent of their wealth (or debts) often surprises their legatees. This secrecy extends to government (The Official Secrets Act 1911) and to most social or business activities.

This culture leads to governance by discretion rather than by rules. The UK has no written constitution and our governance at all levels is pragmatic rather than codified. The City of London has been run largely by self-regulation, relying on a club culture to keep individuals in line. This has begun to fail, most notably in the collapse of Lloyds as a result of systematic abuse within certain syndicates, and in fraud cases such as Distillers. It is also noteworthy that prosecutions for fraud involving City institutions have largely failed, leaving the Serious Fraud Office with a tarnished record.

TRIBAL LOYALTIES

British society is as tribal as most but differs from some in the 'class' structure of its tribalism. This has created governance structures which tend to rely heavily on the 'great and good' of society. These are people of similar background and education and who find it easy to work together. Unfortunately this creates a false loyalty in many cases, leading to the protection of those who have failed and to the covering up of fraud in some cases. It is to help the discovery of fraud and to protect 'whistle-blowers' that a Public Interest Disclosure Bill is being sponsored in Parliament with Government support. This will detail 'qualifying disclosures' which will give protection to the 'whistleblowers'. Such protection will depend largely on having acted in good faith.

Even when companies fail dramatically, it is unusual for directors to be sued successfully in the absence of fraud. John Crowther expanded Coloroll at an unsustainable pace and drove his company into administration. Like many directors in such a situation his loss was little more than a damaged career. Are all parties involved in the excitement of the rise of businesses like Coloroll in some way implicated in their subsequent failure, so that they share the group hangover that follows the party as an alternative to assaulting their host?

LEGISLATIVE WEAKNESSES

The outcome of trials under English law has been very unpredictable. This is due in part to a legal structure which is heavily dependent on case law, and also to the difficulty of securing convictions in criminal cases, where juries are involved. The discharge of the Maxwell brothers on a charge of fraud in respect of the Mirror Group Pensions Fund was a surprise to all who were spectators. Pensions law itself depends on the imperfect structure of English trust law: under present pensions law companies may claw back 'surpluses' in their pension funds identified by actuaries, even though pension funds are legally independent of the companies whose employees they serve. Companies like Lucas/Varity and W H Smith have taken refunds from their pension funds rather than adjust their contributions to future needs. Many companies do not have separate bank accounts for their pension funds; those that do are often heavily in arrears in funding pensions.

English insolvency laws are also open to manipulation. The complexity of this area of law has been compounded by case law and has been exploited by some unscrupulous operators. Many have been very skilful in moving assets from sinking companies to secure havens and it has even been possible for 'rogue' directors to escape both legal liability and pursuit by the DTI. One extreme example was the provision by Xchange Corporate Services of 'substitute directors' resident overseas to replace the directors of sinking companies and to take legal responsibility for the inevitable insolvency of those companies. This service has been stopped by intervention by the Insolvency Practitioners Association, but similar ways to manipulate the insolvency laws remain.

Another major area of weakness is the structure of accounting regulations which shape financial reporting by companies. In his book *Accounting for Growth* (Century Business, 1992), Terry Smith illustrates the various techniques used to camouflage weaknesses in company operations in presenting their accounts. So controversial was this book that the author lost his job in the City. At one extreme the book illustrates how companies like Polly Peck can declare profits and be in receivership within a few days; at the other extreme routine window-dressing techniques, such as capitalizing costs, are examined. Accounting standards are issued by the Accounting Standards Board, following a process of discussion through the Accounting Standards Committee based on Exposure Drafts issued by the Institute of Chartered Accountants. This process is very thorough but, like the 'mills of God', it grinds slowly, so that 'creative accounting' is invariably one step at least ahead of the regulatory process. It was, in part, for these reasons that the Cadbury Committee focused on the financial aspects of corporate governance.

One area of law which has been changed to reflect a general desire for greater accountability is the scope of criminal responsibility. English law has traditionally maintained that only a natural person can have criminal responsibility so that for every major disaster a scapegoat has needed to be found. When the 'Herald of Free Enterprise' sank in the Channel because of failure to close its bow doors before departure, the blame was laid initially on the crew until further investigation revealed a reckless attitude to safety in pursuit of profitability which pervaded the whole operating company, Townsend Thoresen. Out of this incident came a change in the law which created corporate criminal responsibility, making the directors jointly and severally liable to prosecution. Companies have always been open to actions in tort, but the risk of criminal responsibility now forces directors to improve governance processes throughout their business operations since they can no longer pass criminal responsibility down to operating levels of the company without challenge.

LACK OF COMMITMENT

Stakeholders in a company have always had their individual agendas and have tended to use that company to serve their ends. Employees were 'loyal' to the company while it offered lifetime employment and promotion prospects, but tended to live their real lives outside their working environment. Customers had a growing range of choice and would only remain with the company if it offered exceptional value and service. Suppliers were eager to work with the company on their terms but resentful of pressure and arbitrary demands. Directors saw their role as 'empire builders' in preparation for their next career move. Shareholders, by now predominantly institutions, saw their investment as a 'punt' – to be retained while building short-term value and sold at the first sign of difficulty.

These different agendas have created a lack of commitment to the company on the part of its stakeholders. Even the so-called 'company man' of the 1960s was not loyal but basically self-serving. Customers and suppliers have tended to see their relationship with the company as something to be exploited rather than nurtured. Directors have been inclined to see their role as one of short-term maximization rather than as a stewardship for the long-term. In the UK there have been few strategic investors like Berkshire Hathaway in the USA; the growth of venture capitalism in the UK has brought some commitment for that sector, but an exit strategy is the first consideration of any investment.

THE CADBURY COMMITTEE

The Cadbury Committee was established in May 1991 by the Financial Reporting Council of the London Stock Exchange and the accountancy profession in order to address the financial aspects of corporate governance. The terms of reference of the Committee were:

> To consider the following issues in relation to financial reporting and accountability and to make recommendations on good practice:

(a) the responsibilities of executive and non-executive directors for reviewing and reporting on performance to shareholders and other financially interested parties; and the frequency, clarity and form in which information should be provided;

(b) the case for audit committees of the board, including their composition and role;

(c) the principal responsibilities of auditors and the extent and value of the audit;

(d) the links between shareholders, boards and auditors;

(e) and other relevant matters.

When it reported in December 1992 the Committee recommended a Code of Best Practice in the following terms:

1   The Board of Directors

1.1 The board should meet regularly, retain full and effective control over the company and monitor the executive management.

1.2 There should be a clearly accepted division of responsibilities at the head of a company, which will ensure a balance of power and authority, such that no one individual has unfettered powers of decision. Where the chairman is also the chief executive, it is essential that there should be a strong and independent element on the board, with a recognised senior member.

1.3 The board should include non-executive directors of sufficient calibre and number for their views to carry significant weight in the board's decisions.

1.4 The board should have a formal schedule of matters specifically reserved to it for decisions to ensure that the direction and control of the company is firmly in its hands.

1.5 There should be an agreed procedure for directors in the furtherance of their duties to take independent professional advice if necessary, at the company's expense.

1.6 All directors should have access to the advice and services of the company secretary, who is responsible to the board for ensuring that board procedures are followed and that applicable rules and regulations are complied with. Any question of the removal of the company secretary should be a matter for the board as a whole.

2   Non-Executive Directors

2.1 Non-executive directors should bring an independent judgement to bear on issues of strategy, performance, resources, including key appointments, and standards of conduct.

2.2 The majority should be independent of management and free from any business or other relationship which could materially interfere with the exercise of their independent judgement, apart from their fees and shareholding. Their fees should reflect the time which they commit to the company.

2.3 Non-executive directors should be appointed for specified terms and reappointment should not be automatic.

2.4 Non-executive directors should be selected through a formal process and both this process and their appointment should be a matter for the board as a whole.

3   Executive Directors

3.1 Directors' service contracts should not exceed three years without shareholders' approval.

3.2 There should be full and clear disclosure of directors' total emoluments and those of the chairman and highest-paid UK director, including pension contributions and stock options. Separate figures should be given for salary and performance-related elements and the basis on which performance is measured should be explained.

3.3 Executive directors' pay should be subject to the recommendations of a remuneration committee made up wholly or mainly of non-executive directors.

4. Reporting and Controls

4.1 It is the board's duty to present a balanced and understandable assessment of the company's position.

4.2 The board should ensure that an objective and professional relationship is maintained with the auditors.

4.3 The board should establish an audit committee of at least 3 non-executive directors with written terms of reference which deal clearly with its authority and duties.

4.4 The directors should explain their responsibility for preparing the accounts next to a statement by the auditors about their reporting responsibilities.

4.5 The directors should report on the effectiveness of the company's system of internal control.

4.6 The directors should report that the business is a going concern, with supporting assumptions or qualifications as necessary.

Companies quoted on the London Stock Exchange are now required to report annually to shareholders on their conformity with the Code. After an initial period of indifference institutional investors are increasingly taking note of areas of non-compliance. The Code is beginning to be seen as a 'floor' rather than as a 'ceiling', and the better companies now seek to set best practice in key areas. For example, the Code recommends a maximum period of three years for executive directors' contracts: best practice is now one year or less.

Sir Adrian Cadbury recognized when the Committee was formed that finance was not the sole dimension to governance, but that it was the most urgent area to codify in the wake of the scandals of the late 1980s. Wider issues of governance have been explored by the RSA's 'Tomorrow's Company' enquiry, in default of a Cadbury II study, which is examined in Case Study 5.1.

The work of the Cadbury Committee now appears to have laid a foundation on which others can build. This process has proceeded in three directions: first, the further development of codes of practice; second, the exploration of wider governance issues; and, third, the drive for better practice from enlightened company directors. The process is given added impetus by activists such as PIRC (see Case Study 4.2), who are concerned to improve shareholder value. The further development of codes of practice has been spearheaded by the Greenbury and Hampel Committees.

THE GREENBURY COMMITTEE

The impetus for the Greenbury Report came from public disgust at the large increases in remuneration which the boards of newly-privatized utilities appeared to be awarding themselves. The Cadbury Report had addressed remuneration in general terms; the Greenbury Committee was asked to explore issues of directors' remuneration in greater detail.

The Cadbury Committee took two years to report, and the later Hampel Committee deliberated for nearly three years, whereas Sir Richard Greenbury and his team had a deadline which gave them only five months to prepare their report.

The Greenbury Report addressed the remit 'to identify good practice in determining Directors' remuneration and prepare a Code of such practice for use by UK PLCs'. The Code of Best Practice produced by the Committee may be summarized as follows:

O   Code provisions to apply to large companies and principles to apply to smaller companies.

O   Listed companies to report annually compliance with the Code; Remuneration Committees to report on remuneration issues covered by the Code.

O   Remuneration Committee of the Board to comprise solely non-executive directors and to account directly to shareholders annually.

O   The Board to determine the fees of non-executive directors.

O   The Remuneration Committee report to give full details of all elements of remuneration, including basic salary, benefits in kind, annual bonuses and long-term incentive salaries, including share options.

O   The report to detail pension entitlements earned during the year, justifying any entitlements linked other than to basic salary.

O   The report to disclose any service contracts with notice in excess of one year.

O   Shareholders to approve any awards which commit shareholders' funds beyond one year or dilute equity.

O   Remuneration to be judged by performance relative to other companies.

O   Bonuses to be challenging and upper limits considered.

O   Share options and share awards not to vest in less than three years.

O   Share options never to be issued at a discount and normally to be phased over time.

O   The consequences of salary increases on pension entitlement for older directors to be considered.

O   If service contracts of over one year's notice are needed to recruit key directors the notice period to decline to one year after an initial period.

O Compensation for loss of office to reflect the need to mitigate loss, where appropriate, and to be payable in instalments.

Companies listed on the London Stock Exchange are now requested to report performance against the Code's recommendations but, like Cadbury, compliance is not mandatory. It is too early to judge how effective the Greenbury recommendations will be, as they were strongly resisted at the time of publication by a number of interested parties and have been ignored by some companies, such as British Gas. The issue of share options has been contentious, involving technical considerations of taxation and of 'phantom options', which have not been well understood or accurately reported. Pension payments have been even more contentious because of the large sums needed to fund big awards late in life.

The Greenbury Report has unleashed a range of concerns and emotions which is greater than the impact of Cadbury. It is still too early to judge the long-term effect of Greenbury, but it has begun to force greater openness into the issue of remuneration and will, it is to be hoped, bring greater account-ability in time. Public concern with fairness often masks envy, but there is a sense that Greenbury has forced the debate on rewards into the public arena and that doubtful practice will be easier to challenge in future if shareholders are motivated to do so. If they do not do so on a consistent basis, high profile rewards like Martin Sorrell's £25 million, 3-year package for rescuing WPP will continue to distort the real agenda of corporate governance.

Both the Cadbury and Greenbury Reports recommended the establish-ment of a committee to assess progress with their implementation in due time. The Hampel Committee started work in November 1995 on this study.

THE HAMPEL COMMITTEE

The focus of the Hampel Committee enquiry was firmly on the financial issues addressed by Cadbury and Greenbury. The terms of its remit were:

> The committee will seek to promote high standards of corporate gover-nance in the interests of investor protection and in order to preserve and enhance the standing of companies listed on the Stock Exchange. The committee's remit will extend to listed companies only.
>
> Against this background the committee will:
>
> (a) conduct a review of the Cadbury code and its implementation to ensure that the original purpose is being achieved, proposing amendments to and deletions from the code as necessary;
> (b) keep under review the role of directors, executive and non-executive, recognising the need for board cohesion and the common legal responsibilities of all directors;

(c) be prepared to pursue any relevant matters arising from the report of the Study Group on directors' Remuneration chaired by Sir Richard Greenbury;

(d) address as necessary the role of shareholders in corporate governance issues;

(e) address as necessary the role of auditors in corporate governance issues; and

(f) deal with any other relevant matters.

Without impairing investor protection the committee will always keep in mind the need to restrict the regulatory burden on companies, for example, by substituting principles for detail wherever possible.

When the Hampel Committee started work there was a sense in some quarters that the earlier committees' findings had been too prescriptive and that an approach based on principles, such as that of the Nolan Committee on 'Standards in Public Life' was more appropriate. The Nolan Committee has distilled the following 'Seven Principles of Public Life':

1   Selflessness
2   Integrity
3   Objectivity
4   Openness
5   Honesty
6   Leadership
7   Accountability.

Whether these principles would be heartily embraced by company directors in their entirety may be open to discussion; where principles are subject to equivocation, the need for regulation becomes more compelling.

In the event the Hampel Committee tried to address the positive aspect of self-regulation, rather than the negative influences which had preoccupied Cadbury and Greenbury. They saw the need for the board of directors to enhance the prosperity of the business over time and 'to take into account' the relevant interests of stakeholders in the company's business. There is some dilution of the Cadbury emphasis on separating the roles of chairman and chief executive, and the independence of non-executive directors and recognition of the dubiousness of paying them partially in company shares. A set of principles and code of practice were published in June 1998 which recommend that 'box ticking' as required by Cadbury and Greenbury be dropped in favour of a 'narrative account' of how the Hampel principles are applied. If we consider that many of the biggest rogues have been fluent and convincing writers, it has to be questionable whether Hampel has advanced the work of Cadbury and Greenbury, or merely made it easier to avoid specific accountability. It is significant that Margaret Beckett, the Industry Secretary, has been critical of the lack of strategic emphasis in the Hampel Report at the draft stage. This raises the spectre of legislation if corporate governance does not become 'more open, transparent and accountable'. Since those criticisms, the National Association of Pension Funds has moved to improve self-regulation in order to reduce the risk of legislation to enforce better governance.

BEYOND HAMPEL

In the same way that Sir Adrian Cadbury saw the need for a wider approach to corporate governance beyond the focus on financial issues in the Cadbury Report, the Hampel Committee saw a need to use governance to build 'business prosperity', but did not address the question of how it would be done, or how the different stakeholders in the company would be 'taken into account'. After three major enquiries the financial issues of corporate governance have been identified and explored, largely from a standpoint of improving controls and board processes rather than from a conviction that continuous improvement in governance can be a powerful competitive weapon. A challenging view of the way forward for corporate governance is given by LEX of *Financial Times* in Case Study 4.1 in Part II of this book.

Beyond Hampel there lie a number of opportunities for better corporate governance which may include:

O   a convergence of governance criteria with the public sector to reflect a more integrated modern world;

O   the chance to reach beyond the shareholder/board of directors relationship to include customers, employees, suppliers and others who deliver results for the company;

O   the chance to use good governance to build competitive advantage in the long-term;

O   the chance to widen stewardship to build a platform for a long-term sustainable growth of profits.

CONVERGENCE WITH PUBLIC SECTOR GOVERNANCE

The process of globalization is breaking down barriers within and across societies. In the nineteenth century those who were 'in trade' were despised by the intellectuals and amateurs who ran society. Business developed as a separate activity and culture from public service and the voluntary sector. In practice the distinction was less than absolute and diminished over time. Business often supported politicians who allowed it to make monopoly profits, as happened under Hitler, and developed a culture of flaunting wealth – Sir Thomas Lipton was by no means unique in this respect. This urge to flaunt wealth in order to achieve acceptance in society may be seen today in the antics of some trading 'stars' in the City of London; it certainly played a major role in the tragedy of Robert Maxwell.

The public sector has seen many examples of greed and corruption, many of them surrounding the granting of contracts and planning permissions. Some offenders, such as T. Dan Smith, have been successfully prosecuted, but most have not. It was concern about the standard of conduct of holders of public office which led John Major to commission the Nolan enquiry which now continues its work under the chairmanship of Lord Neill. The Seven Principles distilled by Nolan were quoted earlier and have enjoyed considerable support. Given that the distinctions between the public and private sectors are diminishing as societies become more integrated, is it too much to expect that 'selflessness' and 'objectivity' may be adopted by company directors as well as town clerks? Company directors are only stewards and have no proprietorial rights over their jobs; non-executive directors are expected to provide 'objectivity', but does this license executive directors to exercise bias?

It would be fruitful to consider the findings of the Nolan Committee in the context of the private sector. If we seek an integrated and contented society, does it not make sense to play to the same rules? Milton Friedman saw the role of the board of directors as seeking to increase profits while remaining within 'the rules of the game'. As companies and society become more interdependent it will surely become increasingly impossible to play different games!

REACHING OUT TO OTHER STAKEHOLDERS

Cadbury, Greenbury and Hampel all focus on the board of directors and its relationship with shareholders. This is the area defined by the Companies Acts and is perceived to be the area in which governance is exercised. With the growth and increasing complexity of companies it is no longer possible to manage a business from the boardroom (if it ever was), as results are achieved by people who work with customers, suppliers and others, supported by employees inside the business. Without the active support of employees, customers, suppliers, distributors and others a company cannot sustain and develop its business. Modern companies have become a widespread and complex business system which extends well beyond the boundaries of the company itself. The success of the company depends on the effectiveness of the whole system.

The 'Tomorrow's Company' movement, examined in Case Study 5.1, has begun to address the wider agenda of corporate governance. Despite strong opposition from 'traditionalist' thinkers and many company chairmen, such as Sir Stanley Kalms of Dixons, there appears to be a growing acceptance of the need to develop a more inclusive approach to corporate governance if it is to be effective as well as ethical.

BUILDING LONG-TERM COMPETITIVE ADVANTAGE

British business has been accused for many years of 'short termism'. Memories of damage done to profits in the years after the war by trades union militancy and of occasional but limited bursts of inflation seem to linger in the minds of managers and investors. Even today, with inflation at a low level and profitability rising for some years, investment hurdle rates remain at 15/20 per cent and levels of investment in Britain remain low relative to most other markets. Where companies have failed to deliver constantly growing returns on shareholders' funds, year after year, companies have been subjected to 'downsizing' or have been dismembered.

Corporate governance is not a mechanism for feeding higher annual dividends to institutional investors. It has a strategic dimension which has not been developed by the earlier enquiries, which have been City-sponsored. In the same way that shareholder value thinking has begun to focus on long-term growth of value, it must now be time for corporate governance to focus on building long-term competitive advantage. Few company directors see beyond their tenure of office; it may be one of the strengths of family-owned companies that there is as much concern for a healthy inheritance as there is for immediate benefits. Company directors need to think like farmers and plan their stewardship to pass on a stronger business to their successors.

In order to achieve long-term competitive advantage, companies will need to prioritize strategic management and run operationally within a strong strategic framework. This issue is crucial for continued success, and it will be important to involve all stakeholders in the process of developing and delivering strategy. Chapter 7 addresses this matter in more detail.

WIDER STEWARDSHIP AND SUSTAINABLE PROFITS

As a company improves its control of its internal processes, it will become increasingly aware of the factors outside its boundaries which it cannot control. Many of these factors, such as government, are stakeholders with whom it must negotiate. Beyond these lie issues such as poverty, health, law and order, education, defence, culture and the environment which impact on the company, often in unwelcome ways. In his book *The Hungry Spirit* (Hutchinson, 1997) Charles Handy envisages the 'Citizen Company' which would engage in some of these issues in order to make a contribution to the society in which it operates. Such an approach would also help to compensate for the progressive withdrawal of government from the structures of the 'nanny' state. The growing complexity of modern society makes it difficult for governments, even at a devolved level, to understand local issues and manage them economically. If they try to do so, the costs fall on companies as taxation; if it allows companies to involve themselves, where appropriate, the results may be more satisfactory.

Many companies are already active in their local communities. 'Business in the Community' is a movement which was founded 15 years ago and is now active throughout the UK. The main objective of the movement is to achieve the social and economic regeneration of blighted communities. Much of this is done by task forces from companies, supported by member company donations, and new issues such as the environment and opportunities for minorities are being addressed. 'Business in the Community' is a beginning but not the final answer. A MORI poll in 1997 showed that 68 per cent of the general public believed that business did not pay enough attention to its social responsibilities. The evidence from the limited involvement to date is that it is building bridges between companies and their local communities, removing distrust and creating goodwill. A survey done in 1996 showed that 86 per cent of consumers would be more likely to buy a product associated with a cause they support, and that 33 per cent actually had done so.

It would seem that companies are increasingly reliant on the wider community which surrounds them, which in turn needs the support and resources which few others apart from companies can give. This is a stakeholding relationship which good governance needs to recognize and which can make a company distinctive to those who deal with it. Companies which share values with their wider communities are likely to generate sustainable profitability to share with them also.

KEY ISSUES

1   Governance is threatened by secrecy, tribalism, poor legislation and lack of commitment – do we understand the implications for our organization?
2   How does our organization rate in respect of the Cadbury, Greenbury and Hampel codes?
3   Are we thinking beyond Hampel to wider issues of governance?

What action am I committing myself to take? _____

5

OTHER MODELS OF CORPORATE GOVERNANCE

❖

In his book *Managing for the Future* (Butterworth Heinemann, 1992), Peter Drucker refers back to the model of 'corporate capitalism' which was in vogue in the 1960s. Corporate capitalism was aimed at the creation of a limited number of huge multinational corporations which would be run by autonomous managements in the best interests of all stakeholders and society as a whole. This model never really existed except in glossy annual reports, since managements found that they were not autonomous and were increasingly obliged to report higher earnings each quarter in order to satisfy Wall Street. When managements stumbled, they became easy targets for the corporate raiders – speculative capitalism took over from corporate capitalism. Nevertheless Peter Drucker feels that corporate capitalism, even though it found the wrong answers, probably asked the right questions.

THE AMERICAN MODEL

Corporate governance has developed in the USA along lines not dissimilar to those in the UK. Many Continentals talk of an 'Anglo-Saxon' model of corporate governance, seeing the US and British regimes as interchangeable. There are, however, some significant differences:

- An open society
- Stronger regulation
- The relative success of US capitalism
- The role of the corporate raiders and junk bonds.

49

It may be interesting to explore these differences in more detail:

AN OPEN SOCIETY

The USA was established as an open society, with a written constitution which protects freedom in all its aspects. Although less class-conscious than British society, the USA has its own tribes and its own inter-group rivalries. Because of its strong libertarian tradition the USA developed a challenging Press before the UK and there is a Freedom of Information Act which militates against the secrecy which damages British society.

STRONGER REGULATION

The threat to American society from the concentrated power of the large industrial trusts at the end of the last century created a culture where business is respected but not trusted. This has led to a strong framework of laws to control companies and an independent organ for regulating investments, the Securities and Exchange Commission. Regulation is also strong in areas of safety, health and the environment. Regulation in the USA is effected both at federal and state level in many instances. The failure of the regulation of the Savings and Loan institutions caused losses of up to $80 billion. This has given a timely warning of the need to match regulation with consistent objectives.

THE RELATIVE SUCCESS OF US CAPITALISM

The USA has the largest economy in the world and the highest concentration of companies quoted on stock exchanges. It also has the most entrepreneurial economy, creating 900 000 new businesses each year but seeing 800 000 die in the same period. In 1996 $10 billion venture capital was raised, of which 37 per cent went into start-ups (Europe only invested 12 per cent of venture capital raised in start-ups). One in four American households owns a business or has an interest in someone else's business.

THE ROLE OF THE CORPORATE RAIDERS AND JUNK BONDS

Aggressive takeover bids are a feature of Anglo-Saxon corporate life, but in the USA they were stimulated by shareholder value analysis techniques which produced blueprints for corporate breakups. This enabled corporate raiders to attack companies in order to release value for shareholders, adding to the existing hazard of aggressive bids from other companies. This phenomenon became highly geared when 'junk bonds' were used to fund ever-higher bids. Michael Milken, the creator of 'junk bonds', was jailed for fraud but not before considerable damage was done. The positive outcome of the corporate raids was a growing recognition of the need for American business to focus on shareholder value or face the consequences.

One other significant change as a result of the activities of the corporate raiders was an increase in the involvement of institutional shareholders in the governance of the companies where they had significant stakes. This led to greater pressure on boards to generate long-term value and to cope with crises. Shareholder intervention unseated a growing number of CEOs, notably at General Motors, IBM, Kodak and American Express.

As a result of bruising competition with the Japanese and other Asians, US companies have been forced to re-engineer themselves to reduce costs and to concentrate on their core competences. In some areas, such as defence, there has been devastating rationalization and this process has been driven largely by a search for shareholder value. American boards have focused on becoming more professional. As Ira M. Millstein says in an article 'The Professional Board' in *The Business Lawyer* (November 1995).

> Increased professionalism in the boardroom is at the core of the important role directors play, not only in the corporation but – through the corporation – in the wider economy .... Viewed from this perspective, boards of directors are not only fiduciaries for their respective owners and less directly accountable to other corporate constituents, but they are also responsible, in effect, for their nation's economic wellbeing.

Pressure for better governance is coming not only from institutions and pension funds, like Calpers, but from the Conference Board, the American Bar Association and others. Suggested improvements include: (a) the separation of power between chairman and CEO; (b) board control over the nomination and retention of independent directors; and (c) the evaluation of CEO performance solely by independent directors in a separate meeting from that of the board.

THE GERMAN MODEL

Germany industrialized later than Britain, France and the United States and its laws and structures were designed to facilitate a rapid catching up with its rivals. Many of the models used were based on the efficient war machine developed by Prussia; for example, the *Sekretariat* of the larger German banks is modelled on the Prussian general staff. Every encouragement was given to German industrialists to invest and develop their businesses rapidly and the banks had a very material hand in that process, taking significant equity stakes in the process. It is not without significance that the German *Hausbank* system was invented by Georg Siemens and the symbiotic relationship between banks and industry has developed at all levels and over a wide range of services.

According to Peter Drucker, Konrad Adenauer detested the materialistic Germany of the Weimar Republic but reinstated it after the war because it was the only model that Germans then alive had seen to be workable. He also pointed out that Germany had suffered from corporate raiders in the 1920s, including Hugo Stinnes, Alfred Hugenberg, Friedrich Flick and the Krupp empire. Only Flick was able to survive and rebuild his empire, the others being dispossessed, made bankrupt or, in the case of Krupp, destroyed by weight of heterogeneous businesses and sold off to the Shah of Iran. It is not surprising, therefore, that Germans have been nervous of merger booms and corporate aggression ever since!

The 'German model' has evolved out of the *Hausbank* system to include in its governance its investors, both banks and strategic crossholdings, and its employee representatives. The three major banks control some 60 per cent of the share capital of Germany's large companies, either directly or through the voting rights which the banks have for shares held by their customers. Germany has various types of company structure; larger companies tend to be limited liability companies but most medium and smaller companies are private companies (*Gesellschaft mit beschränkter Haftung*) run by a manager appointed by shareholders. Germany has a two-tier board system for limited liability companies (*Aktiengesellschaften*) in which the supervisory board (*Aufsichtsrat*) comprises shareholder and employee nominees, usually in equal proportions. The second tier is the management board (*Vorstand*) which comprises solely executive directors. The role and functions of the supervisory board are clearly defined in German law and distinct from those of the management board. The function of corporate governance encompasses both boards, with the supervisory board setting strategic direction and broad policy and the management board making the plans and carrying out the functions needed to implement them. Ada Demb and Friedrich Neubauer (*The Corporate Board*, Oxford University Press, 1992) see the German model of governance as stronger than that of the USA, UK and France because of the built-in accountability to shareholders, banks and employees created by the supervisory board. In the other countries the boards are seen as weak, putting a greater onus on regulators and society to enforce good governance. In many cases, however, supervisory boards meet infrequently and are made ineffectual by their use by trades unions for purposes not connected with company policy.

For many years the German model has been given credit for the economic success of Germany since the war – the *Wirtschaftswunder*. German banks did not press for high dividends, labour unions were kept in thrall and everybody became richer every year. Takeover bids were not necessary due to cross-shareholding with key associated companies. Below the large firms was the solid and successful *Mittelstand* – largely family-owned and very conservatively managed.

In recent times German industry has seen its own scandals, notably at Metallgesellschaft and Schneider. Daimler Benz has had to be restructured due to over-expansion. It has to be asked what Deutsche Bank's representative on the different supervisory boards was doing, particularly with the detailed briefing he might have expected from his *Sekretariat*, who would have been aware of all banking transactions by the company. At one time the European Commission was interested in using the two-tier board as a model for all companies in the European Union, but questions are increasingly being asked about its effectiveness. From the research done by Demb and Neubauer it was found that supervisory and management boards often meet together. One German director was quoted thus:

> Regarding the existence of both supervisory and management boards, I think there is an advantage in the Anglo-Saxon situation where the non-executive advice is more available. They meet more frequently. On the other hand, the separation of the two boards may mean that management gets more strong criticism.

It would seem that the two-tier and single-tier models could converge over time. If they do so it should be possible to discharge their shared responsibility for governance more effectively.

THE FRENCH MODEL

The state has always been a major factor in the French business sector since Colbert established the system which supported the rule of Louis XIV. Manufacturing has traditionally been controlled by licences, with key sectors being run by the state. In the nineteenth century French industry expanded to compete with the British, using the same system of colonial markets to feed its manufacturers. This expansion was increasingly done by entrepreneurs, with state investment being concentrated on railways, roads and utilities. It was the French who pioneered the management of assets owned by local municipalities – a business which laid the foundations for the success of Société Générale des Eaux (now named Vivendi) and Société Lyonnaise des Eaux in world markets.

The state sector has tended to grow in order to underpin France's search for a leading role in the world. Vast sums have been spent to maintain an independent defence industry, to develop independence of fuel supply through having a predominantly nuclear power industry and to create world-scale financial services giants, such as Crédit Lyonnais. The private sector has grown in the shadow of this phenomenon and has tended to be defensive and undercapitalized in many key sectors. French business has traditionally used a network of crossholdings to protect itself from uncontrolled competition or takeover.

France uses a unitary board structure for limited liability companies (*sociétés anonymes*) and has a considerable number of private companies

(*sociétés à responsabilité limitée*) run by a manager responsible to shareholders, as in Germany. French boards comprise executive and non-executive directors in varying proportions. Most of the non-executive directors are
from the boards of share-linked companies or are appointed by a system of
pantouflage, in which members of the elite group of alumni of the *grandes
écoles* are placed selectively, often with government awareness.

This cosy approach to governance has been subjected to review in the
Viénot Report, issued in July 1995, which examined the working arrangements of French boards. The report is critical of the cross-shareholding
arrangements in French business and of the excessive numbers of non-executive directorships which they create. There is a call for more independent
directors and for the creation of audit, remuneration and appointment sub-
committees of the board. Comparisons with Cadbury are discounted by the
French but, with foreigners owing a third of quoted equity on the Bourse,
the impetus for change may not be solely domestic. This will be important
since the 1998 International Survey of Institutional Investors for Russell
Reynolds Associates finds that the French institutions are the least active in
corporate governance of those of any major economy.

THE JAPANESE MODEL

The classic Japanese model is that of the *zaibatsu*, the totally integrated
group engaged in manufacture, distribution, trading and finance across a
wide range of activities. This structure was adopted in order to allow Japan
to modernize quickly and to catch up economically with the West. It also
served to produce the war machine which defeated Russia in 1905 and was
itself defeated in 1945. After the 1941/45 war Japanese business groups were
broken up but they have gradually been reintegrating over the past fifty
years.

Today's Japanese model comprises a small number of *keiretsu*, the new
business groups, which are less integrated but linked by cross-shareholdings
and relationships, together with considerable numbers of smaller businesses
which supply their needs. These groups are close to government, often
employing civil servants after their retirement, and work together on gov-
ernment-sponsored committees where guidance can be given. In recent
years Japanese groups have competed vigorously between themselves, but
the Japanese model has made it difficult for foreigners to succeed in the
Japanese market.

The implications of the Japanese model for governance have been to
concentrate power in the groups of top executives, with boards acting as
conduits for the relationships with cross-shareholdings, and the network of
committees which links groups to government feeding both the board and

executive committees. Comparisons with Germany's two-tier system are too facile, since labour is not a prime stakeholder in Japanese companies and most banks are affiliates of *keiretsu* groups, not the heart of the system.

The Japanese model has had difficulties in the last few years, due to an excessive over-reliance on loans at interest rates reflecting government pressure on the savings market. Over-investment by banks in property and property loans has compounded the problem. The high value of the yen caused companies to invest heavily overseas and recent financial problems in Asia have increased their difficulties. As a result, the first cracks have been appearing in the Japanese model; bankruptcies have occurred in the shipbuilding and construction industries and have now reached the financial sector.

It is too early to assume that the Japanese model will break down totally, leading to an economy run on classical liberal principles. Japan retains a very cohesive society and the individualism which drives Anglo-Saxon economies is largely unacceptable to it. It is more likely that a new, slightly more open, model will emerge, based on Confucian principles and with the steering hand of the Ministry of Finance more discreetly on the tiller. Japan's 'big bang' is likely to be a strictly-controlled explosion.

THE RUSSIAN MODEL

It is too early to identify a distinctive Russian model of corporate governance. At this stage there are three models: (a) the earlier Soviet state-owned model, providing employment and a whole range of social services, answerable only to a relevant state ministry; (b) the privatized companies, many controlled by Russian 'banks'; and (c) new entrepreneurial businesses. Many of the present and former state-owned companies are effectively controlled by their managers, in some cases through manipulated purchases of shares, and regional governments often exercise considerable influence over companies in their domain.

Owing to the lack of relevant or enforceable laws, Russian governance is almost a misnomer. Many foreign investors have tried to buy into the privatization process and have found it very difficult to exercise any shareholder rights. Following a number of scandals, including dealings by Yukos, the oil company, with minority shareholders, the chairman of the Federal Commission for the Securities Market, Dmitry Vasiliev, has stepped in to try and impose some discipline on share dealings. The IMF is backing Vasiliev's drive for better corporate governance but, until there are greater powers of sanction, the Russian model will remain unpalatable.

THE ITALIAN MODEL

In some ways Italian capitalism reflects one of the potential outcomes of the Russian model. Italy nationalized most of its major business groups in the 1920s and is slowly privatizing them. The powerhouse of Italian success has been the dynamic small business sector, entrepreneurial and often family-controlled, which sets its own rules of corporate governance. A third sector, involving major groups like Fiat and Assicurazioni Generali, is quoted on the Stock Exchange but has most of its shares in cross-holdings which have been too labyrinthine to penetrate. At the core of most of this network lies Mediobanca, the merchant bank of the Italian establishment.

The process of globalization is forcing Italian companies to raise risk capital and to adapt their governance to meet the standards of international investors. A scandal caused by analysts' exposure of false accounting in the Mediobanca's takeover vehicle, Gemina, has further damaged Italy's 'crony capitalism', and investors have been directing capital towards medium-sized companies rather than the large holding companies whose governance remains opaque. It can only be a matter of time before the 'spider's web' of Italian shareholdings is untangled and minority shareholders are given the protection which the Italian financial markets regulator, Consob, has been promising for so long.

In Part 8 of the *Financial Times*' 'Mastering Global Business' survey (20 March 1998) Rory Knight of Templeton College points out the competitive advantage which Continental companies have enjoyed due to limited regulation. This allows companies to create pyramid ownership structures which multiply their control leverage on a limited investment base. Such arrangements are now under threat both from Brussels and from globalization, so that the competitive advantage in home markets is likely to be lost as markets become global. The future pattern of ownership seems likely to be more direct and transparent, opening the door to greater shareholder power.

THE AUSTRALIAN MODEL

For many people the Australian model of corporate governance reflects the aggressiveness of empire-builders such as Alan Bond and Rupert Murdoch, and the scams which characterized the sale of shares in 'mushroom' mining companies.

According to the 1998 International Survey of Institutional Investors carried out for Russell Reynolds Associates, the institutions have set high standards of corporate governance in Australia using the Code of Corporate Practices and Conduct as their basic model. Earlier scandals seem to have made investors more punctilious in monitoring board composition and processes and Cadbury-style rules are supported. Convergence with UK practice seems likely to continue.

As Australian companies begin to have global dimensions, as for example in the flotation of AMP, the pressure for good governance may be expected to increase.

THE LATIN AMERICAN AND DEVELOPING ECONOMY MODEL

The developing world has many economies which have been nurtured behind tariff walls and which are driven by family-based business groups. Often such economies are controlled by the issue of manufacturing licences, as in India, which favour the family groups which are close to the government. In extreme cases, such as China and Indonesia, the ruling elite are themselves involved in business, raising governance issues which can only freely be discussed outside the countries concerned.

Latin American business has been developed largely through family-based companies, the largest of which have become conglomerate empires. Bunge y Born originated in Argentina and is now based in Brazil. The Alfa Group dominates the Mexican economy and the Luksic and Anadeto Angelini family groups have a pervasive presence in Chile. In the earlier years of this century governments created a corporatist economy, with a dominant state sector which overshadowed the family groups for a number of years. This state sector is being dismantled and privatized progressively, allowing foreign capital to enter most markets. According to *The Economist* (6 December 1997) 279 companies have been sold in Latin America in the last ten years for £90 billion. Most of the privatizations have improved managerial performance and may be putting pressure on family-based groups to change their attitude to governance. *The Economist* quotes Lomnitz and Lizaure on the subject of a prominent Mexican business dynasty: 'There is no clear cut separation between family interest and business interest, or between the person of the owner and the legal personality of the firm.' More recently Alfa Group's chairman chose a nephew with degrees from Harvard and Stamford to succeed him, rather than his son. It is to be hoped that family-based groups will be freed by competition to attract the best managers to run their businesses and that a clear separation between family and business interests can be achieved.

CORPORATE GOVERNANCE IN OTHER FORMS OF ASSOCIATION

We have seen that joint stock companies are not the only form of association which can realize human aspirations. They are seen, however, as the archetypal model for corporate governance since most of the failures of governance in recent times are believed to have occurred in companies. Companies quoted on the Stock Exchange are more exposed to external scrutiny than private companies in which power is more concentrated and less publicly accountable. It may be timely and salutary to consider some other models.

PUBLIC SECTOR ORGANIZATIONS

Before the present century public sector organizations were largely major utilities or providers of material needed to support the state, such as arsenals, roads and bridges. The depression in the 1920s and 1930s, coupled with the foundation of the Soviet Union, encouraged the absorbtion of private companies into major state corporations along the lines pioneered by Mussolini in Italy. Following the 1939–45 war a further wave of nationalizations in Europe increased the state sector to a preponderant position in many economies.

In his book *A Stake in the Future* (Nicholas Brealey, 1997) John Plender sees nationalization as a policy aimed at achieving greater efficiency in key areas of the economy:

> Under the Attlee government nationalization was, in effect, a public sector version of the stakeholder concept. It was designed to offer the public a stake in industries that were expected to become more efficient, while striking a more equitable balance between the interests of workers, tax payers and consumers.

In the event this balance was not maintained and the interests of workers took precedence over those of the other stakeholders. This drove up costs and prices, causing significant long-term damage to many industries such as steel, and driving the coal industry into terminal decline. The history of nationalization shows that governance becomes unrealistic when state enterprises are insulated from the marketplace and are run to achieve political rather than commercial objectives. The demise of the nationalized industry model was, in fact, more attributable to government interference than to abuse by trades unions.

Privatization has now reduced the size of the state sector in the UK, leaving a core built round the health service, social services provision and local government. Parts of the state sector exposed in some measure to competition, such as the Post Office, have taken considerable trouble to improve their governance. The Citizens' Charter initiative, sponsored by John Major, has had some effect in improving performance standards in dealing with the public; its focus on the rights of the public, rather than a balanced list of rights and responsibilities, has made it less than effective as a tool of governance. The commissioning by John Major of the Nolan

Committee to produce standards for those in public life has been more successful so far; views on progress made are expressed in Case Study 1.2 in Part II of this book.

COOPERATIVES AND MUTUAL ORGANIZATIONS

The first cooperative was founded by the Rochdale pioneers in 1844. Its objective was to protect members from exploitation by giving them access to food and other essentials at realistic prices. The movement became national in 1863 and stimulated legislation to create industrial and provident societies with mutual ownership. In parallel with this development a separate building society and friendly society movement developed which was given legal protection by laws passed in 1874.

The governance of these societies is focused on mutuality. Ownership and custom are shared, minimizing the conflict between shareholder and customer interests which can make corporate governance difficult for normal businesses. While societies retain their local presence they are likely to have support from local interests, which also facilitates governance, particularly if some of these are suppliers. In theory, therefore, the mutual society should be a favoured model for corporate governance. In fact the cooperative movement has declined strongly in recent years and other societies have been abandoning mutuality – why? Some of the issues around mutuality emerge in case studies of Equitable Life and Birmingham Midshires in Part II of this book (3.2 and 3.3).

The decline in the cooperative movement seems to have been driven by competition from the major retail groups. One major weakness of the cooperative movement has been its use of committees of members to oversee management decisions. This democratic structure has made the cooperatives slow to react to changes in the marketplace and hampered development. An excess of democracy has also led to a growing number of farmers' cooperatives converting to private companies in order to separate more sharply the functions of ownership and management.

The abandonment of mutuality by many building societies and mutual insurers has been for the same reason as farmers' cooperatives have converted to company status, together with the desire to avoid some of the restrictions of mutual status, in particular the lack of access to loan capital to fund rapid expansion. Nevertheless, many mutual societies are adopting the disciplines of limited liability companies while building on their loyalty base. Bradford and Bingley Building Society has been successful so far with this approach. The Nationwide Building Society and others are struggling to find an accommodation between embattled members. The prospect of the release of accumulated reserves as 'windfall' payouts is irresistible to most members, particularly those who only joined to share the plunder!

EMPLOYEE-OWNED ORGANIZATIONS

Cooperatives are owned by their members, often their customers, and not usually by their employees. There are some long-standing employee cooperatives in Northern Spain which have been successful, but the most outstanding employee-owned business in the UK is the John Lewis Partnership. Full details of John Lewis are given in Case Study 3.1.

There have been other employee-owned businesses, but few have enjoyed the sustained success of John Lewis. An example on a smaller scale is Baxi Partnership Limited, a small engineering business in Lancashire, which was able to rescue itself through the willingness of the owners to undergo a severe programme of re-engineering. Unipart encourages its employees to own shares and has a share bonus scheme but remains an unquoted company. This avoids the dilution of employee share ownership seen by the National Freight Corporation since flotation.

The key challenge for an employee-owned business is to commit to the high degree of customer focus needed to succeed in modern business. Much of the public sector has been effectively employee-owned for many years, and privatized organizations have had considerable difficulty in changing to a customer-orientated culture.

CHARITIES

Charities were for many years run on amateur lines with a minimum of structure and controls. Lack of accountability to donors led to growing dissatisfaction and the passing of various Charities Acts. The increasing importance of tax exemption to charities and the need for effective regulation led to the establishment of the Charity Commission, which registers and regulates charities of all sorts and sizes. The views of Lynne Berry of the Charity Commission are examined in Case Study 2.1.

The governance issues of the voluntary sector have been thoroughly researched and analysed by the Ford Partnership in its 1997 report *Under Pressure: Trends in the governance of large charities for the 21st Century*. The findings of the report are very detailed but may be summarized as follows:

O   The charity sector is poorly defined but is a significant part of national activity.

O   With the constraints on Government spending the voluntary sector, including charities, may be expected to grow in scale.

O   Many charities now have the dimensions of sizeable businesses and handle significant resources.

O   With the growth of demands on charities and the growing gap between those demands and resources, charities need to improve efficiency.

O   Demand pressures and competition make the old amateur approach to the governance of charities unsustainable.

O   Charities will need to focus on delivering value to users rather than serve the agendas of helpers.

O   Charities need to attract motivated and trained trustees and adopt governance policies which are more businesslike.

O   Governance in the charity sector needs to become more strategic, while remaining responsive to their users.

A beginning has been made with this process of change by some of the larger charities and by many housing associations. Many now have a core of key executives who are paid meaningful salaries and are given clear mandates.

In studying large charities, the report identifies four cultures of governance:

1   **Trust culture:** Charities run by a body of unpaid trustees, with shared accountability, and regulated by the Charity Commission and the Courts. Their focus is on beneficiary benefit.

2   **Membership culture:** Charities run with membership control, through elected governing bodies. These are political systems and accountabilities are not in line with charity law, which demands personal accountability and not constituency mandates.

3   **Stakeholder culture:** This is typically used by charities providing services to empower all stakeholders and is a fluid, consensus-building culture, rather than a bureaucratic one.

4   **Strategic culture:** Large charities are adopting private sector models, concentrating power in the board and the Chief Executive and focusing on strategic direction. Amateurism is at a discount.

The Ford Partnership report sees a growing tension between devolved power, especially in federal or branch structures, and centralized power. Given the personal accountability of trustees, centralized structures allow an apparent increase in control, which must be tempting. Certainly charities need to embrace strategic leadership in order to survive, a process which needs to be driven from the centre but which must involve all parts of the organization if it is to be effective. Some charities are demonstrating strategic leadership, but there is not yet general support within the charities sector to encourage wide acceptance of the need for professional management of all major charities.

KEY ISSUES

1   Do I understand the different models of corporate governance and are any features relevant to my organization?

2   Is our present organizational structure the best model for our future development?

3   If we are a joint stock company, should we be quoted on the Stock Exchange or not?

What action am I committing myself to take? _____

6

HOW IS EFFECTIVE CORPORATE GOVERNANCE TO BE ACHIEVED?

❖

In most cases it is likely that the achievement of effective corporate governance will need to be driven by the board of directors. Shareholders delegate the direction of their company to the board and should only need to intervene in the process of governance if it is not working. Other stakeholders will influence the process and should be encouraged to do so, but leadership of the process lies with the board of directors. In approaching this task directors need to heed the words of Dr Bruce Lloyd: 'A power driven approach tends to be preoccupied with the short term while a responsibility approach is more concerned with long term issues' (Briefing: *Professional Manager*, March 1996). The choice of approach will be crucial to the long-term health of the company; power-driven boards of directors see corporate governance as an obstacle not as a platform for competitive advantage.

There are a number of approaches to achieving good governance which we need to examine in turn.

THE COMPLIANCE APPROACH

The compliance approach focuses on the regulatory requirements for corporate governance. At its most basic it sees the issue as one of 'ticking boxes' and being able to make the declarations in respect of the Cadbury, Greenbury and now Hampel Codes which are required by the Listing Rules of the London Stock Exchange. There may be more codes in future which may not be helpful. The Institute of Chartered Accountants in England and

Wales has put forward a set of five principles for company boards to follow. These focus on the mix of skills, the role of non-executive directors in making executive directors accountable, dilution of power round the boardroom, professional relations with auditors and open accounting for the board's stewardship. Mere compliance with these codes provides a 'lowest common denominator' approach to governance which wins no distinction for the company concerned. Distinction comes to those companies which seek to establish best practice in corporate governance and move beyond the codes into areas such as environmental protection.

The compliance approach was typically taken by privatized companies seeking to adjust to a new set of opportunities and responsibilities. For many there was also a market regulator with whom to contend. For many such companies testing the mettle of the regulators was a key area of learning; it is no coincidence that the main cause of the Greenbury Report was the uproar caused by large increases in remuneration for directors of former utilities. The battles for effective rather than ritualistic governance continue, with British Gas only an extreme example of the clash between the old and the new attitudes to stewardship.

There is no evidence that the pure compliance approach endows its followers with any competitive advantage. For external parties assessing a company simple compliance with the Cadbury, Greenbury and Hampel Codes is a 'hygiene factor', not a mark of distinction. On the other hand, considerable progress has been made in achieving compliance by activists such as PIRC, whose achievements are examined in Case Study 4.2. Some of the problems faced by smaller quoted companies in coping with the demands of regulation are raised in Case Study 3.6.

THE 'BEST PRACTICE' APPROACH

One of the pioneers of 'best practice' in the USA is Calpers, the largest US public pension fund. Since 1984 Calpers has targeted underperforming US corporations, demanding changes in their corporate governance as a driver for improved profitability. Calpers now recommends the foundation of a British institute for corporate governance backed by institutional investors. Such an institute would spearhead a drive to bring 'best practice' to bear on underperforming British companies.

Some companies also see significant advantage in recognizing the need for better corporate governance and in creating a process to achieve 'best practice' levels of achievement. British Telecom has appointed a Corporate Governance Director, Luke March, and its approach is examined in detail in Case Study 3.4. Such a degree of public commitment to 'best practice' has its dangers; Shell has for many years published its 'Statement of General

Business Principles' which has been used to pillory its development plans in Nigeria and its plans for disposing of the redundant Piper Alpha oil rig. The 'Statement of General Business Principles' is shown in Case Study 1.3.

Companies such as Shell have also taken corporate governance into the arena of environmental protection by establishing demanding standards for controlling the impact of their operations on the environment. Health and safety are often included in this domain of governance; Zeneca has been more active than most companies in setting demanding standards in safety, health and the environment. Their approach is explained more fully in Case Study 5.2.

The 'best practice' model for improving corporate governance makes little impact in isolation from the wider strategy of the company. It may be noticed by the specialist consultancies and parts of the media, but the real benefit is obtained by gearing the search for 'best practice' to the strategies for growing the business. It is in the daily relationship with stakeholders that the real benefits of 'best practice' in corporate governance are delivered.

THE EMPOWERMENT APPROACH

Even in smaller companies the board of directors cannot manage the company in detail, nor should it attempt to do so. Corporate governance is concerned with the responsible use of power and all boards of directors face the need to delegate some of their powers in order to achieve results. In the case of large and/or global businesses the challenges to the span of control risk being unsustainable and power needs to be delegated on a systematic and controlled basis. Delegation is not abdication; directors need to be seen to support those whom they have empowered. This support may take different forms; the directors of Burger King are expected to spend time occasionally working with staff in company restaurants.

Many businesses, such as ITT under Geneen, GEC under Weinstock, have attempted to centralize power and delegate responsibility. The sophistication of modern computers makes such an approach very tempting, but it ignores the potential for releasing the creativity and energy of employees at the heart of the business.

A growing number of businesses recognize the value of delegating power to employees on a mutually negotiated basis. This requires a clear mandate for action, supported by the personal development opportunities needed to deliver the mandate effectively. Empowerment is really workable only within a framework of shared values, such as Shell's 'Statement of General Business Principles' (Case Study 1.3). This framework enables the employee to react with confidence to situations not foreseen in their mandate, in the knowledge that the decision taken is in harmony with the values of the company.

A strong set of values, properly monitored, also helps to avoid the bullying and abuse which some managers seek to justify as 'robust management' needed to meet stretching targets. Empowerment will need to be legitimized by making it open to all qualified employees, irrespective of gender, colour or creed. To do this successfully requires not only the removal of 'glass ceilings', but also the adaption of work patterns to meet the requirements of individual lives. As a result the structured order of 'command and control' companies will need to give way to freer and more energizing approaches to achieving results.

The strength of empowerment can be gauged from 'Fortune's 100 Best Companies' survey (12 January 1998). An employee in SouthWest Airlines says: 'Working here is truly an unbelievable experience. They treat you with respect, pay you well, and empower you. They use your ideas to solve problems. They encourage you to be yourself. I love going to work.' The survey shows empowerment as a key feature of company policies aimed at attracting, developing and retaining the best staff. The role of empowerment in a global company can be seen in a study of Morgan Crucible (Case Study 3.5).

THE STAKEHOLDER APPROACH

The role of stakeholders has not figured largely in strategic planning to date and this may be a significant reason for the frequent failure of companies to implement plans successfully. A recent book *Real-World Corporate Governance* by Nigel and Arthur Kendall (Pitman Publishing, 1998) seeks to expand the strategy process to include stakeholder analysis. They propose a five-step process as follows:

1   Internal analysis (resources, value chain, strengths/weaknesses, culture and so on).
2   External analysis (business environment, markets, competitors, actual and potential customers and so on).
3   Stakeholder analysis (customers, employees, owners, suppliers, community).
4   Confirm or change goal (strengths, weaknesses, opportunities, threats + stakeholder input).
5   Formulating strategy (evaluating strategic options, choosing and planning implementation).

Stakeholder analysis is seen to comprise quantitative and qualitative research among stakeholders covering ethical issues, congruence of goals, organization and reporting. All results are built into a stakeholder model in order to gauge the likely impact of stakeholder views on the company.

This approach is a considerable advance on the haphazard involvement of stakeholders practised by most companies. The difficulty of any process which takes the initiative in stakeholder relations is to know the point at which being inclusive becomes being intrusive. Where information is sought from stakeholders, its objectivity is always in question. Building models from such data may well be a step too far, although the thinking involved is probably useful. The model does not include involuntary stakeholders, such as media and pressure groups, and these often have an impact on the business out of all proportion to their legitimate interest in its fortunes.

This approach seems to be moving in the right direction and has some common ground with that of 'Tomorrow's Company'. The danger of any inclusive approach is that it blurs the focus of strategic direction; shareholder value is a simple goal and stakeholder value is elusive.

None of these approaches will deliver perfect corporate governance which is in any case not a strategic goal. A process to use effective corporate governance to optimize the chances of long-term survival of the company will be examined later. It is important to recognize that corporate governance comprises both formal and informal practices. With growing empowerment and stakeholder involvement the scope for informal practices will increase. This is healthy and controllable provided that the shared system of values remains the touchstone for informal practices.

STRATEGIC LEADERSHIP FROM THE BOARD

As I pointed out in my book *Strategic Leadership* (Simon and Schuster, 1991) the performance of company boards in recent years has been less than adequate. It is interesting that Peter Drucker's early books never mention the board but focus on management. Boards of directors have achieved a higher profile in the last ten years thanks to their role in initiating or defending hostile bids, their ability to survive while their managers are decimated by re-engineering projects, and the moves taken to protect directors as individuals rather than the interests of their company. When the chairman of General Motors doubles his pension on the threshold of retirement and the company is in dire straits, board leadership has reached a very low level. The situation is even worse when directors confuse their roles as directors and shareholders and forget their customers, as the Chairman and Deputy Chairman of Newcastle United plc have done. Directors are stewards not monarchs.

Effective board leadership involves the creation and maintenance of a dynamic and innovative board of directors. The process of building and managing the board is one of the key roles of the chairman. It is well described in Sir Adrian Cadbury's book *The Company Chairman* (Director Books, 1990) and by Sir John Harvey-Jones in *Making it Happen* (Fontana,

1989). Both men basically see chairmanship as picking individual directors, with a range of skills and views, who are able to interact with each other to create value for the company.

FOUNDATIONS OF STRATEGIC LEADERSHIP

The key foundations for strategic leadership are:

○   a soundly built and effective board of directors;
○   a shared strategic direction and commitment to pursue it;
○   strong processes to effect strategic management.

These foundations may be examined in turn:

A soundly built and effective board

In building the board a chairman should consider the resources and competences needed to reach the goals set for the company. These may be deployed by the company itself or made available to it from external sources. The decision about which resources and competences are 'at the core' of company success and which may be obtained externally is obviously crucial. The decision about the competences needed round the board table is a key element of building the board.

A report *Good Practice for Directors* was published by the IOD in 1995, following intensive research and testing by Henley Management College of a set of 'standards for the board' in which I was personally involved. This report addressed:

○   the clarification of board and management responsibilities;
○   board composition and organization;
○   planning and managing board meetings;
○   improving board effectiveness.

In examining the issue of building an effective board, the report highlighted the following key competences of directors:

○   Strategic perception and decision making
○   Analytical understanding
○   Skill in communication
○   Effective interaction with others
○   Ability to plan, delegate, appraise and develop others
○   Focus on achievement, through risk taking
○   Resilience
○   Integrity
○   Independence (especially for non-executive directors).

It is recognized that not every director will have these competences, and that younger directors will need to build them up over time. The real need is to have a board which can 'cover the field' and a chairman who ensures that these competences are brought to bear on issues when needed. It is interesting that the 1998 International Survey of Institutional Investors for Russell Reynolds Associates emphasizes that institutional investors prefer directors to have strategic skills and experience to match the needs of their company, not just a large portfolio of board appointments.

One fundamental danger is the disparity of company knowledge between executive and non-executive directors. Some boards treat non-executive directors with disdain or pick them for their pliability. Such was the case at Lonrho and seems to be so at Disney. Frequently executives hold 'pre-board meetings' in order to decide the outcome of the board meeting resolutions. Even where companies take care to brief their non-executive directors and keep them informed, the executive directors will always be more knowledgeable about the company's internal operations and it will be difficult to challenge them on matters of detail. Most effective non-executive directors seek to contribute from their wider knowledge and experience, but this can easily be discounted unless the board is minded to listen. Occasionally non-executive directors challenge their colleagues on matters of principle, though even here they will not always succeed, as evidenced by the battle against remodelling the Emap board in 1996.

The balance of UK boards is often cited as a reason for adopting a two-tier board model. This would avoid the mixing of executive and non-executive directors and the potential for difficulties between them. On the other hand, recent experience in Germany has shown that supervisory boards are not always kept well-informed, if only to avoid feeding ammunition to the trades unions, and disasters can strike without warning, such as the heavy losses at Daimler Benz in 1995. It was the trades unions which were able to block Thyssens bid for Krupp in 1997.

A key part of the process of building an effective board is to subject it to review at regular intervals. Many company boards examine their performance at 'away days', but few have yet subjected themselves to independent, external review. Such an appraisal should not only bring out criticisms of the board's performance by individual directors, but also enable those who work with the board to air their views.

An important dimension of developing the board is the creation and use of board committees. The Cadbury Report has codified a need for an audit committee, a nominations committee and a remuneration committee, all controlled by non-executive directors. Cadbury saw the role of non-executive directors as bringing 'an independent judgement to bear on issues of strategy, performance, resources, including key appointments and standards of conduct' (Code, paragraph 2). The three Cadbury-recommended committees enable the non-executive directors to exercise untrammelled control over resources (audit committee), performance (remuneration committee), key appointments (nomination committee). Standards of conduct will, at the extreme, emerge through the audit committee after the event (fraud, evading trading limits and so on) has occurred. There is no vehicle in most companies for non-executive directors to ensure that the strategic management of the company is not suborned or neglected. As, increasingly, executive directors are being paid to achieve short-term objectives, the risk of mortgaging the company's strategic future increases. In *Strategic Leadership* (Simon and Schuster, 1991) I call for the creation of a 'strategy committee' of the board, under the control of non-executive directors. This was an idea which appealed to Sir Adrian Cadbury at the time, but did not fit the strictly financial focus of his remit. Such a committee would complete the equipment of non-executive directors to carry out their mandate in Para. 2.1 of the Cadbury Code.

In time it is likely that other board committees will be needed in order to make the board more effective overall. The whole area of stakeholder relations remains underdeveloped and as companies have to respond to a widening audience, the value of contributions from non-executive directors with extended contacts and experience will increase.

An interesting experiment in long-term board development is the creation by Sanmex, a Glasgow-based detergent and household products manufacturer, of a 'shadow board'. This operates in tandem with the main board and each of the younger people on the six strong 'shadow board' understudies a main board director. The link is provided by Steven Grodon, who is business development director on the Sanmex board and chairs the 'shadow board'. In addition to shadowing the main board the 'shadow board' works on development projects which, if successful, will be submitted to the main board. Full details of this novel approach are in the *Financial Times* of 29 July 1997.

Developing an effective board requires commitment and a sustainable process. One approach to this challenge is that of Bob Garrett who has developed the idea of 'The Learning Board'. This tackles the problem perceived by Reg Revans whereby organizations can only survive and grow by learning faster than the rate of change in their environment. Based on ideas derived from his book *The Learning Organization* (Harper Collins, 1994) the development of 'The Learning Board' is shown in detail in Bob Garrett's latest book *The Fish Rots from the Head* (Harper Collins, 1996).

Shared strategic direction

Boards exist to direct companies, not to manage them. Too often boards allow themselves to be overladen with what Sir John Harvey-Jones calls 'boilerplate' matters. Setting the strategic direction of the company and controlling progress towards it are the prime tasks of a board. Without a clear sense of direction the managers of the business cannot produce the results which the board expects from them.

The process of setting and monitoring strategic direction is linked into the strategic planning process of the company. Leadership comes from the board in establishing a vision and values which set the target and tone of the company. Strategy is best decided through a process which involves the people in the business who have to deliver it. The board decides how the resources needed to deliver the strategy will be provided. The whole strategy process is examined in Chapter 7.

Part of the board's role in setting strategic direction is to relate to the external stakeholders who will be involved. Companies have traditionally been secretive about their ambitions and strategic plans; the results have often been less than satisfactory. As Campbell and Alexander show in their article 'What's wrong with strategy?' (*Harvard Business Review*, November/December 1997) companies need to develop 'stakeholder value' as well as shareholder value if they are to be successful. Part of the creation of stakeholder value should be the involvement of stakeholders in developing strategy. Openness has its risks, but lack of openness is a one-way bet on failure. In his article 'Opening the Books' (*Harvard Business Review*, March/April 1997) John Case demonstrates the power of 'open-book management' in winning employee commitment to achieving business success. The principles behind 'open-book' management can apply to other stakeholders and to strategic management, provided that involvement is balanced by education and that there are clear benefits for delivering business goals. 'Stakeholder value' will be an important concept, but much remains to be done to make it workable and not just intrusive.

Strategic management processes

Although boards of directors do not manage their companies, they need to be sure that their strategies are effectively delivered. Leadership to achieve this is usually given through a strategic management process, in which the board sets the strategic direction of the company and the business units contribute their plans and strategies. The process of developing strategies must be balanced by processes to monitor their implementation and to react to emergent opportunities and threats. The crucial role of marketing in this process is examined in my book *Strategic Marketing* (McGraw Hill, 1995). The board is responsible for creating and maintaining processes to achieve effective strategic management. In decentralized groups a key part of the process is for the board to challenge the 'received wisdom' of individual businesses so that innovation triumphs over staid thinking. This has been done very successfully by, among others, Granada.

Failures of management control processes have been dramatic in recent years. The demise of Barings is an extreme example, but many companies have been damaged by strategic and operational errors, including NatWest by the 'Blue Arrow' scandal. Many of the problems have been associated with banks who need to empower dealers if they are to be effective. Similar challenges will face international businesses as globalization forces devolution of authority. In an article in *Harvard Business Review* (March/April 1995) 'Control in an Age of Empowerment', Professor Robert Simons develops a system of controls to cope with the growth of empowerment. He seeks to harness creativity while providing four control levels:

Table 1   Empowerment Control Levels

Potential	Organizational blocks	Managerial solution	Control lever
To contribute	Uncertainty about purpose	Communicate core values and mission	Beliefs system
To do right	Pressure or temptation	Specify and enforce the rules of the game	Boundary systems
To achieve	Lack of focus or resources	Build and support clear targets	Diagnostic control systems
To create	Lack of opportunity or fear of risk	Open organizational dialogue to encourage learning	Interactive control systems

Such a system requires clear leadership from the board and appropriate managers, together with wide but defined discretion and clear rewards or sanctions.

NON-EXECUTIVE DIRECTORS

Having examined how a board can provide strategic leadership, the potential importance of non-executive directors can clearly be seen. As the Institute of Directors states in its *Guidelines for Directors* (1991):

> The present legal framework in Great Britain for appointing boards of directors permits the creation of boards composed wholly of fulltime executives. This can be a source of weakness if such boards become inbred, lacking both the wider perspectives and the domestic stimuli to perform that which an external presence might provide.

Even today there are companies which have no external directors; a survey by MORI in 1997 showed five companies out of 305 respondents having no non-executive directors, with an average of four non-executive directors for all companies.

The role of non-executive directors is both to act as fully participating members of the board in executing its duty to direct the company and to bring wider experience and new ideas to its discussions, to monitor and challenge the performance of executive directors and management, and to ensure that there are adequate control systems in place to protect the company's interests. In the past non-executive directors have too often been beholden to the chairman or managing director and few have successfully challenged abusive management; the success of Angus Murray in defeating Alan Bartlett at Newman Industries is a rare example. It was this situation in part which led the Cadbury Committee to place great emphasis on the appointment of non-executive directors through open processes and on their effective use when appointed. Hampel seems concerned to avoid any divergence in role between executive and non-executive directors in order to build harmonious boards. This is a mistake, which is partially recognized in the concept of the 'lead non-executive director' to act as watchman when the roles of chairman and chief executive are combined. Non-executive directors have a duty to be independent, challenging and watchful of the personal agendas of their executive colleagues – they need to generate creative tension, not harmony, in board deliberations. An interesting article in the *Financial Times* (17 May 1995) features the need for non-executive directors to be sensitive to circumstances which may favour fraud and the work done by KPMG in countering this risk.

Non-executive directors have often been the representatives of special interests on the board. Major shareholders have often appointed directors, and institutional investors such as 3I always reserve the right to do so. This conflicts with the legal duty of the board to act in the interest of all shareholders, a conflict which is compounded by the practice of briefing institutional shareholders between normal reporting dates. In practice, non-executive directors with special interests normally declare them and do not vote on issues where those interests may conflict with wider concerns.

Another issue which needs to be addressed is the practice of appointing executive directors of other companies as non-executive directors. This has the attraction of bringing active practitioners from other companies to interact with the executive directors, but may have significant disadvantages. Executive directors often find difficulty in giving sufficient time and attention to external appointments and in some cases their involvement may raise conflicts of interest. This issue is more prevalent in France where the Viénot Report was highly critical of cross-linked directorships. Another aspect of the use of outside executive directors as non-executive members of the board is the tendency for remuneration committees to act as a ratchet to drive up remuneration packages through inter-company comparisons. It is difficult for those concerned not to establish benchmarks which may be used by their own remuneration committees in reviewing their packages.

Another questionable practice is that of appointing former executive directors to be non-executive directors. Not only does this carry the risk of perpetuating influence from the past but it negates the independence and fresh outlook required of non-executive directors. It may be a sign of new thinking that Cor Herkströter has declared himself unwilling to move from Chairman of the Executive Committee to be a non-executive director of the Supervisory Board of Shell. This breaks a long tradition in Shell and can only be a healthy development.

The new Combined Code, which integrates Cadbury, Greenbury and Hampel Committee recommendations, creates a new role of 'Senior' non-executive director in cases where the roles of chairman and chief executive are exercised by one person. This represents a retreat from the Cadbury Code's requirement to separate those roles and may create divisive pressures on the working of the board.

While companies have been able or content to operate as closed systems, the appointment of non-executive directors has been optional. It is probably for this reason that many smaller companies still avoid such appointments. Where the shareholders are remote from company operations the case for non-executive directors is stronger. There have been a number of high profile cases of chief executives being forced out of office in the USA (General Motors, IBM, American Express, and so on) and the same imposition of accountability may be increasing in the UK companies. In recent months alone we have seen new chief executives at Dalgety and Stavely, so that non-executives may be having some influence on accountability, even if, as in the case of Sears, shareholder and media pressure may be needed to help them. At the same time non-executive directors are losing some high profile battles, as at Emap, or winning Pyrrhic victories as with resistance to the Emerson attempt to control Astec (BSR) with a bullying, cheap bid.

With the opening of markets and greater demand for company performance it is likely that the value of good non-executives will grow. As companies have to come to terms with new markets, new competitors, new challenges and new cultures they will value the experience and contacts of people who are at home in a wider world and who may have gone through similar changes. Such people will need to include female directors and a spectrum of different nationalities, races and ages to reflect the company's varied stakeholders, rather than the clones of the chairman which most non-executive directors still remain. In dealing with a growing number of stakeholders and constituencies, the company will need whole new areas of competence and understanding and the non-executives may be very valuable in facilitating some of those relationships.

SMALL AND MEDIUM-SIZED ENTERPRISES

The use of non-executive directors has become more widespread in recent years, but their employment in smaller companies remains less usual and inconsistent. A survey commissioned by 3I in 1994 showed independent directors in a small majority on the average board of companies with a turnover exceeding £1 billion/year, in balance with executive directors on average for boards of companies with turnovers between £500 million and £1 billion, and a significant growth in executive director preponderance as companies had a diminishing level of turnover. As the number of non-executive directors and their time commitment have increased, average per diem remuneration has fallen and one-third of non-executive directors have no letter of appointment. It would seem that smaller companies have yet to learn how to manage non-executive directors.

Following the spate of buyouts and buy-ins in recent years a growing number of non-executive directors are being remunerated in shares or share options. At the same time 'company angels' are increasingly appearing on the board of companies in which they invest (this affected over one-third of the companies in the 3I survey), so that strict independence for small company non-executive directors is no longer reflected in payment solely in fees.

The Cadbury Code is intended for use by companies of all sizes even though compliance is only required for those quoted on the London Stock Exchange. It requires that 'non-executive directors should bring an independent judgement to bear on issues of strategy performance, resources, including key appointments and standards of conduct'. The Cadbury Code states that 'the majority should be independent of management and free from any business or other relationship which could materially interfere with the exercise of their independent judgement, apart from their fees and shareholding'. Is independent judgement a sufficient reason for a smaller company to appoint a non-executive director?

Smaller companies are usually fragile and exposed to uncertain market forces which are beyond their control. Most smaller companies will have started as an idea in the head of their founder, supported by a small group of trusted followers and funded on the back of a business plan which is rapidly overtaken by events. Many smaller companies will be undercapitalized and hampered by debt financing, usually by overdraft. A fierce attention to cashflow will be essential to ensure month to month survival, so that inessential costs are to be avoided. In such a situation why would a company seek to appoint a non-executive director?

The rationale for appointing a non-executive director to the board of a smaller company will usually lie in having some access to skills and experience which the company cannot afford on a full-time basis. For larger companies a clear distinction is supposed to be drawn between direction and management. Smaller companies rarely have a full range of competences below board level, so that executive directors will be more closely involved in daily management decisions. Such companies can usually deploy the basic competences required for routine operations, but frequently lack the strategic, financial, legal and other intermittent skills and experience needed for longer-term survival. A non-executive director can often bring such competences on a quasi-executive basis and coach members of the board in order to transfer some skills. Such an arrangement is usually cheaper and less threatening than using consultants!

The Cadbury Report is concerned to have effective controls in place to ensure that the board can assess the company's position with reasonable confidence and protect shareholder interests. In a smaller company executive directors will be able to exert a considerable degree of control themselves; in many cases they will be substantial shareholders and be directly motivated to do so. Control may also be a more complex issue in smaller companies, particularly where they have family shareholdings. Family businesses are not always run at arm's length from the private agendas of family members, often producing conflicts of interest which the directors may not wish to share with a non-executive director. It is, however, in such situations that an independent non-executive director can help to avoid situations developing which can damage the company's image and effectiveness over the longer term.

The Cadbury Report favours the use of a nomination committee with a majority of non-executive directors in order to process board appointments. For smaller companies the potential damage done by a 'bad apple' is proportionately higher than for quoted companies and yet the process of selection is often not as rigorous as the appointment would warrant. It is likely that a non-executive director could bring considerable value to the process of selecting executive directors and senior staff in smaller companies but there is little evidence that this resource is used systematically.

Many small businesses are started by entrepreneurs who may be more concerned to realize their pressing ambitions than to create sustainable relationships inside and outside their business. Such entrepreneurs often see little value in having non-executive directors to challenge their authority, yet often they can obtain more value from such an appointment than a board with more widely diffused power. Entrepreneurs usually succeed because they have a clear vision and an appetite for risk in achieving it. In practice a vision needs to be shared in order to achieve it on any significant scale, and risks are best evaluated by those who have experienced them and know how to mitigate their potential impact. A well-chosen non-executive director should be the ideal foil for a forceful entrepreneur.

Small businesses are often too focused on internal issues and not alert to the system of dependencies in which they operate. 'Tomorrow's Company' has brought the concept of stakeholders into the consciousness of larger businesses, but smaller companies are often unconscious of the external relationships which have to be managed in order to achieve sustainable success. An effective non-executive director can help to identify such relationships and suggest how they can best be managed.

Finance is often the Achilles' heel of smaller companies and disinterested advice is not always readily available. In a smaller company the only direc-tor who is financially literate is often the finance director (though even today some small companies do not have their financial controller on the board). Finance is an art rather than a science, and it is unwise to leave its management to one person. A non-executive director should normally bring financial skills to his appointment and be able to ensure that finan-cial issues are examined from all angles by the board. Even a skilled finance director can miss important options when briefing the board on finance issues.

Skills are the lifeblood of a business and, like blood, need regular renewal. Directors involved in a company's operations cannot always see the gaps in its skills or their pending obsolescence. A struggling company can too easily ignore training or fail to recognize the skills which will enable it to compete more successfully. Like generals who prepare to fight yesterday's battles, too many smaller company directors try to win market share with obsolete equipment and skills. An effective non-executive director would be aware of the need to develop and nurture core competences and of the competitive advantage to be gained by doing so.

Smaller businesses grow by being focused on short-term objectives and by managing their operations in the tightest detail to achieve them. Often their growth is not well controlled and many over-trade and become insolvent. Even when growth is properly paced, it can be hampered by external events which are often predictable if proper plans have been made. Directors of smaller companies often boast that they do not need a strategy to succeed, since on their scale progress can be micromanaged. Most smaller businesses fail within their first five years, and a number of surveys have shown that a majority of those who survive have made some attempt to plan strategically. Strategic direction is one of the key responsibilities of any company board but few smaller companies have directors with strategic skills. The use of outside consultants by smaller companies to develop strategy is limited and frequently unsuccessful, since strategy has to be 'owned' by those who have to deliver it rather than handed down as 'tablets of stone'. Some consultants are successful in facilitating the development of strategy by smaller company boards but even this process requires some degree of educated response by the board. Where there is a non-executive director with strategy-making competence, the value to a smaller company is immense. Such a director may lead the board in a process of developing strategy and, as an 'insider', may be more successful in obtaining commitment than an external consul-tant who will not work with them to implement the strategy. Having led such a process myself as a non-executive director of smaller companies, I can confirm that the results can be very far-reaching, even revolutionary on occasions.

KEY ISSUES

1   What are the advantages/disadvantages for our organization in the different approaches to corporate governance?

2   How does the board provide leadership in effecting corporate governance?

3   What is the special role of non-executive directors?

What action am I committing myself to take? _____

7

HOW EFFECTIVE CORPORATE GOVERNANCE CAN CREATE COMPETITIVE ADVANTAGE

In the view of Michael Porter, (*Competitive Advantage*, Free Press, 1991) competitive advantage grows fundamentally out of the value a firm is able to create for its buyers. Where a firm enjoys competitive advantage, buyers will prefer its products to those of its competitors. Where there are repeat purchases, the firm will have the opportunity of creating an ever-closer relationship with the buyer, built on growing knowledge of his needs and increasing competence in meeting them. Where the product is sold in volume to a wide range of consumers, it becomes possible to develop brand values attaching to it, enabling a premium price to be maintained in the marketplace.

Michael Porter warns against a simplistic view of competitive advantage. 'Competitive advantage cannot be understood by looking at a firm as a whole. It stems from the many discrete activities a firm performs in designing, producing, marketing, delivering and supporting its product.' Hamel and Pralahad found highly complex competitive advantages in their research: 'Flexibility advantages were built atop speed advantages, which were built atop supplier-management advantages, which were built atop quality advantages.' Competitive advantage is, therefore, multifaceted – perhaps, like a diamond, its value rises with the number of facets! Certainly its value depends on the sharpness of each facet; one weak cut destroys the total value.

It is fashionable to talk of sustainable competitive advantage in the belief that there is some way of avoiding competitor catch-up or even leapfrogging. Competitive advantage is no stasis: to continue to enjoy competitive advantage it is essential to recreate it and to reposition it into the future

repetitively. The holder of competitive advantage is the target for the inge-
nuity of all his competitors; as any soldier will tell you, only mobile targets
are likely to survive. The Japanese consumer goods companies developed a
technique of continuous improvement (*kaizan*) as a means of renewing
competitive advantage. This has led to a growing wealth of extra features on
consumer products and a constant increase in value to their buyers.

Creating competitive advantage requires both the vision to innovate and
the ability to manage in detail the complex processes of delivering value.
Michael Porter's technique for analysing the value chain of a given product
or service demonstrates the complexity of the process and the number of
persons involved in each stage. The scope for wastage is enormous, yet even
well-tuned processes can yield savings if those involved are fully motivated.
Such savings become essential if value is constantly being increased for the
buyer in order to recreate competitive advantage.

COMPETITIVE FORCES AND STRATEGY

Michael Porter defined a model of the competitive forces affecting profitability, which comprised five forces:

1   Competition within the industry
2   Pressure from and on buyers
3   Pressure from and on suppliers
4   The threat of potential market entrants
5   The threat of substitute products and services.

In many cases this model needs to be modified to include the dimension of
distribution which is critical in most marketplaces. In some cases – for
instance, food products, the distributors have won market leadership from
manufacturers. In the insurance industry the independent financial advisers
have retained a strong market position despite the growth of other distribution channels.

Due to the increasing relative power of buyers in an increasingly open and
competitive marketplace and to the accelerating pace of change, driven by
technology, by lifestyle and by productivity, the model is out of balance in
most industries and firms involved need imagination and adaptability in formulating their strategies.

Michael Porter identifies three generic strategies which he sees as the
framework for strategies tailored for individual businesses. These are:

1   to seek overall cost leadership (low price/high volume)
2   to seek differentiation (premium price/medium volume)
3   to seek focus by combining 1 and 2, targeting a specific market
     segment.

Within this framework there will be a number of specific strategies supporting the main thrust of corporate strategy, which will include planned strategies and those which Professor Mintzberg terms 'emergent strategies' ('Crafting Strategy', *Harvard Business Review* July/August 1987). These are strategies crafted from opportunities or threats which may not have been foreseen when strategic plans were formulated. Businesses which explore their future environment carefully in preparing plans, using techniques such as scenario planning to try to foresee potential changes, are less likely to be surprised by events. Companies which develop their strategies by involving at all levels the people who will have to implement them, are also more likely to avoid surprises and to have widespread commitment to make them succeed.

COMPETING FOR THE FUTURE

In developing strategies companies are not working in isolation. It is too easy to forget that competitors are also developing strategies and that they may have a ready counterstrategy to meet the challenge offered to them. Too often strategies assume too slow a pace of change in the marketplace and are left to fight yesterday's battles. We have seen that differentiation is often the most rewarding strategy, even if the most difficult to bring to fruition. One very challenging but potentially extremely rewarding strategy is to compete for the future.

Competing for the Future (Harvard Business School Press, 1994) by Gary Hamel and C. K. Pralahad is a detailed examination of the crafting of breakthrough strategies aimed at redefining and winning a leadership position in the markets of tomorrow. The kind of questions which it addresses include:

> How influential is my company in setting the new rules of competition within its industry? Is it regularly defining new ways of doing business, building new capabilities, and setting new standards of customer satisfaction? Is it more a rule-maker than a rule-taker within its industry? Is it more intent on challenging the industry *status quo* than protecting it?

These are questions which challenge not only the company but also the environment in which it works – its customers, its suppliers, its competitors and above all, its employees. To turn such a challenge into a competitive opportunity requires the involvement of all of these stakeholders and probably some others. Ideally all those needed to deliver the future should be involved in the process of imagining it and shaping the strategies to create it. There will, of course, be pragmatic limits to involvement; competitors are not likely to be directly involved, for example, unless some of them are seen as strategic partners in some of the initiatives which are to be undertaken. Such initiatives occur with increasing frequency; one of the most wide-ranging is General

Magic, a consortium involving Apple, Sony, Mitsushita, Philips, Motorola, AT and T, France Telecom, NTT and Fujitsu, in an attempt to create the communication and software standards for hand-held communication equipment. At a more basic level companies are recognizing the importance of committed collaboration with suppliers, both in sharing the design and development processes and in ensuring seamless quality control through to the end product. This approach has led vehicle manufacturers to increase outsourcing of components and to focus on their 'systems integration' function. Many companies which downsized to meet competitive conditions have found that working with former business units as alliance partners is more effective; IBM was one of the largest of these 'exploded' companies. The key message from such experiences is that tomorrow's core competencies will differ from those of today. Competing for the future demands the imagination and creativity, what Walt Disney called 'imagineering', to realize tomorrow before other companies have left the mental comfort of today.

Differentiation is a key strategy for businesses which are in crowded markets. Many companies seek to differentiate by service – both WalMart and British Airways have done so successfully in different sectors. Others seek to be distinguished on ethical grounds; the Body Shop has created a cult following thanks to a strong ethical stance on animal testing and environmental issues. Other companies seek to build brand preference around lifestyle; Virgin has been successful in stretching its brand over a range of businesses serving a hedonistic and non-conforming clientele. Some companies compete successfully by creating a reputation for innovation: Minnesota Mining and Manufacturing is an icon of innovation, and Gillette and Sony have also built their businesses on sustained programmes of new product introductions. A strategy of opposing received wisdom can also be successful: Ted Turner ignored conventional media thinking in creating CNN, Nicolas Hayek proved that the Swiss could make affordable watches as well as luxury timepieces.

Is it possible that a company could use effective corporate governance to create competitive advantage? Would this be achievable by projecting a value system which included and balanced the claims of stakeholders, or would the process of inclusion itself enable the company to be more effective in the marketplace? Let us consider these two questions separately, even though they are the mirror image of each other.

PROJECTING A VALUE SYSTEM

Branding is the most effective way to project a value system. In building a brand a company is making a promise to customers to deliver a consistent set of satisfactions associated with the product, and hence with the brand itself. The world's most powerful brand, Coca Cola, reflects 'American' values to its drinkers worldwide, an attraction which is shared to a lesser extent by Levi's, Nike, Pepsi and others. Coca Cola's stakeholders may include its bottlers, whom it enriches, its other suppliers, the governments who tax its profits, advertising agents, retailers and, naturally, its employees, customers and shareholders. Although Coca Cola has been driven for the past 16 years to maximize 'share owner value' (to use the late Roberto Goizueta's special phrase) and its market value has increased by over $175 billion in that time, the company has managed to grow its brand value at the same time. Even though Coke made mistakes, as with the New Coke launch in the 1980s, it was quick to recognize that it had damaged brand values and to return to keeping faith with its aficionados, people of all ages and interests in most countries of the world. Strong brands can tolerate honest mistakes if they are recognized quickly and frankly.

Another company which has built its distinctiveness on values is Disney. When Walt Disney started making cartoon films he had a sixth sense of the tastes of 'Middle America'. He developed characters to whom Americans and, later, others could relate and built a reputation for wholesome fun. Since the death of Walt Disney the company has managed to upset radical Christians and now faces attack from a shareholding pension fund, TIAA-Cref, the largest in the USA, because its board largely comprises cronies of Michael Eisner, the chairman, who has turned the company into a money machine. Values must be practised consistently or credibility, let alone distinctiveness, is lost.

Marks and Spencer is a company which has developed through practising a discrete set of values consistently. It has an open management style and takes great trouble to communicate its value to staff. M & S has a policy of buying in the UK where possible and its overseas sales make it a significant exporter of British goods and values. Customers find M & S a consistent source of value for money, even though its goods are not cheap. Its policy of freely exchanging goods which are not suitable makes it attractive to those who make speculative purchases. Out of this customer interface has come a reputation for fairness and straight dealing which M & S has now used to move successfully into financial services. Even the Arab boycott of Israeli/Jewish products has failed to disturb the steady growth of M & S and its significant sales to Arab customers! In its 1990 Annual Report M & S admitted that it needed to move from paternalism to partnership with its stakeholders; since then it has moved significantly in that direction and strengthened its claim to be Britain's most admired company.

WIDENING INCLUSION

The classical economic model is based on transactions not relationships. Sales are made on the basis of price and fitness for purpose and there is no supposition of repeat transactions. This rather arid model assumes a balance of power between buyer and seller which rarely occurs in practice. The growth of the consumer economies in most countries of the world has shifted the balance of power away from most suppliers, except for some monopolists such as Microsoft, and has opened up a wide range of choice to buyers. Companies can no longer prosper by expecting the public 'to beat a path to their door'; in times of intensifying competition the initiative for building success in the marketplace lies firmly with suppliers.

One form this initiative might take would be to seek closer relationships with the stakeholders in the supplying company's business in order to understand more fully how best to meet real and potential market needs and how to involve the stakeholders in that process. At a basic level this is the process of marketing, but marketing can be intrusive and counterproductive if taken to extreme limits. At a higher level this process of inclusion becomes a shared value system, involving the supplier, customers, employees, its suppliers, the local communities in which it operates and its shareholders. The 'Tomorrow's Company' Centre, mentioned in Case Study 5.1, is championing the process of inclusion and defines its approach to inclusiveness as follows:

○ clearly defines its purpose and values, and communicates them in a consistent manner to all those important to the company's success
○ uses its stated purpose and values, and its understanding of the importance of each relationship, to develop its own success model from which it can generate a meaningful framework for performance measurement
○ values reciprocal relationships, understanding that, by focusing on learning from all those who contribute to the business, it will best be able to improve returns to shareholders
○ works actively to build reciprocal relationships with customers, suppliers and other key stakeholders, through a partnership approach
○ expects its relationships to overlap and acts, with others where necessary, to maintain a strong *licence to operate*.

A fuller examination of the 'Tomorrow's Company' movement may be found in Case Study 5.1.

This approach translates into a business agenda which is wider than that of companies focused on 'shareholder value'. Profit becomes a means to deliver the wider agenda, rather than the end purpose of the company. The human body needs blood in order to function effectively, but maximizing blood levels is not a sensible purpose! This approach may be seen in Hewlett Packard's corporate objectives:

Profit To achieve sufficient profit to finance our company growth and to provide the resources we need to achieve our other corporate objectives.
Customers To provide products and services of the highest quality and the greatest possible value to our customers, thereby gaining and holding their respect and loyalty.

Fields of interest   To participate in those fields of interest that build upon our technology and customer base, that offer opportunities for continuing growth, and that enable us to make a needed and profitable contribution.

Growth   To let our growth be limited only by our profits and our ability to develop and produce innovative products that satisfy real customer needs.

Our people   To help HP people share in the company's success which they make possible; to provide employment security based on performance; to ensure them a safe and pleasant work environment; to recognize their individual achievements; to value their diversity; and to help them gain a sense of satisfaction and accomplishment from their work.

Management   To foster initiative and creativity by allowing the individual freedom of action in attaining well-defined objectives.

Citizenship   To honor our obligations to society by being an economic, intellectual and social asset to each nation and each community in which we operate.

Improvement is accomplished by better methods, better techniques, better machinery and equipment and by people continually finding better ways to do their jobs and to work together as a team. I will never see the day when there is not yet room for improvement. Dave Packard, 1957.

Widening inclusion has strengthened other companies; Unipart has grown in part by developing its employees' competences through its 'University', Grand Met has been strengthened by 'corporate citizenship' and Marks and Spencer by close cooperation with its suppliers. By widening inclusion, companies increase awareness of their products and services and build a larger platform of stakeholdings which can sustain and expand their business. A strategy of inclusion can be incrementally powerful but depends fundamentally on continuous renewal of trust among the stakeholders. One mistake may be one too many as Gerald Ratner found to his cost.

COST LEADERSHIP

Cost leadership is not synonymous with price leadership. Cost leadership comes from being the lowest cost producer of a specific product or service. To achieve cost leadership a company needs to focus obsessively on its input costs and the build-up of costs right along the supply chain to end users. The process may be undertaken in a draconian manner, by bullying suppliers and exploiting employees, but this has rarely been a sustainable strategy in a free society. Working with suppliers and employees, and sharing some of the fruits of cost-saving, has usually been more productive. Cost leadership is usually achieved by avoiding waste of resources and by focusing on productivity gains, while maintaining or improving quality levels and innovating continuously. An example of successful cost leadership is Tesco, which has built market share and managed to strengthen its operating margins at the same time. Success in this endeavour came not only from cost control, but also through widening Tesco's franchise by moving the image of the company upmarket. Cost leadership can only be sustained by an inclusive approach to all stakeholders. People only rush to have Tesco's loyalty card because they believe it has value for them.

FOCUSED STRATEGY

Differentiation and cost leadership are not mutually exclusive strategies. We have seen in the case of Tesco how cost leadership can provide the platform from which a business can develop its own market posture. The cost of doing this and of building the brand preference which sustains the distinct market position is considerable. For smaller companies there is the strategic option of focusing their cost leadership into market niches where they can outclass companies with a broader strategy.

To succeed in a strategy focused on niche markets, companies need considerable discipline in 'sticking to their knitting'. Most achieve this by creating a cult round their specialism. Filofax had been in existence for many years until it was marketed as a cult product for up-and-coming executives and achieved a worldwide niche for itself. For such companies success depends on creating a small world in which customers, employees, suppliers, distributors and media combine to promote and sustain the 'superproduct'. This cannot be done in isolation from a wide range of stakeholders, though it may be boosted by subtle techniques, as Morgan has done by creating a waiting list for its cars.

When this strategy is successful it can create 'spoiling' competition – for example, Redex was a very successful engine performance booster until the oil companies added a booster to their petrol. Success can also lead to takeover – although the shareholders of Lotus may have been thankful to IBM!

Not all businesses succeed through an inclusive approach to governance. As markets have become open to competition, consumers have become used to choice and most businesses have succeeded through greater efficiency and market impact. Monopoly remains the secret desire of most businessmen, and the battle against market manipulation remains one of the greatest challenges to good governance. Companies such as Microsoft seem to have manoeuvred to achieve quasi-monopoly based on a technical lockout of competitors. News Corporation seems also to have been adept at building quasi-monopolistic market positions in many countries. It may be argued that this is no different from the patent monopoly granted to pharmaceutical and other technical companies to enable them to recoup the sunk costs of innovation. Other businesses face high investment costs without monopoly: some such as Eurotunnel struggle to survive; Rolls Royce is more successful, but regularly pledges the future of its business with new aero engine development costs.

Professor Andrew Cox believes that businessmen should seek to create monopoly situations as they have always done in the past. His book *Business Success: A way of thinking about business strategy, critical supply chain assets and operational best practice* (Earlsgate Press, 1997) focuses on strategies to monopolize the supply chain and maximize profitability through meeting 'customer utility'. He believes that all innovation is driven by supply, never by demand, so that control of supply can generate monopoly profits. Professor Cox sees Microsoft as a model for his theory of innovation. He criticizes most companies for giving away value to customers and stakeholders; effective strategy lies in monopoly profits for shareholders. Despite the views of Professor Cox, as globalization advances it will be increasingly important to stimulate and support innovation without allowing competition to be manipulated. This will be one of the greatest challenges to corporate governance and to the governments which create the framework for it to flourish.

HOW DOES THE BOARD MAKE THE GOVERNANCE OF THE COMPANY MORE EFFECTIVE?

We have examined the principles of good corporate governance but not the processes involved in making them work. There are *two* basic approaches to reviewing the governance requirements of a company and installing a system to deliver them, which we can examine in detail. These approaches must be closely interlinked with those for developing and delivering strategy in order to create the potential for competitive advantage.

THE FUNCTIONAL APPROACH

This involves the creation of a functional department to spearhead the establishment and maintenance of good governance practices. We referred earlier to the appointment of Luke March as Director of Corporate Governance of British Telecom, and Case Study 3.4 shows how he is approaching his role in the specific context of the telecommunications industry.

In a more general context a newly-appointed functional head might approach the task in the following manner:

1.1   Make a presentation to the board on the key elements of corporate governance and why it is important for the company's future success. (This presentation should focus on the board's role as trustee

for shareholders in ensuring that the purpose of the company is ful-
filled. Key areas of focus are likely to be purpose, values, strategy,
processes and implementation.)

1.2   Interview the board members and other top managers on a non-
attributable basis in order to draw out their views on the present
state of governance in the company.

1.3   Feed back the findings of the interviews and discuss them in a
workshop involving all interviewees, relating them to best practice
in the company's sector.

1.4   Interview the previous respondents again without attribution to
elicit their views on how the company could use corporate governance to improve its performance.

1.5   Feed back the findings of the interviews and discuss them in a
workshop involving all interviewees. Establish an agreed model for
corporate governance and a programme for achieving its realization. Identify the company's stakeholders and agree how to involve
them in its strategic agenda.

1.6   Establish a programme of key stakeholder visits in order to discuss
and evaluate their relationship with the company and how it can be
developed for mutual benefit. Discuss and agree a shared set of values, align purposes and strategy and agree how processes can be
optimized.

1.7   Work to tune the value system of the company to the achievement
of its long-term purpose (benchmarking it against best relevant
practice elsewhere).

1.8   Tackle areas where values may conflict with short-term objectives –
for example, the sales team may meet short-term targets at the
expense of long-term customer relationships. (This often involves a
significant shift in reward systems.)

1.9   Develop a model for corporate governance which can be used to
drive the achievement of effective governance. Identify the key indicators of success and establish targets for each.

1.10   Evaluate the structure, systems and processes within the company
to ensure that they do not inhibit good governance, are open and
controllable and subject to regular internal audit. Look for improvements which will enhance performance – for example, tighten
review processes for project management. Benchmark against best
relevant practice elsewhere.

1.11   Work with managers and planners in monitoring the key action programmes which drive the implementation of strategies. Review and
tune performance criteria and reward systems, benchmarking
against best relevant practice elsewhere.

1.12   Revisit key stakeholders to retune and realign values, strategy and
processes.

This approach will take at least one planning cycle to be completed and will
need to be adapted to changes in the company's plans and operations.
Particular care is needed to protect and develop stakeholder relations and to
monitor the consistent practice of corporate values. Any failure in this area is
as dangerous as leaving a bad apple in the storage barrel.

A key part of the maintenance of effective corporate governance is the use
of a code of business practice, reflecting relationships inside and outside the
company and the values to be shared with those stakeholders. The Shell
Statement of General Business Principles is shown in Case Study 1.3. BT is
another company which has such a code – its Statement of Business Practice
is reproduced in its current form in Case Study 3.4 and is presently undergo-
ing a review which will involve all stakeholder groups. Such codes are valuable if they reflect the views of all stakeholders, balance rights and
obligations and are used daily in managing the business. Shell has now
made its code a condition of employment and codes which are not observed
consistently lose credibility very fast.

While the working of this governance system will require constant monitoring and adjustment for internal change it will also be extremely important
to continue to seek out and adopt best practice outside the company. This
will build and maintain the reputation of the company as being 'good to do
business with'.

The advantages of creating a corporate governance function are found to
be that:

1   responsibility for success is focused on one person and their staff;
2   the process can be developed and maintained without distraction
from urgent priorities;
3   one focused person can more easily keep up-to-date with new legislation and jurisprudence affecting the company;
4   one focused person can more easily develop and maintain the
external contacts needed to benchmark best performance;
5   an established function provides a sole authoritative source of
advice to the board on issues involving corporate governance.

For smaller companies there may be the danger of creating a bureaucracy
round an area of the business which involves everybody. In the case of BT it
must be recognized that the Director of Corporate Governance has a special

responsibility for corporate governance issues involving the telecommunications regulator.

THE 'COLLEGIATE' APPROACH

The 'collegiate' approach to establishing effective corporate governance is spearheaded by the board itself and involves all directors equally in the process. It is usually appropriate to have the process administered by the company secretary, particularly as the company secretary will probably be responsible for maintaining it when it is established. The developmental process itself benefits in most cases from skilled external facilitation and has steps which parallel those in the 'functional' approach:

2.1   A board presentation to emphasize the importance of corporate governance, what it comprises and how it may effectively be established.

2.2   Unattributable interviews of all directors and top managers to establish their views on the present state of governance in the company.

2.3   Feed back the key context of the interviews to a workshop involving all interviewees and discuss the implications, relating them to best practice in the company's sector.

2.4   Further unattributable interviews with the previous respondents to seek views on how corporate governance might be used to enhance the company's performance.

2.5   Feed back the key content of the interviews and discuss them in a workshop involving all interviewees. Establish an agreed model for corporate governance and a programme to realize it over time. Identify the company's stakeholders and agree how to involve them in its strategic agenda. Set up a small team to drive the realization programme, possibly led by the company secretary. This team will report back regularly to the board on progress and involve directors as appropriate.

2.6   Establish a programme of key stakeholder visits in order to discuss and evaluate their relationship with the company and how it can be developed for mutual benefit. Discuss and agree a shared set of values, align purposes and strategy and agree how processes can be optimized.

2.7   Work to tune the value system of the company to the achievement of its long-term purpose (benchmarking it against best relevant practice elsewhere).

2.8   Tackle areas where values may conflict with short-term objectives – for example, the sales team may meet short-term targets at the expense of long-term customer relationships. (This often involves a significant shift in reward systems.)

2.9   Develop a model for corporate governance which can be used to drive the achievement of effective governance. Identify the key indicators of success and establish targets for each.

2.10   Evaluate the structure, systems and processes within the company to ensure that they do not inhibit good governance, are open and controllable and subject to regular internal audit. Look for improvements which will enhance performance: for example, tighten review processes for project management. Benchmark against best relevant practice elsewhere.

2.11   Work with managers and planners in monitoring the key action programmes which drive the implementation of strategies. Review and tune performance criteria and reward systems, benchmarking against best relevant practice elsewhere.

2.12   Revisit key stakeholders to retune and realign values, strategy and processes.

The maintenance and further development of the corporate governance system will involve the same alertness and disciplines as needed in the 'functional' approach.

The 'collegiate' approach can have some advantages over the 'functional' approach which may include the following:

1   Directors may be more involved both collectively and individually in the implementation and maintenance of the process of corporate governance.

2   Greater direct involvement by all directors may create a higher level of ownership and commitment, especially in 'living the values', than the 'functional' approach can achieve.

3   People outside the board may perceive the process as having the direct commitment of the whole board rather than being the preoccupation of a functional executive.

The decision to use one or other of these approaches is less critical than the commitment to build effective corporate governance into the heart of the company and to maintain and upgrade it to levels of best practice. Careful attention will also need to be given to reporting on corporate governance both to the board and to shareholders. This issue is addressed below. In approaching the task of using corporate governance to win and maintain competitive advantage the board should see it as an investment in health.

In the same way that the discipline of healthy living helps to prevent or delay sickness and degeneration, the discipline of corporate governance provides a bodily tone which enables the company to compete more effectively in the marketplace and to prevent the infection of sloth and corruption which destroys so many businesses from the inside.

REPORTING ON CORPORATE GOVERNANCE

In addition to its obligation to maintain and improve the effectiveness of corporate governance in the company, the board of any company quoted on the London Stock Exchange already has to meet the requirement for an annual report on its compliance with the Code of Best practice established by the Cadbury Committee and now consolidated into the code of the Hampel Committee.

This procedure is focused primarily on larger companies (although Sir Adrian Cadbury sees it as applicable to smaller companies also) and is limited in scope to the financial aspects of governance, leaving wider issues of accountability without a structured framework for reporting.

It is suggested that a more comprehensive annual report on governance would add to the Cadbury/Hampel issues the following key areas of accountability:

1   The views of customers, suppliers, employees and other stakeholders on the company's quality of governance (obtained by independent survey).
2   Validation that the long-term health of the company was not threatened by short-term actions.
3   Certification that the competences and knowledge base needed to develop the company were in place (provided, following an independent assessment).
4   A statement of progress made in the year towards achieving the company's purpose.
5   An annual audit of processes (both inside and outside the company).
6   A statement of progress made in the year towards building long-term shareholder value.

Responsibility for reporting to shareholders would lie with the board; items 2, 4 and 6 would be prepared by the Strategy Committee of the board, led by non-executive directors, while the audit of processes could be undertaken by the internal or external auditor, or an independent consultant, reporting to the Audit Committee.

The main focus of each item in the report would be as follows:

O   **Views on quality of governance** – soundness of strategy, consistency of values and operating effectiveness.
O   **Validation of long-term health** – proper long-term investment in physical and intellectual assets, short-term results consistent with strategic plans.
O   **Competences and knowledge base** – tuning skills to present and future opportunities and building a focused knowledge base to support consistency of results. Long-term corporate self-renewal.

O **Progress towards purpose** – pinpointing progress towards immediate and medium-term milestones laid down in the strategic plan.

O **Audit of processes (inside/outside the company)** – ensuring that key processes needed to build the business are in place and are effective – for example, total supply chain.

O **Shareholder value** – monitoring consistency of progress in building long-term shareholder value (using EVA or some other relevant measure).

It is unlikely that the Stock Exchange would see immediate value in adding wider dimensions to its requirement for reporting on corporate governance, although such reporting does need to be integrated to maximize effectiveness. It may be that the CBI or Tomorrow's Company will champion this extension of annual reporting, initially by quoted companies, but in the longer term by the thrusting smaller companies which are likely to build Britain's long-term future.

KEY ISSUES

1   What creates competitive advantage and how can it be sustained?
2   How can differentiation create competitive advantage?
3   How can values be used to create competitive advantage?
4   How do corporate governance and strategy work together to create competitive advantage?

What action am I committing myself to take? _____

8

HOW IS EFFECTIVE CORPORATE GOVERNANCE TO BE SUSTAINED?

A company is inanimate and yet has many of the characteristics of a living organism. It requires considerable nurture in order to survive and develop and will age and die unless helped in the process of self-renewal. For many years Texas Instruments has had an active process of self-renewal in its business, driven by a board director dedicated to that task. In recent years other companies, such as Unipart and Equitable Life, have seen the importance of having a process of self-renewal. Some, such as Birmingham Midshires Building Society, have engineered internal revolutions to avoid the risk of sclerosis. The Japanese have made self-renewal a slow but ongoing process through *Kaizan* or continuous improvement techniques. Whatever the method used, self-renewal is a continuous journey undertaken with no expectation of ever arriving at a final destination.

Many journeys of self-renewal have continued for centuries. In his book *The Living Company* (Harvard Business School Press, 1998) Arie de Geus examines the sources of company longevity. He shows how companies such as Stora Kopparberg have lasted for centuries thanks to a culture of adaptability. Stora started some 700 years ago as a medieval copper mine; since that time it has had a series of reincarnations, successively as a forestry company, an iron smelter, a hydro power business and, finally, a papermaker.

ACHIEVING SELF-RENEWAL

What are the processes involved in achieving self-renewal? These are, in essence, the following:

○   Understanding better the different future environments in which the company is likely to operate.
○   Identifying and exploring the threats and opportunities which changes in the environment may bring for the company.
○   Assessing the company's present businesses in a potentially changed environment.
○   Understanding the potential need for new competences and resources for a changed future.
○   Developing a strategy for self-renewal.

It may be useful to examine these processes in more detail.

FUTURE ENVIRONMENT

It is rarely possible to forecast the future, but skilled use of scenario planning can enable the future to be explored in an imaginative way which will bring out the factors likely to shape it. Differences in the weighting, timing and vector of these factors may bring about a number of different futures. The detailed picture of these futures is called a 'scenario'. Scenario planning will also bring out the issues which may affect the marketplace in which the company engages.

THREATS AND OPPORTUNITIES

From the work done on scenario planning it will be possible to identify a number of threats and opportunities which may affect the company's present and related businesses. One key factor which is present in most scenario planning is the increasing possibility of businesses converging as markets open up and former boundaries between businesses disappear. Technology is enabling new initiatives to be taken in established marketplaces, such as retailing goods on the Internet or selling financial services on the telephone. Often the greater danger to a company comes from unexpected new market entrants than from existing competitors.

ASSESSING PRESENT AND POTENTIAL BUSINESSES

The scenario planning process will produce a limited number of scenarios, which will be of considerable value for testing present and potential businesses for robustness into the future. It may be found that businesses that are profitable today are threatened tomorrow; an early warning can be very salutary. Potential businesses will also need to be tested rigorously. Where the future promise is obvious there may be a rush of investment which will reduce the potential profitability. Where the promise emerges from lengthy debate it may be possible to achieve 'first mover' advantage. A major insurance company identified the 'care in old age' market by such a process a few years ago and achieved a winning lead by prompt action.

Most companies take a 'scientific' approach to identifying business opportunities. Because scenario planning engages the right hand side of the brain, the intuitive and creative area, it can enable businesses to be seen in a new light and new opportunities created. Richard D'Aveni and Gary Hamel see business as an art not a science. Failure to think imaginatively led IBM to allow Microsoft to build the business which it should have created for itself. Amazon has used the Internet to outflank traditional booksellers. Thinking like an artist is something that Gary Hamel believes can be taught – 'Most famous artists went to art school'. This approach, detailed in an article in the *Financial Times* (1 September 1997), adds a new dimension to the learning process for business people.

COMPETENCES AND RESOURCES

It is almost axiomatic that the competences needed for a given business will be different in the future in markets where considerable change is expected. Too often companies train their employees to fight yesterday's war. Considerable care and insight are needed to anticipate the competences required for future success. Ten years ago it would have been considered fanciful to develop competence in facilitation and mentoring and yet these are becoming core competences for any successful business. Resources have traditionally been led by finance, but it is now becoming clear that knowledge will be the differentiating resource for most businesses.

SELF-RENEWAL STRATEGY

When this diagnosis has been completed and its implications digested, it will be necessary to develop strategies to reposition the company to compete for the future. For most companies this will require new ideas and new skills to be grafted onto a business that is in danger of rejecting them. The board will need to be convinced of its mandate for change and be patient and unrelenting in sponsoring the changes needed. For some companies the process of self-renewal will entail the death of its present persona and the creation of a new entity out of the ashes. The process may take years, if time allows, but it must be driven through purposefully; Smiths Industries took ten years to evolve out of the motor parts industry into a high technology company, but it was able to renew itself from a marginal position into industry leadership. Like Stora and others it had sloughed off its old skin more than once and will have to do so again in due season.

UNDERPINNING SELF-RENEWAL

To be successful, and to be able to repeat itself in due time, the process of self-renewal needs to be underpinned in the following ways:

O   Vestiges of the past which cannot support the future must be removed.

O   All stakeholders must have an appropriate input into strategy.

O   The company should aim to create new standards for the businesses in which it engages.

O   Stakeholders, in particular employees, need to be encouraged to learn and to take reasonable risks to do so.

O   Reward systems need to reflect the wider, long-term needs of the business.

O   The process of communicating with stakeholders needs to be totally and continuously open.

O   Regular independent review processes need to ensure the integrity and functionality of the self-renewal process.

Each of these facilitating factors needs to be examined in more detail.

VESTIGES OF THE PAST

In making changes to a company care must be taken not 'to throw the baby out with the bath water'. Companies depend on their history, and the longest living companies have survived through adapting their past, not destroying it. On the other hand many companies have failed to implement change programmes successfully because of entrenched but skilful internal opposition. British Telecom needed three waves of redundancy in order to break the mould of its old business, and many other companies have failed to force the issue. In all self-renewal programmes there will be people who will be temperamentally incapable of adaptation. At the end of one of the most successful change programmes in the UK, that of Equitable Life, the Managing Director, Roy Ranson, had to retire early a hard core of recidivists. Had they stayed, the success of the whole programme would have been at risk.

In making radical changes care needs to be taken not to lose core competences. Midland Bank went through successive changes in the late 1980s and early 1990s, and removed most of its older employees. When Brian Pearce came from Barclays to take over as Chief Executive of Midland Bank he was incredulous – 'Where are the lending bankers we need to build the business?'

STAKEHOLDERS' INPUT INTO STRATEGY

'Investors in People' is a national standard for promoting learning and employee involvement in their companies. Those who achieve the standard have the right to use the 'Investors in People' logo to promote themselves as progressive businesses. The commitment made is to develop employee skills, knowledge and qualifications and so increase motivation, commitment and loyalty, leading to job satisfaction and better career prospects. To achieve and maintain the 'Investors in People' standard, employers have to involve their staff in the decision-making processes of their company, including corporate plans. Rather than merely inform staff about company plans, many companies practising 'Investors in People' policies are seeking their input into strategy through 'bottom-up' planning processes, workshops and other media. The evidence of 'Investors in People' to date is largely positive, particularly where it is used not just as a standard but as a committed way of working with employees.

Customers have increasingly been influential in shaping strategy, largely through the activities of the marketing department (advertising and impact analysis, focus groups, independent surveys, and so on). Relationship marketing offers the opportunity to invite more specific input into strategy with the prospect of shared benefits. It is becoming more usual to talk through strategic ideas with customers, particularly as the original stimulus may have come from customer suggestions. This process can build trust, particularly where benefits are shared. It is probably more advanced in technology markets than elsewhere; vehicle manufacturers have reduced their design cycles from four to two years in part due to close cooperation with key suppliers.

This kind of partnership can be seen in other markets where time and/or cost are making cooperation essential. Marks and Spencer relies heavily on the suppliers (who have 140 000 employees to its 80 000) and it buys preponderantly in the UK. There are 250 M and S technologists travelling the world to find new material sources for its suppliers to use. M and S fixes the specification and price and the suppliers contract. M and S takes the commercial risk with the final product which it will have designed in association with its supplier. Each has the benefits of an integrated unit, but each preserves its independence.

In small companies shareholders often have a strong input into strategy. For large quoted companies the input of analysts is beginning to be matched by that of institutional investors. Warren Buffet created a model of the strategic investor, buying major stakes in a few companies and working closely with their top managers. Pension funds, such as Calpers, have become more interventionist with managements of companies whose shares they hold, usually for between six and ten years. Calpers advised Sears and Westinghouse to divest themselves of poorly performing divisions and pays close attention to wider issues of corporate governance. Where companies fail to listen to major investors, pain is likely to ensue. James Robinson III was bundled out of his job as CEO of American Express without ceremony. In the UK major companies take increasing trouble to talk to institutional investors. Where their views are ignored, action is beginning to follow: Liam Strong was forced out of his job as Chief Executive of Sears after the institutions lost patience with poor results.

NEW STANDARDS

In the 1960s the car industry indulged in a strategy of 'planned obsolescence'. Each model change was designed to be superseded in a short time, forcing the sensitive car owner to change his car more frequently than physical wear required. This strategy rebounded in time, but car manufacturers remain under its spell. A strategy of creating new standards would also fail if it shared the same cynical motivation as 'planned obsolescence'.

Strategies to create new standards should be the stepping-stones of progress. Where such standards are technical in nature they are usually protected by a patent for up to 16 years. This allows time to recoup the costs of invention and development and provide cashflows to fund the next new standard. In many cases sharing the standard with others will accelerate market development. Matsushita licensed its VHS standard for video recorders fairly widely and defeated the more tightly controlled Sony JCG standard. Microsoft has positioned its operating system for PCs so advantageously that it has 82 per cent market share of a 20-million/year units market priced at $13 per unit. Strategies to set technical standards are therefore very powerful and create the opportunity to make the next strategic step at the right moment.

Setting standards also applies to non-technical areas of business. Companies have striven to achieve quality standards such as ISO 9000, and the more ambitious have competed for a Deming Award. Standards for environmental protection (ISO 14 000) and for employee development ('Investors in People') have demonstrated that superior achievement is required in intangible areas of excellence as well as in the more readily measurable factors of technical and financial performance. It is likely that competitiveness will increasingly be sought in the intangible areas, such as service and quality, which are evaluated by customers and delivered by employees and suppliers.

Strategic benchmarking is a technique for harnessing the strategy process in pursuit of outstanding standards. Companies have used operational benchmarking as a means of seeking out best practice in key performance areas where they find a need for improvement. Strategic benchmarking applies the same techniques to the pursuit of a better understanding of strategic factors which can generate competitive advantage. GE has been active in developing strategic benchmarking and has defined a world-class competitor in the following terms:

○   Knows its processes better than its competitors know their processes.
○   Knows the industry competitors better than its competitors know them.

O Knows its customers better than its competitors know their customers.
O Responds more rapidly to customer behaviour than do competitors.
O Uses employees more effectively than do competitors.
O Competes for market share on a customer-by-customer basis.
   (Quoted in Watson *Strategic Benchmarking* [Wiley, 1993])

This definition shows that the pursuit of outstanding standards requires a relentless search for better understanding of customers and competitors and a rigorous adaptation of the company, its employees and processes, to win and retain competitive advantage. Best practice in strategic benchmarking looks beyond the company's own industry to find models which can be adapted. Watson quotes the lessons learned by Xerox from L. L. Bean in the area of warehouse management. Such cross-boundary studies are not yet numerous, but are likely to become more valuable; the search for best practice in organizing call centres involves banks, insurance companies, utilities and many others.

Another approach to setting new standards is to create a 'virtual company'. Traditional companies have employees and assets; virtual companies outsource every activity except coordination. A model for the virtual company featured in the the *Financial Times* (12 January 1998) is Protodigm, an operation established by Roche in order to accelerate the process of developing drugs and to reduce the cost of doing so by 40 per cent. All work is subcontracted and tightly controlled by a team of nine people. The contractors who do the work are small entrepreneurial businesses who specialize in fast, efficient and cheap processing. A typical British example is Oxford Assymetry.

Results for Protodigm so far have been encouraging, and the virtual company may be a model for reducing overheads and bureaucracy as well as a means of harnessing entrepreneurial skills to the needs of large companies with powerful marketing structures. Virtual companies do, however, depend crucially on stakeholder relationships of a very high order.

ENCOURAGEMENT OF RISK-TAKING AND LEARNING

The saying that 'you can't put an old head on young shoulders' seems self-evident, but it begs the question of how 'old heads' are developed. Too often companies 'empower' people without equipping them to exercise the responsibility they are given. Few companies have proper processes of induction for recruits, of development for existing employees or of coaching for those taking on new responsibilities. Staff are expected to know what to do and are often penalized if they fail.

Self-renewal is not automatic, but has to be facilitated. The renewal of a company's physical assets is normally easier to achieve than the renewal of the assets which do not figure specifically on the balance sheet, but are reflected only in stock market valuations. Employees are usually the largest asset of any company, and like any asset are more valuable when properly nurtured. Employees bring skills, knowledge and character to support a company's growth. Where employees are given the chance to learn, with support from experienced colleagues, they will take risks and may make mistakes, but will become more valuable to the company and enriched in themselves. Learning reaches the parts which training will never touch, since learning is committed, not passive.

Companies have taken increasing interest in the encouragement of learning. Younger employees are given challenges which would once have been thought unrealistic but are supported by mentors ('old hands' who are not competing for their job) as well as by their managers. Some companies, such as Motorola, have created 'universities' to provide wider facilitation of learning among groups and between individuals. Employees are encouraged to develop and practice new skills and competences and to exchange knowledge and experience. Nowhere has this frenetic learning process been more developed and successful than in Silicon Valley. Fuelled by a risk-taking culture and incessant innovation, the market value of quoted companies in Silicon Valley is now nearly $450 billion. Some 50 000 new jobs are created each year and a dozen or so new ventures started each week according to the *Financial Times* (25 August 1997).

The waves of downsizing which hit companies in recent years have highlighted the loss of knowledge and experience caused by making older employees redundant. Many companies have lost their 'corporate memory' and have found themselves repeating errors made in the past. There is a growing awareness of the value of knowledge and experience and of the need to capture it for the company to use when the people in which it resides have left its employment. 'Knowledge management' is now seeking both to marshal the knowledge among a company's employees and to use it to win competitive advantage. A growing number of companies have appointed executives to develop knowledge-management programmes; one of the pioneers in this endeavour is ICL. Elizabeth Lank, Programme Director – Knowledge Management, is spearheading a drive to make ICL a 'knowledge-based organization'. Details of this programme and of its impact on corporate governance are given in Case Study 5.3.

A different approach to learning is taken in Danah Zohar's book, *Rewiring the Corporate Brain* (Berrett-Koehler, 1997). Three types of thinking are identified: rational and linear thinking; parallel thinking (doing several things at once); and 'quantum thinking'. Most people have little experience of quantum thinking, which is focused on creativity and values and thrives on uncertainty. Danah Zohar sees Volvo and Motorola as quantum-thinking companies, which have empowered their employees and see them in the context of their whole lives, not just their working role. Without a conscious effort to develop quantum thinking, Danah Zohar sees most human beings and the companies in which they work as coasting into mediocrity and potential failure.

REWARD SYSTEMS

Reward systems are one of the weakest areas of governance but are fundamental to achieving long-term success. Reward systems need to include defined sanctions for bad conduct or for failure so that employees are totally clear about what the company expects of them. Shell's 'Statement of General Business Principles' (Case Study 1.3) is now part of every employee's contract of employment and enforceable as a result.

At present most reward systems are geared to meeting targets (usually financial) which are short-term and easily measurable. Reporting of short-term results is much better in most companies than feedback on long-term strategies. For long-term projects rewards are often geared to the achievement of defined milestones but, where the employees concerned have little control of events, as in a complex and politically sensitive project like Eurotunnel, such linkages can be demoralizing. It is interesting that Kaplan and Norton *The Balanced Scorecard* (H & S Press, 1996) find that few companies have successfully linked the 'balanced scorecard' approach of setting strategically balanced objectives to evaluating rewards. They quote the example of Pioneer Petroleum which had been found effective and motivating, using a balance of 60 per cent for financial and 40 per cent for developmental measures:

Table 2   Incentive Compensation Based on the Balanced Scorecard

Category	Measure	Weighting
Financial (60%)	Margin vs. Competition	18.0%
	ROCE vs. Competition	18.0%
	Cost Reduction vs. Plan	18.0%
	New Market Growth	3.0%
	Existing Market Growth	3.0%
Customers (10%)	Market Share	2.5%
	Customer Satisfaction Survey	2.5%
	Dealer Satisfaction Survey	2.5%
	Dealer Profitability	2.5%
Internal (10%)	Community/Environmental Index	10.0%
Learning and Growth (20%)	Employee Climate Survey	10.0%
	Strategic Skill Rating	7.0%
	Strategic Information Availability	3.0%

Most companies working with the 'balanced scorecard' concept have found it very helpful in clarifying strategic objectives and beginning to align employee behaviour with the actions needed to implement them. Tying such results to reward systems depends on the confidence that the scorecard targets and weightings are correct and that the company can measure them properly. This is a step in the process that needs to be taken cautiously and with the confidence of all concerned that it will both motivate and drive the business in the desired strategic direction.

One danger of highly geared reward systems is that they either force the search for short-term profit increases or lead to a transfer of profits from shareholders to employees. This phenomenon has been seen recently in the investment banking sector. Even more destabilizing is the use of stock options on a massive scale to drive business development, as has been happening in Silicon Valley and elsewhere in the USA. It seems that US companies have not recorded these options in their accounts but have treated them as contingent liabilities. Given the recent large rise in share prices it would seem that many US company profits have been massively overstated, according to a recent report by Smither and Company in *Financial Times* (17 April 1998). The average discrepancy is some 21 per cent of declared profits. Were profits to be restated, companies like Microsoft would show a loss.

The public and media outcry over the enhanced rewards taken by directors of privatized utilities, which led to the Greenbury Report, shows that there is wide-ranging interest in reward systems. Greenbury has clarified many of the issues around rewards but, in too many cases, has not stopped directors paying themselves beyond the level of their actual achievements. It is notable that the directors of the failed London and Continental Railway have earmarked £500 000 payment for themselves out of the wreckage. Jeremy Marshal, former Chief Executive of de la Rue, is expected to receive a payoff of some £600 000 having led the company into disaster. It is reassuring to see an increasing number of failing directors forced out of office by shareholder pressure, but there are as yet few examples of directors feeling financial pain as they oversee the destruction of shareholder value. Directors of Barclays Bank have recently taken increased bonuses despite poor results; directors of Cadbury Schweppes have adjusted results to remove exchange losses in calculating their bonuses. The pain is passed on to shareholders.

It will be a key sign of effective self-renewal when new directors take the helm and commit themselves to reward systems which truly reflect their status as stewards rather than usurp the wealth which they are charged to create for others.

COMMUNICATING WITH STAKEHOLDERS

In many companies stakeholders are not identified as groups sharing an interest in the company's success but as separate constituencies, with ill-defined relationships and probably conflicting concerns. The Chairman may focus on shareholders, the Marketing Director on customers, the Purchasing Director on suppliers, and so on. This situation has begun to be addressed by the use of public relations agencies to handle external communications and of internal communications specialists to integrate the flow of information within the company. Few companies have yet integrated their communications activities so that all stakeholders receive messages which are consistent. When messages are consistent and responses properly integrated, the company will be at the centre of an extended and more powerful working system; with total openness and continuous information flow the effectiveness and reach of the company will increase dramatically.

REGULAR INDEPENDENT REVIEW

Self-renewal requires both foresight and objectivity. The processes which drive self-renewal need constantly to focus on the longer-term future and to interpret the needs of that longer-term future, in terms of new ideas and competences without bias. Under day-to-day pressure the focus tends to shorten and the needs of the business to be seen in current terms. Most managers are prone to think of themselves as remaining at the helm of the business indefinitely and to see their attributes as the model for their eventual successors. It is to guard against conscious or unconscious distortions of the self-renewal process that regular and independent reviews are needed.

The review process may take a number of forms. It may be a formal process audit or an external assessment of outputs from the process, done by consultants or other external specialists. It may be a self-appraisal process, facilitated by consultants to ensure independence and rigour. In the interest of good corporate governance it will be useful to involve stakeholder representatives in the review process since they will have a real interest in the ability of the company to cope with change and to perpetuate its past success.

It will be seen that good governance and good management are intertwined. The processes which enable a company to ensure its survival are dependent on the same stakeholders who have an interest in its continuing success. Company failure is frequently the result of failing to sustain the synergy between good management and good governance, or of failing to maintain a working balance of interest between stakeholders. Companies are often killed by fraud, but many die a lingering death from complacency and lack of nurture. In corporate governance the sins of commission are dramatic and exciting – those of omission are often unseen and ultimately just as deadly.

KEY ISSUES

1   What is the process of self-renewal and how does it affect my organization?
2   Can we use scenario planning in order to explore the future?
3   What contribution can stakeholders make to our strategy?
4   How can we use learning to make our organization more effective?
5   What contribution could a strategic review make to our organization?

What action am I committing myself to take? _____

9

CORPORATE GOVERNANCE IN THE FUTURE

It is 25 March 2050 at 11.00 in the morning. In front of a bank of video screens sit Joanna Smith, Principal Trustee of the Global Life Sciences Corporation, and the Secretary of the Corporation, Hassan Muhammed. The faces in the video screens reflect the universality of the business: the Board of Trustees comprises representatives of all major world communities, with differing cultures and creeds. Today is important for the corporation as the Board needs to make decisions on a radical new business partnership and on the recommended participations in the profit from the last trading year. To preserve strict accountability decisions are made by the Board alone, but the views of all key stakeholders are sought on the resolutions to be brought to the Board and some may be contacted during the Board meeting to provide specific input needed by Trustees to facilitate their decision-making. Joanna Smith's approach to leadership is moulded by the ideas of Robert Greenleaf in his book *Servant Leadership* (Paulist Press, 1977), using a desire to help others as a means to empower them.

'Good morning, fellow Trustees,' says Joanna, scanning the video cameras with a smiling glance, 'may I welcome you to this 42nd meeting of the Board?' After short formalities, the Secretary reads a number of letters from stakeholders, making suggestions about the proposed business partnership with the Genetic Corporation. One of the corporation's suppliers had learned through contacts in a local university that one of the patents underpinning the partnership was to be contested by a competitor – was the corporation aware of this? Joanna raised the issue with Martha Chang, the Technical Trustee, who indicated that this situation had been admitted by the prospective partner, but that indemnities would be given against the limited risk of patent dilution. Other issues were aired and debated prior to the formal proposal for the partnership being tabled by the Genetics

Division Trustee, Krishna Sharma, with support from the Corporate Governance Trustee, Anna Polovna.

When the partnership proposal had been debated and approved, Joanna Smith called up Keichi Tanaka, High Custodian of the Genetic Corporation, and shared with him the good news. It was agreed to prepare a joint statement immediately for release to the stock exchanges, the media, stakeholders and other interested parties. The Board then proceeded to discuss other business, among which was the allocation of profit from the previous trading year.

Following successive changes in company law in the first half of the 21st Century, different models of company ownership had emerged. Some were based on the cooperative model, with ownership spread among all key stakeholders. Some companies had increased their reliance on debenture funding, so that their shares behaved like bonds rather than equities. Other companies had sought to cement stakeholder relationships through loyalty bonuses to customers, increased payments for results to employees, quality bonuses for suppliers, and so on. Global Life Sciences Corporation had taken the view that share ownership was now widely spread, both directly and through pension funds and other savings media, so that a shareholder value approach to management was not, of itself, prejudicial to other stakeholders. The corporation was managed to achieve long-term shareholder value, subject to a policy of sharing profits with key stakeholders in order to bind them into the corporation's value chain. Profits were shared by issuing equity to all stakeholders, except non-executive directors, who were only paid fees in order to preserve total independence.

The Trustees discussed the proposed appropriation of profits between stakeholders. Shares were to be issued in proportion to the business done with the corporation, or to targets achieved for employees. The Remuneration Committee, entirely comprising non-executive directors, had made proposals to the Board based on balanced scorecard results; the balanced scorecard was also used for senior employees. Joanna Smith directed that the directors' remuneration should be discussed after that of other stakeholders and that the other stakeholders should have priority where awards were constrained.

During the discussion of profit allocation, Carole Pascal, the Research Trustee, spoke of the considerable assistance given by the University of the Gambia in basic research on treating a new strain of swamp fever. The deadlines for the WHO bid would not have been met without the crash programme carried through by the University. Following discussion a special award of 1000 shares was approved.

It was interesting to watch the interaction of the directors and to understand their different backgrounds. None of them was a lawyer (the Secretary was the senior lawyer) and there were many fewer lawyers in society as a whole. Most of the directors had a technical doctorate and had qualified as directors through further examinations and practical experience. Joanna Smith had a PhD in genetics and an MA in molecular biology, followed by an MBA and the Institute of Directors professional qualification. Each director had worked in the charity sector as well as industry; Global Life Sciences worked closely with non-government organizations worldwide and exchanged staff with them as part of their personal development. The corporation also worked with governments; Joanna Smith had been seconded to the White House to work for Jane Munroe when she was President, having had earlier experience as a member of the Think-Tank of the European Commission. One of her main contributions had been the analysis of fraud and deception which had led to the Directive on Whistle-blowing Protection.

One of the areas of business where Global Life Sciences was strong was military applications. War had evolved from major set-piece confrontations to sporadic local conflicts in which physical brutality was supplemented by technical assaults. Germ and chemical warfare had become generalized and great skill and imagination was needed to provide new defences against a rapidly changing range of threats. Global Life Sciences had a division dedicated to defence against germ, chemical and other disabling weapons which was headed by a former soldier, Anna Cerny. One of the proposals before the Board was for a strategic alliance with the British Police Laboratory to develop means to combat chemical warfare at football matches which had now reached epidemic proportions in parts of the country due to the large number of unemployable men in the country.

During the discussion of the alliance with the British Police the Trustee for Public Affairs, a South African named Martha Mayer, recalled the work done in the post-Mandela period to recruit businesses to work with unskilled people. Global Life Sciences had long sponsored charities working with the alienated people in many countries; should the company not tackle the problem directly? Joanna Smith sought views from every Trustee on this issue, and there was a consensus that a pilot project should be established, initially in Scotland, because of its post-independence traumas, as a potential model for a more general drive to tackle alienation. The project would be given to Tom MacLeod, the Steward of Global Life Sciences in Scotland, who had considerable experience of working with recidivists and others at war with society.

The Technical Trustee, Martha Chang, reported that recent work with recombinant DNA had raised the prospect of average life expectancies of over 150 years. The technical issues had largely been settled, but she was concerned about the ethical and societal issues raised by this possibility. Following a lively discussion the Board decided to refer the matter to the Ethics Committee for thorough examination.

And so the Board meeting continued, across time zones, mixing and merging culture in order to give leadership to a business which had been able over the years to generate and share wealth on a steadily increasing scale. What are likely to be the characteristics of a successful company in the mid-21st Century? It seems likely that these will include:

O   meeting expectation by most people worldwide that business is the key generator of wealth;

O   recognition by those involved in generating wealth that they are time-limited custodians of the process on behalf of a wide range of stakeholders in society;

O   an understanding that only open processes and full accountability can create sustainable trust between all stakeholders;

O   commitment to constant self-renewal, to the search for innovation and to consistent improvement through learning;

O   dedication to outstanding performance in the marketplace without having to win by damaging others.

In the late 20th Century business success is often linked to the personality of business leaders. General Electric is deemed to be successful only because of Jack Welch; in the words of Warren Buffet: 'People are voting for the artist, not the painting.' This cult of personality, derived from media focus on pop stars and sports heroes, grossly oversimplifies the processes of business success and leads to unrealistic expectations when star chief executives move into new companies, as with George Fisher at Kodak. For most businessmen their greatest success is often achieved before they become a media idol; this may be true for Warren Buffet, George Soros and even for Bill Gates. In the next century personality will remain important, but as a means of projecting leadership for others to follow, not as a magnet to attract the credit due in large measure to others.

It may be instructive to compare and contrast possible typical business attitudes between the late 20th Century and the early 21st Century:

Table 3   Typical Business Attitudes

Typical 20th Century views	21st Century views may be
success is its own justification (the end justifies the means)	long-term sustainable success depends on an ethical approach
leadership (right or wrong) is all powerful	leadership reaches further by empowering others (in the manner of Robert Greenleaf's 'Servant Leader')
we inform others on a 'need to know' basis	openness is the best long-term policy
business is serious and demands total commitment	business with a shared purpose should be fun

younger employees are better, cheaper and more docile	the old and the young benefit from working together
our tribe is better than your tribe	pool tribal strengths for the benefit of everyone
there are winners and losers (and some survivors)	win/win solutions are better in the long run
not-for-profit activities are second rate	worth is as important as wealth
my importance is proportional to what I take	giving can be a sign of strength

The 20th Century views are redolent of arrogance and of abuse of power. They typify the person who has arrived at greatness by default and who lacks the confidence and humanity to recognize that power is only legitimate when used for the general good. This viewpoint contrasts with that of a leader who has the confidence to recognize their limitations and to work with others openly in order to achieve a shared long-term success. The inadequate leader is driven to fit the stereotype which others have designed; the confident leader works with others to shape a pattern of power and working values which can be effective in the long-term. Where people are eager to go to work there is usually good leadership.

Many models have been devised for governance in the 21st Century. We have already looked at 'Tomorrow's Company', an ethical and inclusive approach to governance which has developed a growing weight of support. The Future Foundation has carried out extensive research, sponsored by BT and has produced a model for 'The Responsible Organization'. This focuses on the expectation of most respondents that companies will take greater responsibility for societal issues in the 21st Century, through the diminishing role of the state and the need to cope with new global challenges. The drivers of this model are ethics, the needs of society and the commercial advantage of the company. Younger people emerge as more concerned about society than those over sixty; people with children are greatly concerned about education and their children's future in a world of obligatory self-reliance. It may be inferred that consumers will be increasingly demanding and will seek relationships with companies which address their wider needs with understanding and creativity. The governance of companies to meet these challenges will need to be outward-looking, sensitive and inclusive of a growing range of stakeholders, yet firm in its resolve to create the wealth needed to meet the long-term needs of those stakeholders in proportion to their contribution to the company. Sound governance will also be expected of the state; in shifting to business the burden of funding pensions and providing more amenities, such as creches, it will need to transfer back the appropriate amounts of tax.

The inclusive models of governance in the future are seen by sections of British business as unrealistic. The CBI favours the focusing effect of shareholder value which might be blurred by equal concern for other stakeholders. The difficulty of accommodating different and often conflicting agendas seems insuperable and too demanding of precious management time. The IOD draws a distinction between 'weak stakeholding', which takes account of legitimate interests, and 'strong stakeholding'. *Business Matters* (January 1998) states: 'we strongly reject the notion of "strong stakeholding" in which the directors should be accountable to all their stakeholders and not just shareholders. This would be quite unworkable, would destroy accountability and would be a recipe for corporate governance anarchy'. Corporate governance is seen by some businessmen as an expensive fad and as a restraint on the natural exuberance of entrepreneurs. There is a danger of a 'nannying' approach to corporate governance which is why effective self-regulation offers a better way forward than excessive legislation. However much some of its critics wish that corporate governance would disappear as an issue of public concern, it is likely to grow in importance for three major reasons – fear, fairness and long-term effectiveness.

Fear is where the concern about governance began, with the scandals which destroyed jobs and damaged confidence in the late 1980s. Lack of openness and accountability created the climate for manipulation and fraud. Even when companies were not wrecked by scandal, there were many which had much to hide and whose employees were not secure in their jobs. Poor governance creates uncertainty, which breeds fear. People who are fearful are incapacitated and lose clarity of values, rather like the Daimler Benz managers in Poland who used condemned Jewish workers in 1942 to overcome a temporary skills shortage and returned them to the SS when no longer needed (Neil Gregor, *Daimler Benz in the Third Reich*, Yale University Press, 1998). The antithesis of fear is fun. When people are confident they can enjoy challenges and manage risk with competence. Release from fear is the first major step towards effective governance, but fear still pervades much of corporate life.

Fairness reflects the trust which grows out of open transactions between people. Where fear reigns, fairness is banished to the back of the mind; where there is no sharing there can be no fairness. As people become more confident they find that they can negotiate workable relationships with others. These relationships depend fundamentally on a shared view of fairness which becomes the key to cooperation and the touchstone for good governance. Fairness is seen in concepts like 'win: win'; lack of fairness led to the Greenbury Report and is manifest in the cynicism which emerges from the one-sided approach to restructuring seen in so many companies in the past ten years.

Long-term effectiveness is the ultimate purpose of corporate governance. In a world which is increasingly open to competition, nations will compete to create the economic, political and social conditions in which their businesses can themselves compete. In the past companies have sought to compete by creating as much monopoly advantage for themselves as possible, damaging others without compunction in doing so. This is as true of Microsoft as it was of Standard Oil or Bell Telephone. In an open, multi-cultural world cooperation is becoming the best way to create sustainable competitive advantage, since few companies will have the resources to do so unaided. This cooperation will be driven by customer needs and will require the active support of employees, suppliers, alliance partners and other stakeholders. Only a system of inclusive corporate governance which can orchestrate and sustain that cooperation will enable the company to adapt and prosper into the future.

The OECD established a study into the role of corporate governance in enhancing economic competitiveness whose results were published in 1998. Its most striking finding is that globalizing markets will increase pressure on companies to be outstanding in order to attract and retain the financial and intellectual capital needed to compete in the long-term. Transparent and motivating corporate governance practices are seen as a major factor in attracting the support needed to prosper in conditions of increasing uncertainty. The report sees no merit in a fixed universal model of corporate governance, but recommends that each company should experiment and adapt to find its own best practice, subject to agreed minimum standards and to universal rules for accounting. This study has integrated best practice from all major economies. It sees shareholder value as being the accepted objective of business, while recognizing the need to be responsive to the demands and expectations of other stakeholders. A convergence between the US philosophy of maximizing shareholder returns over the long-term and the societal focus of German and Japanese companies is expected to occur as globalization forces economies and companies to compete without protection. 'Governments are seen to have a distinct and important responsibility in providing a regulatory framework that allows investors and enterprises to adapt corporate governance practices to rapidly changing circumstances.' The report recommends further work to encourage member nations to establish an enabling regulatory framework to support the improvement of corporate governance. Such work might produce a public policy document, a code of best practice and a set of reporting standards. The need for understanding societal concerns about corporate governance and to clarify responsibilities between the public and private sectors is underlined. Given the likely acceleration of European economic integration arising from the single currency, it may be expected that the present divergence in corporate governance between countries will tend to converge progressively. A member of the OECD Report working party, Jonathan Charkham, has contributed Case Study 1.4 on the issue of globalization.

Many successful businesses of the 19th Century were built by men of vision who took responsibility for communities in order to achieve and sustain their vision. Among many others George Cadbury would have understood and approved of the work begun by his grandson and now expanded by a growing number of enthusiasts. Capitalism may have re-emerged triumphantly from the challenges of the 20th Century, but its triumph will be short-lived unless it adapts to meet the new challenges of globalization, environmental sustainability and interdependence. In a world in which power is increasingly devolved and regulation becomes progressively more difficult, it will fall to companies and other drivers of the microeconomy to build the consensus which will sustain the growth of global capitalism.

Failure to meet this challenge could have dire consequences. In an overpopulated, undernourished and poorly educated world the mature industrial economies have been a source of funding and a model which many emerging nations have begun to adopt for themselves. With less immediate threat of global war and rapid technological advances to cope with diseases and malnutrition there should be an opportunity for sustainable development within the limits of environmental tolerance. Better governance should drive this process, but there remain dictators in parts of the world and reactionary forces which benefit from corruption and abuse. It seems certain that such forces will seek to harness the envy and hatred of those who are alienated from the modern world in order to derail its progress. If global capitalism fails to 'trickle down' to the poorer people who, with modern media, are increasingly aware of a better way of life, the maintenance of the fabric of civilization is at risk. Global capitalism needs to be inclusive in order to be acceptable and will need an inclusive process at the level of each individual business to reach down into society.

Inclusive corporate governance has the potential to become the major instrument for global development and for fulfilling the destiny of companies and of all who work with them. If inclusive corporate governance is used properly, it will help companies to compete for the future by maximizing their effectiveness in understanding and meeting customer needs, using the skills and support of employees, suppliers, distributors and other partners. The success of each company will nourish and support its stakeholders, many of whom will also directly or indirectly be owners of its shares. The success of clusters of companies will contribute substantially to the building of a society in which it will be invigorating and worthwhile to live. This success will, however, need to accommodate the failure of companies and individuals who are unable to adapt and compete in a complex and demanding world. Human beings are imperfect and the groups which they form are subject to the interplay of these imperfections. Effective governance cannot abolish sloth, greed, envy and other 'deadly sins' but, through education and example, must counter them and seek to mitigate imperfection and failure within a society at peace with itself. To adapt another saying, the price of good governance is eternal vigilance.

KEY ISSUES

1   Have we abolished fear, established fairness and set a course towards long-term effectiveness in our organization?
2   Have we developed an open, ethical and inclusive approach to our stakeholder relationships?
3   Do we understand that global capitalism will require us to compete by outstanding example since power will be increasingly diffused?

What action am I committing myself to take? _____

PART II

CASE STUDIES IN CORPORATE GOVERNANCE

❖

INTRODUCTION

In the course of researching for this book a number of individual interviews were granted to me. From these interviews I have been able both to synthesize and test general principles for inclusion in the basic text and to develop specific case studies to illuminate those principles. These case studies are included in this section of the book and fall into the following main groups:

1   Case studies about corporate governance principles
1.1 The Institute of Business Ethics (interview with Stanley Kiaer, Director).
1.2 Standards in Public Life (interview with Peter Rose, Press Officer, Neill Committee).
1.3 Statement of general business principles – Royal Dutch/Shell Group (BT's 'Statement of Business Practice' is shown in Case Study 3.4).
1.4 Corporate Governance and Globalization (interview with Jonathan Charkham – member of the working party on the OECD Report).

2   Case studies of non-trading organizations
2.1 Charities and the Voluntary Sector (interview with Lynne Berry, Charity Commissioner).
2.2 Governance and the professions (interview with Carl Hopkins, Partner, Lawrence Graham, Solicitors).
2.3 Corporate governance in a trade association (interview with Warren Newman, Chief Executive, BACTA).

3   Case studies of various trading organizations
3.1 Governance by and for employees – the John Lewis model (interview with Ken Temple, Chief Registrar, John Lewis Partnership).
3.2 Equitable Life Assurance Society (interview with Roy Ranson, Chief Executive).
3.3 Birmingham Midshires Building Society (interview with Michael Jackson, Chief Executive).

3.4   Corporate governance at British Telecom (interview with Luke March, Director of Corporate Governance).

3.5   Morgan Crucible – governance on a global scale (interview with Dr Bruce Farmer, Chief Executive).

3.6   An SME view of corporate governance (interview with Richard Purdey, Chairman, Merrydown plc).

4   Case studies of bodies defending good corporate governance

4.1   The LEX column – one of the pillars of corporate governance (interview with Hugo Dixon, *Financial Times*).

4.2   Regulation by Research – the role of PIRC (interview with Ann Simpson, Executive Director).

5   Case studies of bodies widening the scope of corporate governance

5.1   'Tomorrow's Company' approach to corporate governance (interview with Nick Obolensky, Director of Centre for Tomorrow's Company).

5.2   Stewardship management in ZENECA Agrichemicals (interview with Andy Coe, Stewardship Analyst).

5.3   Governance and Knowledge (interview with Elizabeth Lank, Programme Director, Knowledge Management, ICL plc).

These case studies largely speak for themselves. Having done them I am aware of countless other nooks and crannies in the world of governance which remain unexplored and which could add further insights into the achieving of better practice in the corporate sector. That is perhaps the raw material for another book …

1.1

THE INSTITUTE OF BUSINESS ETHICS

The Institute of Business Ethics (IBE) was founded in 1986 by the Christian Association of Business Executives with the following aims: 'to emphasize the essentially ethical nature of wealth creation, to encourage the highest standards of behaviour by companies, to publicize the best ethical practices and to demonstrate that business ethics involve positive initiatives, as well as constraints'. The Institute is a multi-faith organization, with charitable status and with wide support from major British companies. A key tenet of the IBE is that 'goodness advances with a mix of altruism and self-interest'.

The Institute's Director is Stanley Kiaer, a former executive in the pharmaceutical industry who has seen the scope of the Institute widen to cover consultations, conferences, research and education. The IBE focuses on the dissemination of best practice and offers models of ethical codes, but without seeking to be prescriptive. The emphasis is on practicality; this is well illustrated by the 'Twelve Steps' process which has helped a growing number of companies.

1   **Integration**   Produce a strategy for integrating the code into the running of the business at the time that it is issued.
2   **Endorsement**   Make sure that the code is endorsed by the Chairman and CEO.
3   **Distribution**   Send the code to all employees in a readable and portable form and give it to all employees joining the company.
4   **Breaches**   Include a short section on how an employee can react if they are faced with a potential breach of the code or are in doubt about a course of action involving an ethical choice.
5   **Personal Response**   Give all staff the personal opportunity to respond to the content of the code.

6   **Affirmation**   Have a procedure for managers and supervisors regularly to state that they and their staff understand and apply the provisions of the code and raise matters not covered by it.

7   **Regular Review**   Have a procedure for regular review and updating of the code.

8   **Contracts**   Consider making adherence to the code obligatory by including reference to it in all contracts of employment and linking it with disciplinary procedures.

9   **Training**   Ask those responsible for company training programmes at all levels to include issues raised by the code in their programmes.

10   **Translation**   See that the code is translated for use in overseas subsidiaries or other place where English is not the principal language.

11   **Distribution**   Make copies of the code available to business partners (suppliers, customers, and so on).

12   **Annual Report**   Reproduce or insert a copy of the code in the Annual Report so that shareholders and a wider public know about the company's position on ethical matters.

In recent times the Institute has been helping businesses to cope with ethical problems in international markets. In this work it has been aided by executives with practical experience of ethical issues in foreign cultures, such as Ken Rushden, Company Secretary of ICI, who spoke at the launch of 'Codes of Ethics and International Business'. It is so important to look to the long-term. Stanley Kiaer cited the case of a Kenyan accountancy firm deciding to create a culture of honesty: initially it was damaging to the business, but their reputation for probity secured for the firm work from the World Bank.

The environment has been of concern to the Institute for many years. A new factor is the strength of NGOs and their access to the Internet, which has put environmental responsibility at the top of the agenda for many of the IBE's subscribers. Help is offered in developing codes of environmental responsibility which give practical guidance to employees.

The 1980s with its emphasis on privatization and maximization of profits has brought its own problems. Downsizing has caused a decline in loyalty both on the part of employer and employee, and corporate memory has in some cases been destroyed, as a whole layer of management has been removed. Shell has sought to counter this with its 'Statement of General Business Principles' which is shown in Case Study 1.3. Not all such codes are mandatory and the best involve extensive consultations; NatWest Bank took two years to negotiate and refine its code of ethics. Having a code is only the first step, but the code can become a vehicle for building trust, if company directors are seen to provide leadership and 'live the code'.

The Institute is becoming involved with schools as an initiative to bring ethical values to young people in their formative years. Role models are important for impressionable youngsters and those provided by *Eastenders* and other television programmes do not necessarily encourage the adoption of ethical values. The approach to schools uses a 'Responsibility, Relationships and Respect' (3Rs) set of teaching aids and the IBE provides training for schools where requested. The Jewish Association of Business Ethics goes further and performs sketches to schools to highlight moral dilemmas, encouraging businessmen to speak of their own experience in this field direct to schools.

The IBE surveys the use of corporate codes of ethics regularly. The 1998 Report shows 57 per cent of large companies having or planning to have codes of conduct, compared with 18 per cent in the 1987 survey. In 1997 replies came 30.7 per cent from Chairmen/Chief Executives and 40.4 per cent from Company Secretaries, marking a progressive shift of accountability from Personnel and Corporate Affairs.

Stanley Kiaer is concerned that it is harder for smaller companies to adopt codes of ethics. Often they take their ethics from the beliefs of the owner, and do not feel they need a code, particularly as they believe it involves both time and money – two precious commodities. He is pondering a model of the 'honest entrepreneur' in order to address this issue. While entrepreneurs are popularly seen as selfish and unaccountable, models such as Anita Roddick may demonstrate that small businesses can prosper on the basis of ethical practices. On the topic of 'whistle-blowing' Stanley Kiaer suggests that the problem often starts where people join the wrong company. Careful assessment of the company during recruitment and questions about codes of ethics and governance processes will often raise warning signals before engagement. He is aware of nine companies which have hot lines to enable people to air their concerns without prejudice. The growing use of mentors for the development of junior staff is also a useful safety valve, particularly as the breakdown of the traditional family has removed the 'Uncle Georges' to whom young people were once able to turn. The IBE has mentoring dinners from time to time and some of the professions are adept at mentoring. An example is IMACE where retired accountants act as mentors to any in the profession who feel the need. The Institute has held conferences on the growing problem of personal debt and the risks to which it exposes those concerned.

The IBE has seen considerable change during its short life. Born on the rising tide of Thatcherism, it has seen its message move from partial rejection to recognized relevance. Now as Thatcherism ebbs, it is well-placed to help to bring back the trust which is essential to enable business to thrive.

1.2

STANDARDS IN PUBLIC LIFE

ETHICAL CHALLENGES IN A TIME OF CHANGE

The Nolan Committee on Standards in Public Life was set up in 1994 by John Major, then Prime Minister, to act as an 'ethical workshop' to clarify and codify ethical standards in the public arena. The terms of reference of the Committee are:

> To examine current concerns about standards of conduct of all holders of public office, including arrangements relating to financial and commercial activities, and make recommendations as to any changes in present arrangements which might be required to ensure the highest standards of propriety in public life.
>
> For these purposes, public office should include: Ministers, civil servants and advisers; Members of Parliament and UK Members of the European Parliament; members and senior officers of all non-departmental public bodies and of NHS bodies; non-Ministerial office holders; members and other senior officers of other bodies discharging publicly-funded functions; and elected members and senior officers of local authorities.

This remit has recently been extended: 'To review issues in relation to the funding of political parties and to make recommendations as to any change in present arrangements.'

The key drivers of the Nolan, now Neill, Committee were initially the concern around payment to MPs to ask Parliamentary Questions, the decentralization of the civil service into agencies (with false analogies with the privatization of utilities), the growth of quangos, the dismantling of local government and the growth of special interest lobbying.

The Committee has examined and reported on Members of Parliament, Ministers and Civil Servants, non-departmental public bodies, and local quangos and local government and has also reviewed progress arising from its report on quangos. It is now mandated to examine the funding of political parties. The Committee's first report distilled 'The Seven Principles of Public Life' which have been adopted by the House of Commons and by many public sector organizations; these principles form the basis for more detailed codes of conduct in each organization.

The Seven Principles of Public Life are:

1   **Selflessness**   Holders of public office should act solely in terms of the public interest. They should not do so in order to gain financial or other material benefits for themselves, their family, or their friends.

2   **Integrity**   Holders of public office should not place themselves under any financial or other obligation to outside individuals or organizations that might seek to influence them in the performance of their official duties.

3   **Objectivity**   In carrying out public business, including making public appointments, awarding contracts, or recommending individuals for rewards and benefits, holders of public office should make choices on merit.

4   **Accountability**   Holders of public office are accountable for their decisions and actions to the public and must submit themselves to whatever scrutiny is appropriate to their office.

5   **Openness**   Holders of public office should be as open as possible about all the decisions and actions that they take. They should give reasons for their decisions and restrict information only when the wider public interest clearly demands.

6   **Honesty**   Holders of public office have a duty to declare any private interests relating to their public duties and to take steps to resolve any conflicts arising in a way that protects the public interest.

7   **Leadership**   Holders of public office should promote and support these principles by leadership and example.

I spoke to Peter Rose, Press Secretary of the Neill Committee, about progress made in the last four years and its enlarged agenda. The Nolan process has begun to reverse earlier attempts to impose codes of behaviour from the centre. These had never been 'owned' by local government and had led to manipulation and misunderstanding. With the reversal of the Thatcherite policy of centralization by John Major the Nolan process had been able to work more effectively with local government and local quangos to develop workable standards. The fourth report shows that departments and local quangos have been trying to implement their codes and guidance notes, although there remain serious problems of communication and some sectors, for instance, older universities and further education colleges, remain recalcitrant. The process is now sufficiently advanced for the Government to issue a Green Paper to move it forward. The OECD has begun to examine the issue of ethics in public life and is relying heavily on UK experience.

Peter Rose believes that further work remains to be done to facilitate whistle-blowing. The traditional civil service approach has been that the Cabinet Secretary's door 'is always open'. This is manifestly inadequate as a safeguard and arrangements for independent advice for civil servants are being examined, possibly some kind of Ombudsman. The same problem exists in local government and quangos and will impede progress if not addressed.

The likelihood of a backlash, such as that which has stalled progress by the Hampel Committee, is not seen to be great by Peter Rose. He finds that the main difficulty is over-slavish interpretation of codes. For example, the new processes for open appointment to quango boards, with a new com-missioner to audit the selection process has led to delays in finalizing appointments. In hybrid organizations, like TECs, there is some resentment by businessmen used to a different culture at what they see as interference. Peter Rose believes that private sector people working with the public sec-tor may need specific training to appreciate the public service ethic.

I asked Peter Rose if there could be a long-term convergence between governance in the public and private sectors. We examined the 'Seven Principles' (to which Lord Nolan might have added Courage) and isolated Selflessness and Objectivity. It was agreed that there were increasing issues around rewards in the public sector – for example, in some cases the chief executives of agencies were running large businesses. The shortage of good leaders would make realistic remuneration an issue in the public sector, balanced by Accountability and those other principles. It was difficult to see entrepreneurs embracing Selflessness, but to do so they would need to understand the difference between their ownership of shares and their stewardship as a director (as demonstrated in the recent conflict at Newcastle United). Objectivity had been found difficult in hybrid organiza-tions. Civil servants were in tune with the principle of objectivity, but per-sonal agendas were more intrusive among business people. Rules on the declaration of interest were tight in the public sector, in particular for local government. Nolan called for the declaration of a 'clear and substantial interest'.

The growth of hybrid organizations and of the Private Funding Initiative, together with globalization and the breakdown of rigid structures are seen by Peter Rose as trends which will lead to a convergence between public and private sector governance. Both have to work in the same society and answer to many of the same stakeholders. In the past the DTI has seen the companies they regulate as different in culture; this misunderstanding led to failure to tackle situations of abuse such as Maxwell. Today there seems to be a growing recognition that 'good ethics are good business', driven by bodies such as The Institute of Business Ethics and policed by PIRC and other watchdog groups.

Peter Rose is interested to see what will be the outcome of the study into the funding of political parties. In the USA there is a clear differentiation between access and influence in respect of contact between lobbyists and politicians. In the 1970s the Federal Electioneering Commission had tried to control the process, but had fallen foul of the First Amendment to the Constitution. Americans not only protect freedom of speech, but are sensitive to freedom of how people spend their own money. As a result US politicians such as Forbes and Perot have been free to spend without limit to buy office. In the UK expenditure is limited to £8500 per candidate and yet the Conservatives spent over £15 million at the last election. The difference is the blanket publicity for the party from which individual candidates benefit indirectly. The Neill Committee is expecting to have an interesting time in its study of political funding!

The process used by the Committee has been a key part of its success. It approaches each study with an open mind and develops with experts an 'issues and questions' paper which allows flexible answers and encourages other thoughts to emerge. The material which has been gathered is then exposed in a number of open hearings which ensures that those involved build ownership of the results through active participation. The process is thorough and develops credibility in the outcome.

1.3

STATEMENT OF GENERAL BUSINESS PRINCIPLES – ROYAL DUTCH/SHELL GROUP

1 Objectives

The objectives of Shell companies are to engage efficiently, responsibly and profitably in the oil, gas, chemicals and other selected businesses and to participate in the search for and development of other sources of energy. Shell companies seek a high standard of performance and aim to maintain a long-term position in their respective competitive environments.

2 Responsibilities

Shell companies recognize five areas of responsibility:

i   *To shareholders*
        To protect shareholders' investment, and provide an acceptable return.

ii   *To customers*
        To win and maintain customers by developing and providing products and services which offer value in terms of price, quality, safety and environmental impact, which are supported by the requisite technological, environmental and commercial expertise.

iii   *To employees*
        To respect the human rights of their employees, to provide their employees with good and safe conditions of work, and good and competitive terms and conditions of service, to promote the development and best use of human talent and equal opportunity employment, and to encourage the involvement of employees in the planning and direction of their work, and in the application of

these principles within their company. It is recognized that commercial success depends on the full commitment of all employees.

iv   *To those with whom they do business*
To seek mutually beneficial relationships with contractors, suppliers and in joint ventures and to promote the application of these principles in so doing. The ability to promote these principles effectively will be an important factor in the decision to enter into or remain in such relationships.

v   *To society*
To conduct business as responsible corporate members of society, to observe the laws of the countries in which they operate, to express support for fundamental human rights in line with the legitimate role of business and to give proper regard to health, safety and the environment consistent with their commitment to contribute to sustainable development.

These five areas of responsibility are seen as inseparable. Therefore it is the duty of management continuously to assess the priorities and discharge its responsibilities as best it can on the basis of that assessment.

3 Economic principles

Profitability is essential to discharging these responsibilities and staying in business. It is a measure both of efficiency and of the value that customers place on Shell products and services. It is essential to the allocation of the necessary corporate resources and to support the continuing investment required to develop and produce future energy supplies to meet consumer needs. Without profits and a strong financial foundation it would not be possible to fulfil the responsibilities outlined above.

Shell companies work in a wide variety of changing social, political and economic environments, but in general they believe that the interests of the community can be served most efficiently by a market economy.

Criteria for investment decisions are not exclusively economic in nature but also take into account social and environmental considerations and an appraisal of the security of the investment.

1.4

CORPORATE GOVERNANCE AND GLOBALIZATION

Jonathan Charkham brings his experience in the Bank of England and as a practising company director to bear on issues of corporate governance in many major world economies. His book *Keeping Good Company* (OUP, 1994) remains an authoritative text on the subject and he was a member of the working party which produced the OECD Report, published in 1998. Jonathan sees corporate governance in a global context and can relate its processes to those of banking supervision where it is useful so to do.

The OECD Report was very comprehensive but it 'papered over the cracks' in respect of the very different national attitudes to the purpose of corporate governance. These range from the 'Chicago School' view that companies exist to maximize profits for shareholders to the Continental tradition in which companies operate in support of the 'public weal'. For economists such as Milton Friedman, social responsibility has no role in the boardroom since it impedes the maximization of profits; the Chicago School stance has been modified more recently to focus on shareholder value, leaving shareholders as the final beneficiaries of company operations while allowing directors more flexibility in how shareholder value is created. Jonathan Charkham illustrates the Continental model with an actual incident in Germany in which a company had too many factories and was concerned to find a socially acceptable way to concentrate production. At a critical moment one factory burned down and the Management Board recommended closing the site. The Supervisory Board opposed this recommendation indicating that the company was morally obliged to use the insurance money to rebuild the factory and continue operations in that community. Would such a decision be acceptable for a US company?

For Jonathan Charkham any process of convergence in corporate governance philosophy and practice in different countries is likely to take a considerable time. He sees a number of dimensions to corporate governance that would need to become aligned or reconciled; these include (a) purpose of governance (b) governance laws and structures (c) accounting conventions.

Another way of expressing the purpose or philosophy of governance in the developed world is to contrast the 'shareholder primacy' and 'stakeholder-focused' approaches. The Anglo-Saxon world has traditionally given primacy to shareholder interests, in order to attract risk capital to support new enterprises. This accorded with the 'laissez faire' philosophy of government and contrasts with the more interventionist model developed on the Continent. The USA has had few government-owned companies; in Europe the 'commanding heights' of most economies have been state-owned in significant proportion at various times. Such economies tend to have a national focus and to be protective of the short-term interests of the different stakeholders in a company.

Jonathan Charkham expressed reservations about shareholder value as the sole business purpose. He finds that board decisions are rarely driven solely by shareholder value considerations. These are always of great importance but shareholders' interests can only be protected in the long-run if other stakeholders – employees, suppliers, bankers, the community, are safeguarded too. It is only by growing the profitability of the business over time that stakeholders can be attracted or retained, but such growth is heavily dependent on the support of stakeholders.

The laws and structure of governance differ markedly between countries. The UK Companies Act is an 'enabling' document, allowing considerable freedom of operation to company directors (boards are not mentioned!). This freedom was sometimes abused and the inaccuracy of reporting in some well-known cases led to the setting up of the Cadbury Committee and the code it produced. German company law is detailed and prescriptive. It was shaped to operate within a closed economy; with globalization it may become burdensome (will the employees of Chrysler and Rover be represented on the Supervisory Board?). The USA has different laws for each state but has tight regulation of the securities market through the SEC. Curiously, Jonathan Charkham finds US directors less sensitive to legal challenge than might be expected in a very litigious country.

The process of globalization does not yet seem to have changed national structures very much. Switzerland has a small market and a disproportionate number of multinational companies (Nestlé sells only 2 per cent of its output in the Swiss market), yet the system of governance remains largely Swiss, with circumscribed voting rights for shareholders and very few non-Swiss directors. One factor which is beginning to change governance in European multinationals is the need to change voting rights and accounting conventions if they wish to trade shares on the New York Stock Exchange.

Nestlé has been obliged to make such changes and Daimler Benz could not have acquired Chrysler without having done so many years ago. Few European companies have yet globalized their board membership to the extent that major Anglo-Saxon companies, such as ICI, have done. This reflects the relative homogeneity of European societies compared to that of the USA. Where people have a shared culture, relationships need less formalization than in 'melting pot' countries, such as the USA, where 'American values' and 'due process' provide unifying factors for differing ethnic cultures. In America recourse to law is endemic; in Japan it is an admission of failure in relationships.

Other significant differences are likely to impede the globalization of corporate governance. Germans and Japanese tend to work in committees, developing solutions through 'group think'; Americans are typically individualistic. In French companies the CEO (PDG) is often all-powerful. German law puts management responsibility solely upon the Management Board (German Company Law is more prescriptive than that of most other countries). The French have the option of using two-tier boards but they are rare, probably because of the separation of powers which they imply. Formal UK company law remains permissive as far as governance is concerned but it has now been much supplemented by 'voluntary' codes which are treated for all intents and purposes like official regulations (except that they are not policed directly by the government or its agencies).

Accounting conventions are the third crucial dimension of corporate governance that needs reconciliation if global convergence is to be achieved, particularly through greater use of the international capital markets. At present attitudes and conventions vary greatly – to the point where 'profit' is calculated on a quite different basis. It is suggested that a lack of clear accounting has been a brake on mergers and acquisitions, not only in markets such as Russia but even in developed markets. German companies, for instance, are allowed to accumulate hidden reserves and to include pension funds in their balance sheets – but what happens if the company is insolvent? Jonathan Charkham sees greater convergence of accounting conventions and rules as a major precondition for achieving the potential benefits of globalization.

The process of globalization seems likely to favour those multinational companies which have learned how to reconcile their codes of conduct with local practices in different markets. The openness and pragmatism of Anglo-Saxon groups has often been an advantage in this respect. Jonathan Charkham does not see any chance for a world authority to monitor corporate governance until there is an agreed purpose and a consistent set of accounting conventions. Given such a framework with clear laws and operating structures, it should become easier to begin to regulate corporate governance on a global basis. Whether it is appropriate to do so is another question: he does not think it would be. In the UK corporate governance of quoted companies is regulated by codes of conduct, leaving the policing largely to market and peer pressure. It may be more appropriate for the WTO or some world body to develop and maintain a code, leaving the regulation largely to market forces and pressure from those affected by poor performance. Certainly Jonathan Charkham sees the prospect of a Universal Companies Act as very distant, since there would be no impulsion to create it unless there had been a major disaster such as the 1930s Depression. Full-scale regulation could only be based on a shared legal structure, which would be preferred by many Europeans but resisted by Anglo-Saxons. In the last analysis the best regulator is the competitive advantage which best practice in corporate governance gives to the company which you fear the most.

2.1

CHARITIES AND THE VOLUNTARY SECTOR

The voluntary sector in the UK makes a very significant contribution to the economy of the country, most of which escapes normal GDP calculations. Over 600 000 paid employees can be identified, but this may be only 3 per cent of the people involved in some degree in voluntary work. The value of this work to the community is incalculable, but its monetary equivalent is likely to be a substantial proportion of Britain's £800 billion recorded GDP even though its financial input is only some £15 billion/year. Charities are a discrete part of the voluntary sector, administered under the Charities Acts and subject to specific rules – for example, that they may not engage in political activity.

The voluntary sector predates the formal economy and is based on the principle of supporting those who are disadvantaged. In origin much of its activity was organized through the churches and it has always had considerable involvement in education. Many early charitable foundations were established by benefactors and administered largely with voluntary support. Over the years there has been a gradual movement towards state involvement in some areas which were voluntary (schooling, Poor Law, housing, and so on) but most successful initiatives in the voluntary sector have always been locally established and maintained.

In the early 1990s it was decided to review the working of the voluntary sector in order to prepare it for the 21st Century. An Independent Commission on the Future of the Voluntary Sector was established by the National Council for Voluntary Organisations (NCVO) chaired by Professor Nicholas Deakin with Lynne Berry as Vice-Chairman. Its report made the following key points:

O   Voluntary and community organizations in all their diversity are a major national resource. Their independence must be safeguarded.

135

○   A single inclusive definition of charity should be introduced, based on a new concept of public benefit.

○   Users are vital stakeholders. Their rights are central to the future role of the sector and their involvement is crucial.

○   The sector should be governed by six basic principles:

1   Public policy needs to recognize the unique qualities of voluntary action.
2   Partnership must be on an equal basis.
3   The role of users is crucial to the sector.
4   Voluntary bodies must always be free to act as advocates.
5   It must be managed professionally without deflecting from the sector's purposes and aims.
6   Diversity of funding sources is one of the best guarantees of independence.

○   The sector should seek to harness the enthusiasm and commitment of young people.

○   Voluntary organizations should work in partnership with other agencies to make their distinctive contribution. But their diversity and the need to preserve independence rule out any 'master plan'.

○   A concordat should be drawn up with government laying down principles for future relations. Government departments should make their requirements and priorities explicit.

○   Voluntary work must not be a substitute for activity that is properly the responsibility of the state or the market.

○   New sources of financial support are needed to supplement funding from government and business.

○   Voluntary organizations must maintain public confidence through recognizing the importance of setting standards of good practice and effectiveness.

During the enquiry there had been considerable sensitivity about the issue of standards for the voluntary sector. Given the importance of achieving maximum effectiveness from the limited resources available to the voluntary sector, it was decided to refer this issue to an Advisory Group, chaired by Lynne Berry and involving representatives of key constituencies within the voluntary sector.

The report of this Advisory Group was published by the Joseph Rowntree Foundation in April 1997. Its title 'Towards Voluntary Sector Code of Practice' underplays the degree of consensus achieved by the group and its constituencies, but leaves the door open for individual organizations to develop their specific codes of practice based on the framework and consensus developed by the Advisory Group. The basic commitments were seen to be to:

O   state our purpose clearly and keep it relevant to current conditions;
O   be explicit about the needs that we intend to meet and how this will be achieved;
O   manage and target resources effectively and do what we say we will do;
O   evaluate the effectiveness of our work, tackle poor performance and respond to complaints fairly and promptly;
O   agree and set out for all those to whom we are accountable how we will fulfil these responsibilities;
O   be clear about the standards to which we will work;
O   be open about our arrangements for involving users;
O   have a systematic and open process for making appointments to our governing body;
O   set out the role and responsibilities of members of our governing body;
O   have clear arrangements for involving, training, supporting and managing volunteers;
O   ensure that our policies and practices do not discriminate unfairly or lead to other forms of unfair treatment;
O   recruit staff openly, remunerate them fairly and be a good employer.

The chapters to which these undertakings refer contain a considerable amount of shared experience and acknowledged best practice. These chapters cover:

O   **Effectiveness** (clear objectives, targeted resources, performance evaluation);
O   **Accountability** (to whom accountable, degrees of accountability, complaints procedure);
O   **Standards** (quality-driven approach, standards for performance and governance, benchmarking);
O   **User involvement** (self-empowerment of users, user choice where possible, openness);
O   **Governance** (managing risk, guarding mission, statutory and codified rules, balancing stakeholders);
O   **Voluntary action** (involving, training, supporting and managing volunteers for focused action);
O   **Equality and fairness** (avoiding discrimination towards users or other stakeholders);

○   **Staff management** (recruiting, training and remunerating staff, relations with volunteers).

In the view of Lynne Berry a key issue facing the voluntary sector is whether it exists to push at users the services which it believes to be appropriate or whether users should be allowed to pull from the sector the services which they wish to have. Many providers do not believe that their users can exercise judgement in respect of services if they are mentally impaired or have significant disabilities. Providers often see themselves as 'special' and find it unseemly to seek commonality of purpose or governance. The 'philanthropic and beneficent' sector ('phil and ben') rarely has problems with cooperation: the large national charities saw the code of practice as an aid to better funding; smaller charities saw it as an unnecessary bureaucracy. It seems that their positions have begun to converge through further work now being done by the Royal Society of Arts (RSA) and the NCVO.

The desire of the Labour Party to reach a concordat with the voluntary sector has forced its constituents to decide how to organize a joint response to Alan Michael, the Minister responsible for the initiative. Following on from the April 1997 report, Rodney Buse of RSA and John Plummer of Demos, who researched for the Nolan Report, have worked for NCVO on mapping all existing codes of practice. Lynne Berry and the Charity Commission are working with them, convinced that a model code needs to be developed without delay, lest the Government seeks to impose its own model on the voluntary sector.

The voluntary sector is focused on immediate action and fiercely independent. Structure, processes and accountability do not come naturally to most workers in the sector. Each participant needs to think through its mission and identify its stakeholders (users, funders, wider public and others) and decide how to structure and weight those relationships. Such thinking helps the organization to campaign more effectively, having clarified its issues and marshalled its evidence. A family health charity might campaign on poverty, not a minimum wage; highlighting problems is usually a better strategy for a charity than advancing solutions (which might cause offence to some potential donors). The power of evidence is stronger when potential donors may draw their own conclusions.

The environment is not a charitable issue so that Greenpeace and other environmental lobbyists cannot have charitable status. The main stream of charity lies in relief of suffering and in education. Educative trusts have charitable status only to the extent that they focus on learning; where education goes beyond diagnosis to indoctrination, it has no charitable status. Such distinctions are often difficult for smaller charities to understand and they usually need improved governance more than the larger charities who support and mostly practise the concept. Good governance begins with clarity about the mission of the organization and about its rules and regulations, derived from its Memorandum and Articles of Association or from the Deed establishing it. There are some 180 000 registered charities in the UK, of which 140 000 have income of less than £10 000/year. Only 20 000 charities have incomes in excess of £100 000/year. This distorted pattern derives from the common custom of supporting local charities and large ones with a high profile. Those in the middle are often struggling to survive.

The Charity Commission is both a registrar and a regulator of charities. It was founded in 1853 with the express purpose of speeding up the working of the Chancery courts which handled disputes over trusts. The focus of the organization was for well over a hundred years strictly legal, primarily on trust law. The concept of charity law is unique to England and Wales and the basic legislation dates from 1601. Charity law is entwined with trust law: both have grown largely out of precedent, with occasional consolidation by statute, and are today very untidy and backward-looking. Trust law remains inadequate for current needs and likely to become increasingly out of touch with the needs of tomorrow's world.

In 1989 the role of the Charity Commission moved away from its emphasis on trust law and its tendency to introspection towards giving more active support to the charity sector. New working models were introduced and new approaches to governance; the Charity Commission began to take a closer interest in the finances and wider issues affecting its registered charities. The Charity Commission is a government department, reporting to the Home Office for the past thirty years, and administering the Charities Acts. The 1993 Charities Act changed the role of the Commission and its operating rules; whereas all Commissioners had previously been required to be legally qualified, the new Commission had three lay commissioners and two lawyers. One of the lay commissioners is now Chief Commissioner and another an accountant. The register has now been established properly for the first time; the database is complete and the first annual returns being made. There are now clear accounting regulations and a watch on solvency. There are now recommended structures for charities, varying by size, and accounting systems are being standardized. The Commission has changed its stance from introspection towards greater involvement in the markets in which the charities it regulates seek to operate.

Charities were furious with the 1993 Charities Act but most are coming to terms with the new regime. From Commission research it is clear that the public does not see charities as necessarily good. There have been some swindlers which masqueraded as charities and a number of 'religious' charities which have had a bad Press. The tide of libertarianism has receded and the case for financial governance and accountability has been won. Now there is a need for greater openness, clearer purpose and wider choice for users. The Commission cannot interfere in the running of charities unless their governance breaks down, in which case trustees may be removed. In the past finding abuse depended on whistle-blowing, but now analysis can point to malpractice. One charity was found to have been gun-running in Bosnia behind the cover of its relief work. The Commission has two forensic accountants and some ex-Customs staff who can expose international manipulations.

In the USA the IRS regulates the voluntary sector. In Europe there is a NGO network to which the Commission has access. The Commission also has a secondee at the European Commission to further its understanding of the process of Europeanization. Charities are an English concept; voluntary work is not common outside the UK. In France cooperatives and collectives do charitable work, but the trustees and workers are also beneficiaries. It is not certain that the altruistic model will be adopted by Europe in the future.

The applications of charity are also changing. There are moves to make urban regeneration charitable, even though it will inevitably create private benefit. There is also a Private Finance Initiative model. One benefit of the new database at the Charity Commission is that themes can easily be pursued (user benefit, trustee benefit, private/public benefit from education, and so on). The Commission also needs answers from Government about charitable status for religious organizations and other groups. Even clubs have now lost their charitable status, which shows how the concept of charity had widened during years of loose regulation. The impact of the National Lottery on the income of charities is not clear, but will need to be watched carefully. The future status of trustees needs to be reviewed; should they be paid in some circumstances? The ability to sue trustees also needs to be re-evaluated. Charities need to become accustomed to regulation and the Commission may need greater power of sanction. Even with the present limited powers the Commission finds itself being sued by Arthur Scargill! The power of local authorities to nominate trustees has been abused on several occasions.

Lynne Berry sees the end of the amateur trustee for charities. This trend is reflected in Kevin Ford's expression 'the era of decent chaps is over' in the Ford Partnership Report *Twenty-one trends for the twenty-first century*. Often trustees are well-intentioned but unbriefed, or 'leave their brains outside the boardroom door'. Trustees need to understand what is expected of them and to be given practical guidance on how to proceed. Charities need to win public confidence and regulation has to be purposeful but helpful, in the manner of Claire Spottiswood at Ofgas. The Charity Commission has been recruiting staff from charities and has a hundred people regularly visiting registered charities. 'Learning on the ground' is the new style of regulation and enables charities to seek help on how they balance calls for attention from their different stakeholders. The Commission can only give limited advice but encourages charities to network with each other and to join the Council of Voluntary Service.

It is possible that the governance of charities will converge with corporate governance over time. Certainly Lynne Berry finds she can relate to the language used by the Prince's Trust which is a bridge between the charitable and business sectors. The Charity Commission is keen on the social audit work done by the New Economics Foundation, BT Forum and others. The BT Forum has helped to improve communications within and between voluntary organizations.

Lynne Berry has studied the not-for-profit sector in Japan. The English model is perplexing to Japanese people who find the role of the Charity Commission hard to understand. With company paternalism waning, Japan will need a third sector to provide social cohesion. Lynne Berry has talked at length with Mrs Shoichiro Toyoda, wife of the Chairman of Toyota, who is active in promoting NGOs in Japan. She sees that, even after forty years' work, it will take another twenty years to achieve real success in Japan, even though the era of jobs for life has passed.

The Charity Commission sees governance as an increasingly important issue. The former lax administration of charities created few major scandals, such as the 'Lady Aberdare' fund raising scam, but probably did a great deal of hidden damage. Today the Commission is developing a 'good nose for bad 'uns' and, through better processes and the taking-up of references, the chances of crooks working for charities is lessened. Lynne Berry sees a need to register charity workers, create curricula vitae and vetting procedures, in order to minimize entryism by undesirables. There have been problems with paedophiles in some charities and the legal grounds for refusing the offer of work are still inadequate. At present the Commission may not access the police computer, but these powers are being sought. Some of the people who work for charities have strange motives, seeking power, prestige or authority. The larger charities are obliged to be accountable but regulating small charities can be unpleasant, suffering threats, hate mail and even physical assault. Charities increasingly deal with a wide range of stakeholders and those running them need considerable skills to cope. Lynne Berry's former charity deals with 28 local authorities, five Government departments, 40 companies, and so on and administers a budget exceeding £6 million. A business of similar size and complexity would be subject to considerable internal and external regulation.

Lynne Berry sees the balance of governance moving towards supporting the needs of users, much as businesses have been obliged to give priority to customer requirements. There remain some charities with monopoly power who cling to the idea of supplier-led offerings, but these will become progressively fewer in number. The pressurizing of donors through incessant mail shots and telephone canvassing will need to be brought under control. Greater coherence will be needed in establishing policy for the voluntary sector, which will need to move beyond efficiency towards effectiveness.

People are increasingly unwilling to tolerate amateurism or poor governance in the charities sector – they want to see the impact of their contribution and will complain if results are not demonstrable. Only good governance can ensure effectiveness.

2.2

GOVERNANCE AND THE PROFESSIONS

If the media are seen as the 'fourth estate' of the realm, it makes eminent sense to identify the professions as another distinct part of society. In many ways the professions are the successors to the monks and nuns who provided solicitude and learning to the outside world prior to the Reformation. Their service was altruistic and required the trust of its recipients to be effective.

Subsequently the needs of society have been met by the public sector, by the voluntary sector and by the professions. Services from the professions have been paid directly or indirectly and the professions have organized themselves into bodies which are in many ways the successors to the medieval guilds. These bodies are self-perpetuating, control admission to each profession, regulate their members and also, in many cases, represent their members' interests to other parties, as if they were a trades union, or regulate markets for their members' services.

The professions face several dilemmas in respect of governance. They have for many years been held up as a model of self-regulation and yet their members have much to gain individually from the extension of bureaucratic regulation. Where there have been failures of governance there have mostly been professional people implicated directly, or mainly indirectly, in the process and this has progressively corroded confidence in the professions. The hidden and rather arcane governance processes of many professional bodies has not inspired confidence in a general public which is increasingly well-educated and demanding of its rights. The reporting in the media of the internal struggles for control of the Law Society did little to help the image of solicitors, although the outcome may be a healthier governance of the profession. Perhaps the most insidious influence has been the tendency of politicians and media to lampoon the professions as lazy, incompetent and self-serving. Given the importance of the professions in serving global businesses investing in the UK or working in the City of London, this stigma cannot be in the long-term interest of the United Kingdom.

Carl Hopkins, a partner in Lawrence Graham, a firm of solicitors, has extensive experience of governance in the public sector and of the problems of achieving an acceptable level of effectiveness. The Widdicombe and Nolan reports have contributed to a more accountable approach to local government and Carl is confident that self-regulation can be made to work, given strong leadership and mutual trust. He recognizes that the external regulation model is seductive, but fears that such models are bureaucratic and self-perpetuating. He believes that all regulators should be time-limited and be committed to working themselves out of a job. This approach may be seen in Don Cruickshank's management of Oftel.

Success in regulation or self-regulation depends crucially on social attitudes. As long as avoiding taxes is seen as smart, the tax regime will need to be unyielding and intrusive. The fight against crime has led to enormous increases in bureaucracy and cost with public support weakened by tales of corruption and excess within the system of the law. Often it is the criminals who are portrayed as heroes; certainly the criminals seem to have more intellectual fire power and to be able to retain the initiative. Carl Hopkins sees a need to break away from the cynicism which has damaged relationships in recent years and to rebuild trust. If it became normal to assume good behaviour, the need for a 'policing' approach to governance would diminish. Peer pressure would move from supporting success at any price to encouraging behaviour which builds sustainable relationships. Disapproval from peer groups would provide the most effective form of regulation for least cost.

Like most professions the Law Society is self-regulating and has clearly defined codes of conduct. A not insignificant number of solicitors are struck off the register for major breaches of the code of conduct. If clients complained more, there would probably be a greater number of ex-solicitors. This is not because solicitors are more wicked than average people, but because strict governance is essential to preserve the professional ethos of putting clients before self.

Regulation by complaint is the lowest level of governance. The Press Complaints Commission fulfils a useful function but does not begin to regulate the Press. On the other hand, heavy-handed regulation on the lines favoured by Lord Irvine would be close to censorship. In the last analysis the public has the Press it wants – the decline in circulation of the 'red top' tabloids in recent years, and the disappearance of *The Sun*'s 'Page Three Girl', are perhaps signs that the British public may be more grown up than the media which serve it.

Carl Hopkins suggested that an umbrella organization might be established by Act of Parliament to regulate all professions. Its role would be to control access to each profession, to provide and monitor quality standards, and to regulate behaviour. At present individual institutions were often allowing their profession to become overcrowded. While a few solicitors earned 'telephone number' salaries, the majority were poorly paid, which made it difficult to impose professional standards. The umbrella organization would have the power to remove poor performers from the register without the concern to maximize its membership income. Carl recognized the problem of a 'pecking order' among professions, although he would welcome teachers and embrace teaching unions provided that each group was committed to professional standards of performance and behaviour. Such a body would, of course, need to embrace EU professional people who wish to practise in the UK.

If a 'Professional Services Authority' were established to regulate the professions, it might be responsible for controlling access to the professions (balancing supply and demand over time), maintaining a register of practising professionals, establishing and overseeing ethical and performance standards and regulating professional bodies. The individual professional bodies would manage their professions under the direction of the PSA, would regulate non-practising members according to PSA guidelines and act where necessary to protect the interests of their profession and its members. In this way regulation and representation would be clearly split and the conflict of interests made more manageable.

Professional compliance depends at present on reacting to complaints and, since there has always been a reluctance by Britons to complain, many professionals must be tempted to take the line of least resistance. When documents from the Cooperative Wholesale Society were produced for analysis by professionals, prior to the recent hostile takeover bid by Andrew Regan, no professional adviser seems to have questioned Regan's right of possession. If professional status were subject to rigorous standards, no professional adviser would touch stolen documents and those involved would have denounced Regan to the police. With questionable conduct being condoned at the top of many professions, unless and until exposed by others, it is unsurprising that less well-paid members of the professions do not always make a stand on questions of principle.

Carl Hopkins was concerned that British professions should set standards which would enable them to compete globally. Failure to set high standards had facilitated the machinations of fraudsters such as Maxwell, aided by the weakness and inconsistency of the English trust law. He recognized the danger of 'whistle-blowing' for those involved, and suggested that quiet diplomacy often produced equal results with less histrionics. Nevertheless the obligation to 'whistle-blow' should be part of the professional code, overseen by his proposed umbrella organization. Carl Hopkins saw value in members of that organization having a distinctive title – he suggested

'Doctor', but a new title might give distinction to the holder, confidence to those working with him or her, and be a cachet which nobody would wish to lose. If Britain could strengthen the external perception of the trustworthiness of its professions, it would achieve a powerful boost to its global competitiveness, not only through the City of London but in all areas of human endeavour.

2.3

CORPORATE GOVERNANCE OF A TRADE ASSOCIATION

Warren Newman is the first Chief Executive of BACTA, the largest of the trade associations in the gaming industry, and brings to his new role a formidable reputation in public and government relations. BACTA was previously 'managed' by a Chairman (President of Council) who was elected every other year, and who also continued to run the business of his member company.

BACTA has moved to a new model of governance, involving a part-time Chairman, with responsibility for building and developing the Council and for top level representation where needed, and a full-time Chief Executive. The role of the Chief Executive is to develop and propose policy and strategy, to manage the affairs of BACTA and to maintain and develop contacts with members. This model of governance was first developed by Marc Boléat for the Association of British Insurers, and has close parallels with company structures and governance, where relevant. Most striking is the recognition of the distinct roles of Chairman and Chief Executive, creating the focus and resource to move forward in two dimensions at the same time – in the building of trust among members at all levels and in the delivery of services to sustain that trust. Much of the Chairman's role is ceremonial and custodial, but it creates and sustains trust among members and key external constituencies, such as government. Individual Chairmen come and go, so that wise Chairmen allow their Chief Executive as much discretion as he can usefully employ within a framework which distinguishes between legislative and executive prerogative but without rigidity.

Before Warren was appointed Chief Executive the Chairman and elected members of BACTA ran the Association with the support of General Secretaries who did his bidding. Not only was such an arrangement unstable in democratic terms, as contact with the full membership occurred only once a year, but it slowed down action by restricting it to the pace of the Committee cycle. A dual top command allows the Chairman more time to consult members and to understand the wider context in which the Association operates, while the Chief Executive can both manage and develop its activities and can interact with the Chairman to shape policy and strategy. Having a dual top resource has enabled BACTA to consolidate its membership into four special interest groups, which meet as a Management Committee to resolve conflicts. The four groups are:

- Manufacturers (12)
- Suppliers/importers
- Family amusement centres
- 'Adult' amusement centres.

The importance of nourishing the grass roots of BACTA may be illustrated by the growing strength of the 'seaside' lobby in securing support for amusement centres as sources of employment and visitor attraction in major resorts. There are half a million gaming machines in the UK and the industry is growing fast, despite the competition from the National Lottery. Gaming is, of course, a major source of revenue for the Government and subject to close regulation by the Gaming Board under the Gaming Act.

The BACTA President of Council is elected for a two-year term alternately from among large members and small members in order to preserve a balance of influence. The membership varies in size from groups like Bass and Rank down to small local amusement centres. The individual agendas of members vary enormously, but all have a major interest in developing their gaming revenue, even if some use gaming to some extent as a 'loss leader'.

One key change in the new structure is the devolution to the four sector groups of responsibility for funding. Each year a budget is agreed and each sector group is responsible for 25 per cent of the total subscription income required. This means that the twelve manufacturers must pay a higher average subscription than the amusement centres in order to command a quarter of BACTA's attention. This is more than repaid by the work done to lobby for the introduction of higher value coins and to press for early clarification of the technical specification of the new euro coins.

One key benefit from the division of responsibilities between the Chairman and Chief Executive at BACTA is increased effectiveness. Mutual organizations have an inbuilt tendency to introspection as members seek to make themselves felt. This problem has been a major driver of the move away from cooperative structures in agriculture, releasing managers to build the business without day-to-day interference. At BACTA the appointment of a Chief Executive has created continuity of management and enabled the public face of BACTA to be identified with one individual. Warren Newman is becoming the face of BACTA, appearing in the media and elsewhere to represent the Association in a manner pioneered by the CBI, Institute of Directors and other influential bodies.

I asked Warren Newman about the conflict of interest within bodies which both represented their members and regulated them. The professions were the most evident example of this issue: the BMA acted both as a trades union for doctors and as a disciplinary body. BACTA members are, in fact, regulated by the Gaming Board and have limited powers of self-regulation. Warren Newman felt that the balance of regulatory power was appropriate for the gaming industry; the only real difficulty was the fact that the Gaming Act was thirty years old and was in growing need of revision. He saw the potential benefits of integrating regulation of financial services through the proposed Financial Services Authority. This overcame the problems of regulating across sector boundaries and should produce greater consistency of regulation.

I asked Warren whether there was a danger that trade associations could facilitate cartelization. He was aware of this potential risk which was significant where the number of members of a group was small. The Bingo Association had two groups (large and small members) and there were now just a few large corporate members. The antidote to the risk of cartelization was to ensure maximum openness of process and of reporting; one advantage of becoming a Company Limited by Guarantee, which Associations are doing increasingly, was that all members had to declare for whom they acted, so that the risks were shared openly. A broad base of membership was also essential in order to preserve shared governance; there were too many small trade associations which were at risk both financially and of being captured by vested interests.

We spoke further about mutuality. Warren indicated that the Consumers' Association was strongly in favour of mutual organizations, both because they were democratic and because they were answerable to members (the public) rather than to employees. When mutuals converted into limited liability companies there was a danger that they could become bureaucratic (Warren felt this might have happened with BUPA). Asked about the future of mutual organizations, Warren believed that many would survive – for example, the NFU Mutual which provided valuable services, such as insurance, to farmers, and had a strong local presence around the country. We discussed the similarity of that model with the new BACTA (the strong-grass roots feeding and being fed through a responsive organization and supporting its lobbying activities with government and other external constituencies). We agreed that these integrating organizations offered a powerful model of effectiveness where members' interests were substantially aligned; in cases where interests diverged or clashed, the leaders of such organizations would find themselves 'trying to herd cats'.

Warren Newman had worked earlier for the John Lewis Partnership and he had found it a unique organization in its totally democratic approach. A key strength of John Lewis was its ability to align the interests of shareholders and employees (the same people), and to take democracy right through the business by establishing distinct structures. The staff at John Lewis could dismiss the Chairman under its constitution and relationships were open and respectful at all levels, controlled by a very strong culture of interdependence. Warren admitted that some external recruits could not adapt to the collegiate culture of John Lewis and left to pursue individualistic careers. It was perhaps significant that John Lewis recruited predominantly from the Civil Service and the armed services where a strong team culture was seen as normal.

Warren expressed concern that many mutuals had not developed a culture of strong management. This was particularly evident in the Cooperative Movement, though the Cooperative Bank was a notable exception. There was, perhaps, a difficulty within a culture of mutual dependence in driving for continually higher levels of performance, such as those demanded by institutional investors in the USA of major corporations. It would be interesting to watch the performance of the newly converted building societies and insurers – how would they adapt to cope with satisfying shareholders who would increasingly be different from their customers and uninterested in the personal relationships over the counter on which the business had originally been built?

Corporate governance was seen by Warren as a complex and shifting series of trade-offs which had to be managed in real time. Success in corporate governance came from lack of incident or friction. Like Sherlock Holmes' 'dog that did not bark' it was remarkable for being unremarked. A great deal of work needed to go into creating effective governance, from establishing an open and workable structure and climate, through transparent and audited processes to recognizing and involving the different constituencies with a stake in the outcome. Like the swan gliding serenely on the smooth pond it managed to draw attention from the hectic paddling below the surface needed to make progress!

3.1

GOVERNANCE BY AND FOR EMPLOYEES – THE JOHN LEWIS MODEL

We examine in Case Studies 3.2 and 3.3 the process of governance in mutual societies, where the members own the business and constitute a large proportion of its customers. It is interesting to examine a different model where the company is owned by its employees and in which the tensions between different stakeholders are also partly defused by mutual interest.

Employee ownership can take a number of forms. Sometimes a failed company can be taken over by its workforce, as with Triumph Motorcycles, or may be bought out, as in the case of some coalmines or, more famously, the National Freight Corporation. Workers 'cooperatives' have quietly flourished in Northern Spain and elsewhere, and in Yugoslavia state factories were effectively run by the workforce. Few of these examples have been successful on a large scale over time and the history of employee share ownership has rarely been stable; the shares of National Freight Corporation are now widely dispersed, with employee share ownership reduced to some 20 per cent.

A model which has proved more robust is that of the John Lewis Partnership. Its shares are held in trust for all employees and the company operates under a constitution comprising 13 Articles, 200 Rules and 600 Regulations, which has provided a firm framework for success by adapting through consensus to meet changing circumstances. John Lewis began in 1864 with a small shop in London selling fabrics. Over time and through the heyday of Victorian prosperity, the shop expanded into a department store dedicated to meeting all the daily needs of its customers. In 1905 John Lewis bought Peter Jones in Sloane Square for cash since the business was losing money and would otherwise have closed.

John Lewis had two sons, one of whom had little influence over the business; the other, John Spedan Lewis transformed it. Spedan Lewis was a typical Victorian manager until a riding accident in 1904 gave him time to think deeply about the business. He was struck by the fact that he, his father and brother were taking as much profit (£16 000/year) from the business as the sum total of the wages of their 300 employees. He came to the conclusion that the contribution to the business of its employees was considerably greater than that of the Lewis family and began to develop alternative models of governance and reward to those of Victorian capitalism.

After some years of losing money at Peter Jones, John Lewis realized that radical remedies were needed to revive its profitability. Aware of the unconventional ideas of Spedan, he decided to give him control of Peter Jones so that his theories could be put to the test. To keep matters in perspective he was expected to work full-time at John Lewis' department store and only start work at Peter Jones after 5pm!

In 1914 Spedan Lewis accepted the challenge from his father and set about turning Peter Jones into a partnership. His objective was stated thus: 'I am trying to build up a system of business which shall serve the public not less well than the ordinary type of the present day, but which shall be carried on ... not for the benefit of the capitalists or yet for the benefit of the managers ... but for the benefit of the staff as a whole, managers and all.' In order to encourage the staff to work as a team, Spedan Lewis pooled all commission payable to salesmen and set up staff committees in which he could meet employees without the presence of managers. This idea of talking directly to sales assistants was revolutionary at the time and led to a strengthening of staff motivation.

In 1918 Spedan Lewis undertook to share profits from Peter Jones with employees once the business had returned to profitable trading. In 1919 he set up a Staff Council at Peter Jones to oversee the development of the business and to integrate the work of its staff committees. In the early 1920s Peter Jones became profitable and Spedan Lewis became confirmed in his belief in the partnership model. He had started his thinking from a sense of guilt but had shaped his ideas to achieve efficiency rather than philanthropy. His mission statement when he formed the partnership in 1928 focused on 'happiness' but in no uncommercial sense: 'the Partnership's supreme purpose is to secure the fairest possible sharing by all its members of the advantages of ownership – gain, knowledge and power; that is to say, their happiness in the broadest sense of that word so far as happiness depends upon gainful occupation'. The focus within the business is then on 'gainful occupation' and on how it can best be achieved. Spedan Lewis' original objective had been 'to build up a system of business which shall serve the public not less well than the ordinary type of the present day', while at the same time 'the business will be run by the staff for the staff subject to scrupulous care of the capital and the dividends'. It would seem that Spedan Lewis' vision for the business was not to create a self-serving and inward-looking system but to create a virtuous circle in which enlightened self-interest led to better service of customers from motivated and knowledge-able employees who themselves benefited from the resultant higher profits and through 'gain, knowledge and power' retained and developed a grow-ing body of committed customers.

'Gain, knowledge and power' are in effect the three pillars which sustain the John Lewis Partnership. The Partnership itself was based on a Trust Settlement made in April 1929 by which all ordinary shares came to be held in trust for the employees. In return Spedan Lewis, now sole owner of the business, took the interest from deferred bonds of a total value of £1 mil-lion, to be repaid out of profits over thirty years. He also retained ordinary shares in a new holding company, John Lewis Partnership Limited, enabling him to exert control over the business, if necessary. A second Trust Settlement in 1950 transferred this holding to a new company, John Lewis Partnership Trust Limited.

The role of 'gain' in the Partnership is important. The constitution pro-vides that all surplus – that is, post-tax – profit shall be allocated either to reserves (for reinvestment) or to Partners' profit-sharing. In recent years Partners have shared just under half of post-tax profits. The basis for profit-sharing was laid down by Spedan Lewis to be the individual contribution of each Partner to the success of the business. He decided that relative pay was the best measure of relative contribution and this has remained the criterion for profit allocation ever since 1929, despite frequent attempts to have a lev-elling formula adopted. In recent years bonus has been paid at rates varying between 24 per cent and 8 per cent of pay, depending on economic circum-stances. Experience has shown that profit-sharing is meaningful to employ-ees and helps to attract and retain motivated staff.

'Knowledge' has been the driver for the intensive internal communication process which characterizes the John Lewis Group. The Partners are seen to be entitled to as much information about the business as is consistent with their ownership, subject only to commercial risk. Few shareholders of lim-ited liability companies are as well informed as John Lewis Partners and the risk of information overload must be high. Today 'knowledge' is seen as an understanding of the products and markets of a business as well as of its performance. This wider concept of 'knowledge', now increasingly evident in the John Lewis communication system and supported by a commitment to training, makes Partners among the best informed of all retail staff.

Much of today's talk about 'empowerment' has little or no substance. At John Lewis 'power' is totally shared and diffused – Partners talk about 'our business' and are able to hold their managers and each other accountable through the constitution. Ultimate power lies with the Central Council which can dismiss the Chairman if it wishes (it has never done so!). Because power is so widely spread, is subject to clear rules and its exercise is open for all to see, there is little danger of abuse of power in the John Lewis Group.

The constitution of the Group is the cornerstone of its power structure. It provides for the establishment and running of a Central Council which succeeded Spedan Lewis' 'staff council' at Peter Jones. It comprises elected representatives from all parts of the Partnership, together with some ex-officio members from the Board. The 130 or so councillors meet six times a year and have the following key functions:

O   To elect five of the twelve members of the Board.
O   To provide a public forum for managers to account for their stewardship.
O   To decide how some profits are spent (pensions, sick pay, subsidies for shopping and social activities).
O   To decide policy on working arrangements (Sunday trading and Christmas/New Year opening hours).

The decision to open on Sundays is taken locally by each Branch Council. This is a local version of the Central Council, and the Managing Director of each store is accountable in detail to his Branch Council. The 'third leg' of the constitution is the network of 'Committees of Communication', some 150 in total, which developed out of Spedan Lewis' 'staff committee' at Peter Jones. These committees are elected by non-managerial Partners, are chaired in turn by four full-time chairmen, and meet four to five times a year. They deal with local grievances and act as a conduit for opinion from the shop floor to Central Management and in reverse. Proceedings are anonymous and questions need to be answered by the appropriate director or manager and remedial action taken. Committees for Communication seem to be very effective and highly prized by all Partners who use them.

The process of anonymous challenge is duplicated through the in-house magazines of the John Lewis Group. There is a weekly Group magazine, *The Gazette* and local newsletters (*Chronicles*) which allow questions and debate on any matter. The appropriate director or manager must reply within 21 days, and both letter and reply are published together. Recent topics in *The Gazette* have included pension arrangements, pay rates, allowing the local hunt to cross the John Lewis estate in Hampshire and how to chop onions!

The relationship between the Partnership and trades unions is tenuous overall, although there are some units with union members (mainly in manufacture and distribution). The relevant rule states: 'Every member of the Partnership has complete freedom to belong to a trade union ... in case of conflict between a trade union and the Partnership, those concerned must remember the special obligations which they have to their Partners'. With the Partners having ownership of the company it must be difficult for trades unions to bring any real extra benefits!

The John Lewis Partnership would seem to be as focused on shareholder value as General Electric or any other 'red raw' capitalist company. Lord Hanson is supposed to have ranked his concern as, shareholders first, customers second, and employees third. The result has not been a sustainable success. In fact the 'employees first' philosophy of the John Lewis Partnership has evolved over time. Concern for customers has strengthened progressively, leading to the famous 'never knowingly undersold' pledge, which is administered with great care. John Lewis lays great emphasis on imaginative buying, focusing on its core clientele in the A, B and C1 categories and seeking to build ongoing relationships with each customer. The John Lewis card (with one million holders) and the skilful promotions supporting it all provide an effective relationship marketing thrust. The relationship with suppliers has moved towards a partnership made with those who can match the Partnership's high standards and bring flair in support of its further development. Other stakeholders in the business, such as local communities, are also cultivated carefully. As evidence of a wider view of its responsibilities and interests, John Lewis has been involved in the 'Tomorrow's Company' study, undertaken by the Royal Society of Arts, and which has broadened the debate on corporate governance.

Is John Lewis a special phenomenon or a model for the future? It has prospered on the back of postwar expansion, settling for steady and sustainable growth rather than the over-expansion and mergers seen elsewhere in retailing. Even John Lewis has begun to need to adapt to changing patterns of footfall; it had to close its branches in Streatham and Holloway Road because they could not justify the new investment needed to sustain them. All staff were offered transfers to other branches and £1 million of surplus staff costs were carried for a year until head counts came into line. John Lewis has to make people redundant from time to time (they are employed by John Lewis plc and this is separate from their membership of the Partnership). Redundancy payments are well above legal limits and the facts are openly communicated to all Partners.

John Lewis has been more successful as a model of employee ownership than share-owning examples, such as NFC, where employee share ownership is now down to some 20 per cent. Another model is that of Tullis Russell, the Scottish paper-maker, where 70 per cent of shares are held in trust and 30 per cent are in circulation. The Baxi Partnership has a similar focus on trustee shareholding. It is possible that fewer mutual societies would have converted to public companies if their shares had been held in a formal trust structure. It must be recognized, however, that trusts are not exempt from the pressures of the market place – the trustees at Wellcome knew when to sell out to Glaxo. How John Lewis would react to a very generous takeover bid is a matter for speculation. The Trust Settlements can only be modified by court order and an application would need Partner support. Unlike mutual society shareholders the Partners of John Lewis would be pledging their jobs as well as their stake in the company. One senses that the temptation would need to be overwhelming to succeed.

It would seem that for John Lewis to be a model for the future, there would need to be significant changes in society and in corporate governance. When the Partnership was formed, most joint stock companies were owned by rich individuals or investor groups; today there are relatively few individual shareholders and most institutional investment is held by pension funds or insurance companies, ultimately on behalf of individuals. Today most employees can prosper without owning their company. Does ownership protect employment when so many companies have 'downsized' with ruthless abandon? John Lewis has shown that it must adapt to the real world and can no longer provide jobs for all for life. Where John Lewis does show itself to be a powerful model is in the three pillars concept (gain, knowledge and power). Each is interdependent, but the integral effect is to produce a system where directors and managers are given the authority to manage the business and are then held accountable in a very open, detailed and pressurized manner. If shareholders were able to hold the directors and managers of quoted public companies accountable in the same degree, the effect on performance could be electrifying! This is, of course, unrealistic, but it does underline three important dimensions of good corporate governance: first, that gain should be proportional to real contribution (and subject to internal challenge); secondly, that the business should be run with full internal disclosure; and thirdly that power should be diffused to those who need to use it and should be matched by full and open accountability. John Lewis does have some important lessons for corporate governance, even though they may be painful for directors and managers who have been able for so long to avoid any searching appraisal of their stewardship.

3.2

EQUITABLE LIFE ASSURANCE SOCIETY

The Equitable Life Assurance Society is the oldest mutual life assurance society in the world. It was founded in 1762 and its title 'equitable' was chosen to emphasize its commitment to fair principles of governance. As the earliest mutual society in life assurance, it is now the standard bearer for the principles and practice of mutuality. More importantly, it has become the life assurance industry benchmark for best performance.

Effective management is now more fundamentally important to the Equitable than mutuality. The Society's Managing Director and Actuary, Roy Ranson, has devoted his whole career to the Equitable since leaving Cambridge. Appointed Managing Director in 1991, he has masterminded a complete transformation of the Society into a high productivity, low-cost operation which is now market leader in annual premium income and capable of processing much larger volumes of business in the future. In doing so, Roy Ranson has focused on four key principles – fairness, order, long-term planning and simplicity.

Fairness is at the heart of the Equitable. In its early days there was considerable effort expended on finding the fairest ways to distribute profits, leading to the concept of 'policy holder expectations'. This must have been one of the earliest manifestations of customer care! In 1765 the Society declined the opportunity to use third party distribution of its policies, preferring to maintain direct contact with its customers. Fairness is also a characteristic of the Society's relationship with its employees. The management process is open and shared fully with employees, pay is above average for the insurance industry, and performance-related bonuses can be earned. There is little emphasis on perquisites, other than use of a car, so that rewards are direct and uncomplicated. The Equitable is sensitive in all that it does to the implications of its name: policy-holders are given more information than is usual in life assurance and their expectations are carefully managed; employees have longer average service than the norm for the industry; even competitors are handled courteously and beaten strictly in terms of performance.

Order is the lifeblood of the Equitable. Order is based on logic, openness and effectiveness. At its heart is the 'management company', a notional trading company set up to drive the Cost Management and Control (CMC) system set up by Roy Ranson in 1992 to monitor all Society activities in the UK and overseas. Monthly profit and loss accounts are prepared for each business, and the marketing and administration activities are reported on in detail. Each quarter a more comprehensive report is prepared, including balance sheets for each business as well as detailed profit and loss accounts.

As the objectives of the CMC system are to drive the business towards agreed goals and not just report results, control is focused on three elements of income:

1   Allowances for new business (current and advanced loadings)
2   Amounts available to meet renewal expenses (based on premiums in force)
3   Management fees for services to subsidiaries (outside the CMC system)

And on three elements of expense:

1   Management expenses (including salesmen's salaries)
2   Chargeback of development expenditure (usually over 5/7 years)
3   Corporate costs (charged out in proportion to turnover).

In calculating expenses development costs are usually capitalized and charged back (under 2 above).

This 'management company' (the 'Equitable Management Company' (EMC)) provides the framework both for control and for awards made under the Business Performance Bonus Scheme. Recipients may include all non-field staff and executive directors; 50 per cent of the profits emerging are passed on to policyholders, so that they also can benefit from productivity gains.

The workings of the EMC are transparent to all staff so that it enjoys ownership and commitment. As the aim of the system is to maximize productivity and its results feed into the Business Performance Bonus Scheme, it is not considered that budgets are helpful in running the Society. The EMC is a flexible, self-correcting system and its workings are open to all staff. For this reason also, Equitable prefers a more constructive approach aimed at helping more managers rather than a formal internal audit function, since staff are motivated to police internal processes for their own benefit.

The benefits of the EMC and of a £50 million investment in computers came through over time in a number of ways. Having fallen from 8.4 per cent in 1986 to 4.3 per cent in 1996, the Society's expense: premium income ratios remain the best in the industry; its investment returns are well above average, and these driving factors have resulted in the highest annual premium income in the industry being achieved. The system is self-reinforcing and self-policing, creating a process capability which now exceeds the volume of policy transactions. The growing likelihood of Government reliance on the private sector, both to handle larger volumes of personal pensions and age care provisions and to process the rump of Government schemes, makes this spare capacity an important potential asset.

Long-term planning has been the basis for 230 years of success in the development of The Equitable. Vision was necessary to create a new industry, and innovation followed quickly with the development by James Dodson of the first life expectancy tables, based on actuarial principles. In 1816 the Society restricted further sales in order to focus on the interests of its existing members and did not resume the general sale of new policies until 1890. This is a profound example of customer care, but also of long-term planning. In more recent times the focus of long-term planning has been on the creation of the most efficient and cost-effective life assurance system in the industry. In the 10 years to 1995 total nett assets increased from £1 billion to £16 billion. Liabilities are currently some £15 billion, reflecting the policy of high payments to policy holders and of limiting free capital levels.

It is in the area of free capital that the battle between mutual and converting societies is being fought. Most of the arguments for conversion turn on wider opportunities for which a larger capital base is seen as essential. Free capital facilitates acquisitions and new ventures, but Roy Ranson sees free capital as potentially a moral hazard in the life assurance industry. He argues that the positive cashflow of the industry enables major capital investments to be funded internally. The new computer system was funded out of premium income, on which interest was paid to policy holders. The maximum level of loan plans interest outstanding peaked in 1993 at £52.9 million and represents only part of the investment book cash allocation.

The other main argument for conversion to a public limited company is the ability to grow faster. The Halifax Building Society has managed to expand by acquisition even as a mutual society but will no doubt feel able to move faster on the growth trail after conversion. Some insurance companies, such as the Norwich Union, have converted for the same reason. In making the case for mutuality, Roy Ranson quotes a Fabian Society pamphlet which identifies three key characteristics of mutual societies:

1   They provide basic services meeting essential needs of members.
2   They normally involve a long-term relationship between the member and the organization providing the service.
3   They generally involve a significant financial commitment by the member.

A key overriding factor is the fact that 'members' are also the largest number of customers of the mutual society, so that the conflict of interest between shareholders and customers, which Companies Act-incorporated businesses face, does not materially affect mutual societies.

Simplicity is the last of Roy Ranson's key precepts. Since he became Managing Director in 1991 he has striven to create a 'paperless office' by integrating computer systems and devolving operating responsibility. This has involved reducing ten departments to one and involving everybody in the EMC system. Products have been made simpler to understand and their inner workings more transparent. Even though the Equitable's customers are largely higher nett worth individuals, simple products create trust which is developed by above-average annual results.

Internally simplicity is now being pursued at all levels, from the setting of business goals to the selling process. The key target for the Society is to continue to drive down the cost: premium income ratio both for new and for renewed business. This demonstrates the achievement of productivity gains and feeds the virtuous circle of higher yields on policies and increasing premium income. Another key target is a steady long-term improvement in investment yields so that the performance of Equitable policies remains unbeatable.

As the Society moves towards the next century it remains true to its founding principles, which are (in modern phraseology):

> To operate as a mutual body providing financial and associated services directly to the policy-holders at cost.

> To run a full distribution of profits policy and to avoid the unfairness created by the retention of profits earned by one generation of policy holders for the benefit of successors. Furthermore to aim at 'fair' bonuses between all classes and durations of policy.

Although the preponderance of its business lies within the UK, the Equitable has a growing volume of expatriate business developed through its branch in Guernsey and has established a network of branches in Germany. The Equitable is one of the ten largest life assurers in Ireland and is actively exploring new opportunities in other overseas markets. While its processing capacity exceeds current internal demand, the Society is servicing the needs of other insurers – for example, Marks and Spencer. Even though such contracts are priced to produce a fair contribution to Equitable members, the low cost base of the business may make it attractive for other insurers to buy a processing service. Great care will need to be exercised in choosing such clients as the industry is attracting many opportunists with recognized brand names but no real stake in life assurance.

The opportunities for growing business in the UK remain considerable. The value of annual premium business is £2.5 billion/year, giving the Equitable 15 per cent market share. Single premium business has risen to some £16.4 billion, giving the Society some 10 per cent market share. Life assurance business had been set back by the scandals surrounding the sale of personal pensions; in 1995 and 1996 the Equitable increased its sales both of annual and single premium policies, vindicating its policy of tight control of its 380 salaried salesmen. Given the large number of life assurers in the UK market, and the entry of a growing number of aggressive foreign companies, such as Axa, Swiss Life and AMP, it is to be expected that there will be a rapid concentration into large groups. The growing integration of financial services product ranges will also help to drive this process of concentration.

Where does this rush towards concentration leave the Equitable? It faces a growing number of giant competitors, like David facing an army of Goliaths, with only its efficiency and its native wit for protection. Its efficiency means that it currently has £9 million of assets per employee, compared with £2.1 million for HSBC, £3.6 million for the Halifax and £1.3 million for GRE. Its native wit has largely been deployed in creating the 'state of the art' system which has brought market leadership. At present the Equitable spends only £3 million each year on advertising, compared with £10 million by Scottish Widows. Most of its business comes by word of mouth and systematic database marketing. Among professional people the Equitable still remains something of a secret – too good to share with others! It has even been seen as the Coutts of life assurance.

As the 'elephant dance' on the financial services stage begins, the Equitable will face mounting assaults on its existing business from giants desperate to break into a market which is increasingly likely to be driven by tax allowances. The Society could diversify to widen its market base, but this would seem to be a hazardous strategy. Given the growth potential in pensions and long-term savings, it will probably make more sense to strengthen its market grip in these sectors. As it faces this challenge the Equitable should feel heartened by the link between mutuality and relationship marketing. The giants wanting to break into the life assurance market will need to invest heavily in database marketing and advertising to make their initial sales; the Equitable is well known in the market and should be able to build on its established reputation for performance and customer care. Many of the quoted insurance companies have lost credibility in the personal pensions debacle and few people love their bank sufficiently to create a long-term investment relationship with it. Parents tell their children about the Equitable and have done so consistently for over a hundred years. Fairness and sustained performance create powerful bonds, especially when cemented by trust.

3.3

BIRMINGHAM MIDSHIRES BUILDING SOCIETY

Effective corporate governance is usually uncomfortable. Rather like Bunyan's *Pilgrim's Progress* it is a compelling search for the 'celestial city' which seems always to be beyond reach. As Pilgrim was never tempted to stay put at any of the places through which he passed on his journey, so the search for effective corporate governance needs constantly to move ahead.

Birmingham Midshires Building Society is regarded as one of the UK's most progressive financial services groups with a passion for delivering excellence in everything it does.

In 1990 Michael Jackson joined Birmingham Midshires – an £8 billion-in-asset business with over 2000 staff and one million savers and borrowers – from Bank of America in the new role of Chief Executive. He found a society which lacked management processes to move it forward. Michael realized that he needed to create an effective board as the basis for galvanizing the Society, and used a programme at Sundridge Park as a catalyst to challenge his colleagues to take stock of the present performance of the board and to set themselves targets which would provide the leadership to set new standards for the building society.

Leadership is the basic fuel of good corporate governance as it sets and maintains an example for others to follow and to build on. As Mike Jackson says 'We have rebuilt our business like a jigsaw. We have laid down the framework, the straight edge pieces, and have encouraged my collcagues to fill in the picture.' Birmingham Midshires has carefully developed its Board structure and processes to match the Cadbury model. This was seen as the minimum requirement and further improvements are continually being worked on by the Board. There is now a practice manual to guide the Board in all its basic processes: for example, there is a full procedure for recruiting non-executive directors which ensures the selection is wide-ranging but focused

163

on the specific skills and experience needed to enhance Board effectiveness. Directors now evaluate each other against agreed criteria and regularly appraise Board papers and information contained therein. Individual Board processes are also evaluated regularly and best practice sought externally. The next logical step is to have an independent external review.

Part of the mutual assessment process of Board members is intended to ensure that the values of the Society are practised by each Director. The maintenance of values is monitored also by a people attitude survey at irregular intervals and customer feedback surveys are carried out by the Society. Complaints are handled fast and openly, with the Board taking a close interest in customer satisfaction levels.

The Society's Annual General Meeting has now been moved into positive mode, not run as a non-event. Displays on company performance, values and products enliven the proceedings. The process is open and unintimidating so that questions are encouraged and issues pursued to the satisfaction of the members concerned. Last year members made visits to the new premises at Pendeford, followed the AGM and saw how a modern and purposeful building society was organized.

The Society has been closely involved in the RSA study on 'Tomorrow's Company' and recognizes the importance of its relations with all stakeholders. Members are seen as prime stakeholders, both as owners and as main customers; Society people follow in order of importance. This is not seen as a problem, since they are trained to put the customer first in all situations and take pride in a culture of helpfulness and friendliness. Business partners, local communities, the City, media and others who impact on the Society's work are all recognized as stakeholders and cultivated positively.

Openness to stakeholders is matched by openness to best practice. Birmingham Midshires is not content to measure itself against the top 10 building societies and top 10 banks but is increasingly looking outside the financial services sector for models – for example, in respect of customer care.

The Society sets itself aggressive annual targets based on simultaneously improving profitability and customer satisfaction. It pays well to recruit good staff but drives performance gains through a universal bonus scheme. On top of a profit-related pay scheme, all Society people have individual or group targets to meet. Bonus is paid for beating the target by bands agreed annually. The union is supportive of the scheme, which has widespread acceptance among the staff.

The importance of learning is recognized at Birmingham Midshires because of the need to differentiate itself from other financial services' organizations by outstanding customer care. Learning is seen as the way to open minds and to give people the extra confidence to be effective in dealing with customers.

Each person is encouraged to work out a personal development plan and to use the tools and resources put at their disposal. Some basic training is on a 'sheepdip' basis – for example, customer satisfaction – but a growing number of development programmes are available on a self-learn basis.

Self-renewal is an article of faith for Mike Jackson. He is committed to constant change as a way of life and is continually on his guard against any hint of corporate sclerosis. He recently sensed that arteries were beginning to harden, and responded by creating a situation which led to a restructuring of the Society. This involved breaking up the hierarchical structure which had driven internal change within Birmingham Midshires, and re-focusing the business on the customer.

The new structure has four main groups:

O   A customer team
O   A development team
O   A servicing team
O   A support group, comprising 'people', finance, systems communications and the corporate risk.

In the new organization the whole structure focuses on the customer; previously the organization had been headed by the Chief Executive, with the result that every action was focused on his top team. The change of focus means that the Chief Executive is a facilitator acting in the interest of the customer, much as a conductor integrates the individual efforts of musicians in an orchestra to produce a memorable experience for the audience.

The new structure shows strength in depth to meet customer needs communicated through different media:

Table 4   Birmingham Midshires – Customer-focused Restructuring

Channel Teams		Product Teams	Information Team
Customers	Post, telephone Personal contact Intermediary	Lending Investment New and emerging products Insurance	Customer needs' identification

The executive team at Birmingham Midshires is structured into support teams, each focused on the customer, to provide:

O   people development
O   business performance
O   managing change
O   managing reputation.

All teams integrate to work on customer management, so that the customer is present at all times in the very heart of the Society.

In the meantime the processes used to manage the Society are being changed to facilitate customer interaction and to bring customers into the inner workings of the business. In too many companies processes are used to keep customers at bay; Birmingham Midshires wants to open up the Society to its customers, most of whom are also its members.

The Society recognizes that every person in the business will have to change, and keep changing. Every process in the Society will need to be changed, and changed repeatedly to meet evolving customer requirements. This process cannot merely be reactive, unless the Society is willing to be uncompetitive. Change needs to be driven if it is to create competitive advantage; it also needs to be steered in order to arrive on time in tomorrow's marketplace.

The Society has adapted the Shell process of scenario planning in order to be able to explore alternative futures and to begin to understand the implications of each for the Society. It is recognized that there is no secure future for any contender in the financial services industry unless it can achieve a sustainable competitive advantage. For Birmingham Midshires the distinguishing factor will be extraordinary customer service which will enable it to survive in a world of relentless competition. The key competitive advantage the Society sees is the ability to anticipate customer needs and to be first in meeting them. This requires the constant 'freeing up' of the structures and attitudes in the Society so that bureaucratic sclerosis can never set in. Mike Jackson sees a recurrent necessity for creating discomfort through positive change in order to generate better morale for those who can meet the challenge. People need to be motivated to achieve ever more demanding goals – and rewarded well for doing so. Birmingham Midshires Building Society has a growing number of processes to encourage people towards achievement, including a 'quality evenings' which seek to set new standards for customer quality. The focus on quality may be gauged by the growth of the Society's suggestions scheme from 74 to 86 suggestions per month, an increase of 16.2 per cent.

Attitudes to change are monitored by regular independent questionnaires. Few respondents are keen on the idea of change and yet 90 per cent have expressed support for more change and a similar number believes that the Society is performing better than before. Only effective leadership can make a transformation which nobody wants into a success which everybody fully owns!

What are the implications of the transformation of Birmingham Midshires Building Society for corporate governance? Much of the emphasis placed on corporate governance is directed towards compliance with regulations and 'good practice' in the terms of the Cadbury and Greenbury Reports.

Birmingham Midshires Building Society is fully compliant with such practices: the main thrust of corporate governance for the Society is to set stretching standards of behaviour and achievement rather than be contented with matching standards set by others. Corporate governance is not just the avoidance of blame, but also an opportunity to create and win prizes.

In recent months the prizes have indeed begun to emerge. A bid for the Society has been made by the Royal Bank of Scotland which has now been 'trumped' by Halifax. Birmingham Midshires may, we hope, only be the first of many companies to win competitive advantage through effective corporate governance.

3.4

CORPORATE GOVERNANCE AT BRITISH TELECOM

British Telecom (BT) has recently appointed what we believe to be the first Director of Corporate Governance of a British public limited company. Luke March, a corporate lawyer, was appointed less to ensure full compliance with the law and Oftel regulations than to achieve competitive advantage. Having been assistant secretary at Thorn EMI and Company Secretary at TSB, Luke has ample experience of legal compliance and has been involved in a fundamental review of BT's relationship with Oftel.

BT has its roots in the Post Office and its present governance regime has remained orientated towards the public sector culture. The BT Board has been structured along public sector lines, with a strong preponderance of non-executive directors and rather unfocused personal accountabilities. A review of the Board's governance practices has been carried out which will change its structure and introduce a complete set of personal accountabilities. The Corporate Scorecard on which executive directors' accountabilities are based is shown in Table 5. Previously the Chief Executive was not totally accountable, since he was required to share even small decisions. His mandate for signature had a ceiling of £30 million and joint signatures were even required at that level.

The public sector ethos affected the Investment Committee where non-executive directors shared executive decisions. There is now a two-stage process for capital investment planning: a capital investment plan provides a framework, with lists of specific projects which are brought forward individually for detailed approval by the Investment Committee. The framework plan earmarks some £5 billion per year, and specific projects are taken first to business unit committees and referred to the Investment Committee if they exceed £50 million in value. Projects with a value in excess of £100 million are brought before the Board. The Capital investment plan is agreed by

Table 5 BT – Corporate Scorecard

Shareholder/Financial	Customer/Key Stakeholder
Improve returns for our shareholders, within a challenging regulatory framework	Win loyalty in chosen markets through valued relationships and the excellence of our customer service
	Ensure BT people feel fulfilled, well managed and recognized as valued partners with a stake in the company's future
	Contribute to the wealth and well-being of the communities in which we do business
Processes	**Organizational Learning**
Grow our business by delivering a worldclass portfolio of telecoms and information products and services, which creates shareholder value	Recruit, develop and deploy the necessary people capability to deliver our strategy
	Share a compelling vision and strategy that drives efforts and activities towards competitive advantage and commercial success
	Inspire BT people by creating a climate for action and enterprise which drives the achievement of corporate goals

the Board and there are now no non-executive directors on the Investment Committee.

The new Board governance arrangements have given back to non-executive directors their essential independence. The process of recruiting non-executive directors has also changed: however well known to the Board candidates may be, they are interviewed and assessed by consultants and alternative candidates brought in to widen the Board's choice. There is now a healthy scepticism about appointing chief executives of other companies as non-executive directors. Experience has shown that they rarely have enough time to commit to their non-executive role. Their independence may be called into question – for example, in assessing the remuneration of their executive peers. The ideal non-executive director should be fiercely independent and willing to resign if not satisfied with answers from executive directors. Ewen Fergusson had been a model non-executive director on the BT Board.

The new governance approach at BT would include stakeholders as far as is reasonable. BT had not recognized the fundamental importance of its relationship with its institutional shareholders and had not enjoyed their support during the MCI difficulties. Sir Peter Bonfield was now spearheading a programme to keep the institutions fully aware of BT's thinking. Luke March was concerned to balance the treatment of shareholders – BT already reported quarterly to all shareholders. Of the total number of 2.1 million shareholders, some 2 million were private shareholders who held some 25 per cent of total equity, and most of them were also customers. In the same way that small investors in insurance and pension plans focused their power through the large institutions, which used their money to build large share-holdings in key companies, might not the smaller shareholders in BT focus their power through an elected body whose representatives would integrate their proxies? The issue of the rights of small shareholders was likely to increase in importance as their numbers grew and as each discovered his relative impotence. With the Halifax having 7 million shareholders, 1997 must have seen an increase in small shareholders in the UK of well over 10 million. Unless they were treated fairly that number might rapidly decrease.

BT saw its stakeholders as the institutions, other shareholders, customers, employees and the local community. Suppliers had not had the same recognition. Considerable work was being done to engage customers (some complained of intrusiveness) and BT took great care with internal communication to and from employees. A community affairs function dealt with local communities and used local advisory groups to raise issues. BT focused considerable attention on education, including the provision of material for use in schools. £15 million was spent annually on community schemes, including help for disabled people. The Board takes a close interest in these matters and in issues of environmental control.

Many of the issues surrounding governance are explored by the BT Forum, which is sponsored by the company to discuss and research matters affecting society and consequently BT's customers. The Forum is chaired by Joanna Foster and makes regular reports which are published by BT.

BT sees governance not as a matter of pure ethics but as a system of shared values at work which are reflected in its 'Statement of Business Practice', a working code of conduct which is shown in Table 6.

Codes of conduct are not difficult to write but much harder to communicate and even harder to monitor. Value systems are easier to share in the UK than in many overseas markets. BT employees outside the UK want a prescriptive regime to protect them from conflicting practices. The real test of governance is to make it work in a multi-cultural world economy.

Table 6   The way we work in BT – our statement of business practice

BT aims to go further than simply complying with the laws and regulations of the territories in which we operate. Our standards of business integrity and professional competence in all activities around the world must be world class. How our customers and shareholders perceive BT's ethical behaviour may affect their willingness to do business with BT.

The BT statement of business practice sets the standards that we require from our employees, agents and contractors when representing BT, group-wide and world-wide.

They should:

o not divulge information obtained through their work except as authorised
o not offer or accept any inducement to obtain or grant preferential treatment
o avoid or declare any situation in which they have a personal interest or conflict.

Customers

We want our customers to enjoy doing business with BT.

BT is committed to providing:

o world class telecommunications services and products
o value for money
o choice and flexibility.

Our main services are backed by guarantee and we compensate our customers if we fail to meet our published standards.

BT will:

o respect the confidentiality of our customers' information
o respect customers' special needs and difficulties, including when we supply on credit and when we collect payments
o be truthful and accurate in all our communications with customers, and be helpful and honest in all our dealings with them
o compete vigorously but fairly in the marketplace
o handle complaints speedily, professionally and courteously.

Employees

BT is an equal opportunities employer.

We will:

o treat our employees fairly and with respect
o reward them appropriately
o make clear what is required of them
o keep them informed and encourage them to give their views
o provide development and training so they can contribute to BT's success
o promote safe working and healthy life-styles

Shareholders

Our shareholders own the company.

We will:

o strive to increase long-term shareholder value
o inform them about BT's objectives and performance
o give them opportunities to express their views
o operate to the highest standards of corporate governance.

Suppliers

We will use our purchasing power fairly and will:

o administer tendering and contracting procedures in good faith
o pay promptly and as agreed.

Community and environment

In the places where we do business, we will:

o support social, economic and cultural well-being
o encourage our employees to contribute to the community
o help to protect the environment, through energy efficiency, recycling and waste reduction.

3.5

MORGAN CRUCIBLE – GOVERNANCE ON A GLOBAL SCALE

❖

Globalization can only fully be realized when larger businesses are effectively managed on a global scale. Even smaller companies, such as Filofax, are likely to have wide international coverage. Even when companies build internationally through franchising, like McDonalds and Marriott Hotels, there remains an issue of governance on a widening basis.

In the 1960s there was concern that the world would become dominated by a small number of megacompanies, mostly controlled from the USA. This concern was expressed most powerfully in the book *The American Challenge*, written by Jean-Jacques Servan-Schreiber, with a view to galvanizing European resistance to American economic domination. In the event American companies have remained the leading force in international business, but have to share world markets with Japanese, European and other businesses. Increasing global competition fed by trade liberalization has forced companies to rationalize in order to remain independent. Major oil companies have sold off investments in coal and minerals to focus on energy; most major banking groups have abandoned ambitions to offer a whole range of financial services on a global scale. Today the emphasis is on maximizing profits from a limited number of areas of core competence. Growing shareholder value is seen as the best protection against takeover in a world where even ICI was not safe from attack.

Where are the models for tomorrow's global company? The Swedish/Swiss giant Asea Brown Boveri (ABB) has been seen as such a model. It operates in 128 countries and has an extremely decentralized structure, with business units being limited in size to some 42 people. As a European company it has been able so far to take a longer-term view of its

175

strategic investments than Anglo-Saxon shareholders would tolerate – it has moved powerfully into Russia at a time when other investors have been more cautious. ABB has been the creation of Percy Barnevik, its visionary and charismatic Chief Executive, who has now returned to Sweden to manage the Wallenberg business empire. It remains to be seen how ABB will now develop into the future.

Morgan Crucible is a British company which has grown over a longer period than ABB and has achieved a similar degree of global coverage. It has 176 companies in 43 countries and trades in over 120 countries. Morgan Crucible has focused its activities on technologically advanced materials, chemicals and components which are used by virtually every industry. These include products such as carbon brushes, ceramic insulators, refractory products and dry film lubricant coatings. The company is structured within four divisions (carbon, technical ceramics, thermal ceramics and speciality materials) each of which operates globally. In certain cases similar competencies exist across divisions – three divisions produce silicon carbide products. Cross-divisional networking is a key strength of the group, whose annual turnover is now some £1 billion.

Morgan Crucible is largely the realization of the vision of Dr Bruce Farmer who has spent 15 years of his working life building the company. Bruce saw the potential for a company able to develop and manufacture a range of high technology essential materials and components which would be needed by a wide range of companies. His objective was to be the prime source for such components, tailoring them as needed, but building close relationships with customers. Bruce saw Morgan Crucible becoming the 'really useful' company whose title Andrew Lloyd Webber preempted. He has managed to persuade some customers to give up making products which Morgan Crucible could supply more economically: GE was even persuaded to outsource to Morgan Crucible the distribution of replacement carbon brushes worldwide. Morgan Crucible has consistently set its face against competing with its customers, a policy which has developed strong trust over the years. Its strategy for expansion is geared to filling out key product ranges; it has the widest range of commutators available and its range of seal faces is so comprehensive that TI Crane buys virtually the full range from Morgan Crucible.

Bruce Farmer takes a long-term view of strategy. He has certain patterns of product competence and market positioning in mind, and works patiently towards their realization. He waited 15 years to acquire a key German family company; Morgan Crucible has bought 130 companies and sold 21 in his time as Managing Director, and only one hostile bid was made. Bruce believes fervently that hostile bids risk damaging the relationships needed to develop the business which has been bought.

Bruce Farmer talks about 'The Morgan family'. This is not the eponymous Welsh family which founded J.P. Morgan, Morgan Grenfell and Morgan

Stanley, and later created Morgan Crucible and Morgan Grampian. For him the 'Morgan family' is the group of people at all levels who share the vision and culture of Morgan Crucible. Great trouble is taken in all parts of the business to recruit people who have affinity with 'the family'. These people need to be creative, flexible, enquiring and responsible. 'The Morgan family' comprises people who are committed to customer service, product quality and working together. Those who have their own agendas or who are morally unsound are rarely recruited – one very senior US director had to be dismissed, but this was very exceptional.

Morgan Crucible does not promulgate fancy mission and values statements, but Bruce Farmer has encouraged the development of a strong Morgan culture by pushing authority and responsibility right down to foreman level. Each division is expected to develop its own vision, which is reconciled with group vision where necessary. The group structure is minimal; a small team in Windsor 'plans and coordinates worldwide business development, monitors performance and controls overall legal, tax, treasury, secretarial and intellectual property matters'. Each company produces its own plans and budgets; the 170 budgets are reviewed annually and strategic plans are reviewed every two years. The review takes place in Windsor in November. At the AGM in June overseas directors and managers are able to meet shareholders and analysts.

Morgan Crucible meets all of the Cadbury recommendations and all Greenbury recommendations apart from maintaining two-year directors' contracts. It has reduced from five-year contracts down to two-year contracts without compensating those concerned. In view of the care taken with recruitment and the relatively long learning curve of a complex business one year contracts are seen as unrealistic. Bruce Farmer is opposed to any watering down of Cadbury through the Hampel Committee enquiry and is conscious of the strong criticisms of British business for its short-termism and greed. He believes that better standards for governance will help to restrain the pressures on British companies to act against their own best long-term interests.

Asked to whom a company belongs, Bruce indicated that in Japan it worked for employees' interests, in Germany for society and in Anglo-Saxon countries for shareholders. His own view was that there was a tripartite stakeholdership – for customers, for shareholders and for employees. He recognized that communities were important, especially in some overseas locations, and that suppliers would be important to many companies who looked to them for design or technological support.

The development of people was a key part of Morgan Crucible's culture. Bruce Farmer had started his time as Managing Director by appointing a HR director, with a free-roaming commission, who reports directly to him. As a result a learning culture had been encouraged throughout the group. All companies organized their own development and training activities, and £1 million/year was spent at the centre on training events. These included interpersonal skills, change management, the management of technology and team-building. The facilities of Outward Bound and the Prince's Youth Trust were used to supplement in-house courses. The company also works with schools: Epsom College teachers have been on Morgan Crucible courses, and local schools are a key source of recruitment. The company is in the Best 100 Employers book and well regarded on the graduate 'milk round'. A number of fast track recruits are brought to the centre annually from North America, Asia and other market areas and given very thorough development programmes. It was significant that 85 per cent of those recruited since 1985 remained with the group. Although Morgan Crucible had a high retention rate in its staff, the emphasis of training was now moving towards self-development as it becomes more usual for young people to manage their own careers.

Morgan Crucible set targets for each company for return on funds employed, for cash flow after capital expenditure (which had to be between 1 and 1.4 x depreciation), for operating margin and for growth in profit before tax. Most companies also had working capital targets to meet. These targets were geared to group targets (25 per cent return on funds, 3 per cent free cash flow, 15 per cent operating margin and 10 per cent pre-tax profits growth). Personal rewards were geared to achieving these targets which, in turn, were geared to achieving long-term development of the group. Any attempt to mortgage future development by maximizing short-term results would quickly be seen and not sanctioned. At group level it would be possible to abandon China and increase short-term profits, but this was not acceptable. Bruce Farmer indicated that the City now trusted Morgan Crucible and was not pressing for short-termism. The company had consistently paid dividends of 40/50 per cent of earnings in good times, and up to 69 per cent when profits were squeezed. The dividend had never been cut in 40 years. Debt varied between 30 per cent and 70 per cent of equity, but interest was well covered even at 70 per cent (7 times), despite City nervousness.

The Top Fifteen institutional investors held 60 per cent of Morgan Crucible's shares and were kept well-informed through presentations twice each year. Bruce Farmer was conscious that individual shareholders were less well-briefed about company prospects, and planned to see how this could be remedied during his Chairmanship. He saw the Chairman's role as that of a facilitator. He wanted to ensure that the company vision remained challenging but realistic and that the complex strategy to realize it was fully understood. He spent much of his thinking time on strategy and had tried to instill this discipline in his colleagues. He saw the Chairman's role as helping to identify acquisitions and disposals; the key task was probably to ensure that self-renewal processes were effective. He saw himself spending more time visiting companies and talking to people at all levels, both to find new ideas and to spot people of potential. He recalled that he had long kept a 'little book' of potential leaders: he had first earmarked his successor as Managing Director, Ian Norris, in 1982.

The detailed attention paid to recruiting and developing employees is reflected in the process of selecting non-executive directors. The Morgan Crucible Board comprises six executive and seven non-executive directors. This ensures that the internal constituencies of a complex and wide-ranging business are fully represented, while allowing a majority of external directors to bring their independent judgement to key issues. Non-executive directors are chosen with a view to bringing regional understanding (an American, a Chinese, a Frenchman and a Swede), City credibility and Government experience. They have two interviews with Bruce Farmer before they meet the executive directors over dinner and the other non-executives informally also. There has to be unanimous enthusiasm for a candidate before he is appointed. The regional non-executives bring a valuable network of contacts in their region and an understanding of how local systems work. The non-executives become committed members of the Morgan family and its culture, but remain constructively critical in Board deliberations.

At present there are no female directors of Morgan Crucible. The business requires a high degree of technical competence and women have not been attracted to the components business. Nevertheless, there are two women managing directors of overseas companies and the Financial Controller in Windsor is female. Bruce Farmer is conscious of the need to provide more opportunities for women at the top of the company.

Bruce Farmer sees his executive colleagues as a team of entrepreneurs. The four divisions compete and cooperate at a breathless pace. Creativity and speed of reaction are critical in a component business – second to market wins no prizes. This hectic pace is carried down into all parts of the business; speed is essential to meet customer demands which are increasingly challenging. Several companies in the group process and ship products within one day to be competitive.

Although the four divisions compete with each other to beat their targets, comparisons are never made country-to-country. Such comparisons would not have any meaning for the business and would risk being gratuitously offensive. Morgan Crucible has never managed by country even though it markets into countries. This gives it total flexibility within its product group; in the 1970s everything sold in Japan was made there, but now products sold in Japan are mainly imported from low-cost sources.

Morgan Crucible has gone a long way towards being a global company. Its skill in grouping products and capturing control of key component areas, together with imaginative trading across boundaries have given it global niche leadership in certain products – for example, crucibles. Having involved and empowered its employees, it remains for them to have the chance to become fully mobile globally and to have their career developed within the worldwide Morgan family as well as in their Chinese, Russian, Brazilian or Zambian homeland.

3.6

AN SME VIEW OF CORPORATE GOVERNANCE

Richard Purdey pointed out the dilemma Merrydown plc faced when it decided to float on the Untitled Shares Market (USM) in 1981 when he was Managing Director. The company had begun in 1946 almost as a hobby shared by three friends and had grown in a club-like atmosphere until it faced the need for major investment to lay the foundations for real growth. There being no sensible borrowing option at the time, its founders had taken the flotation route both to find new funding and to create a market in Merrydown shares.

Flotation moves most owners into a new role – that of custodian. Depending on the level of funding it can also dilute their level of control. The direct control previously exercised is now subject to second-guessing and actions can easily be misinterpreted. To avoid misunderstandings greater regulation is called for: actions have to be explained and accountability is greatly extended. In a smaller company it is possible to work more on trust; a handshake with somebody whom you know well is worth more than the best contract or due diligence. Quoted companies find, however, that they are obliged to wear the regulatory suit designed for members of the FTSE 100. This is burdensome and time-consuming; for many smaller companies the demands of quoted status take valuable top management time which should be devoted to the strategic and operational imperatives of the business.

Another key issue is the different agendas of institutional and private shareholders. Richard Purdey has found private shareholders generally to be very loyal, despite the mixed fortunes of Merrydown, and they have remained consistent holders of over 15 per cent of the company's equity. The institutions remain focused on growth and expect regular private briefings in order to maintain support. Richard Purdey is concerned that private shareholders only meet the Board usually once a year at the AGM and have no means of consolidating their voting power on key issues. A mechanism to pool proxies would be very welcome.

The role of brokers in briefing private shareholders was seen as important but probably underdeveloped. Richard Purdey found that the drinks sector analysts whom he briefed were usually well-informed and quick to understand the issues faced by Merrydown. He enjoyed talking to analysts and found that the time spent was usually well-invested, both in terms of retaining City support and in raising the profile of Merrydown relative to larger competitors. Openness was an essential part of dealing with analysts; issuing a profits warning only eight weeks after a bullish profits statement wins no friends.

He believes that companies should be managed for long-term shareholder value. In doing so, the directors should endeavour to manage stakeholder expectations so that the outcome satisfies the owners. He likens the process to an orchestral performance where the shareholders are the audience and the different instrumentalists are stakeholders. The role of the Chairman is to ensure that the stakeholders are motivated to produce a quality and harmony of sound which shareholders will applaud.

Some concern is felt by Richard Purdey about the City. Its role as a provider of funds is becoming institutionalized so that small companies face processes of due diligence, with obligatory merchant bank, accountant and solicitor involvement which drives up fees to unrealistic levels in proportion to the sums being sought. The City has become a monopoly supplier of capital – perhaps some competition, for example NASDAQ or the Scots after devolution, could challenge them? As a consequence he would advise owners of such businesses to think twice before 'going public'. When the smaller company is quoted, it becomes locked into a very demanding and expensive process that can absorb valuable time and money which, he believes, certainly in the case of Merrydown, would have been better devoted to building the business through greater investment in brand marketing.

Richard Purdey finds the principles behind the Cadbury and subsequent reports acceptable. He is concerned at the level of prescription in some cases when applied to smaller companies. Cadbury calls for at least three non-executive directors who shall be independent. Many smaller companies have minimal-sized boards which would be swamped by three non-executive directors. When companies with family roots expand they are likely to bring in non-executive directors they know and trust, not strangers. The committee structures in Cadbury are excessive for smaller companies, many of whose issues will be sorted out round the family table. For Richard Purdey it would be preferable if corporate governance could depend on the trust which intimate groups of people are able to build naturally by working closely together. Where size weakens intimacy and trust, regulation inevitably becomes necessary. In his view this will always be a poor substitute for real relationships.

4.1

THE LEX COLUMN – ONE OF THE KEY PILLARS OF GOVERNANCE

Hugo Dixon ('LEX' of the *Financial Times*) sees governance as an issue of growing importance in the business world. For him the key principle is to protect the interest of shareholders as owners of the company. This is no longer an Anglo-Saxon issue, but is now emerging strongly in a growing number of countries. In Europe, Germany, France and others are shifting towards an Anglo-Saxon model of governance and an emphasis on share-holder value is starting to be seen.

The LEX view on corporate governance is more comprehensive than the interest in high rates of remuneration which exercises much of the Press. Governance is a means to generate wealth over the long-term. The enlight-ened pursuit of wealth requires good relationships between companies and their shareholders. Shareholder value has to be created in a sustainable manner over the long-term. To achieve this the focus has to be on invest-ment and training as well as on efficiency. Companies with good governance are directed towards profitability but within a strong basic moral framework and with a value-based relationship with the other stakeholders (customers, employees and suppliers principally).

To be successful directors need to focus on one basic target and not be tempted to reconcile all stakeholder agendas. The directors are the agents of shareholders in directing the company and may only act in their interest. Focusing on shareholder value is the best way of fulfilling their mandate.

There are, for LEX, three major issues around the successful pursuit of shareholder value. First, the board needs to be rigorous in choosing the chief executive and ruthless in disposing of any chief executive who is inappropri-ate or unsuccessful. There are some signs, as at Booker, that this discipline is

183

being imposed. Secondly, the board has to be rigorous in judging that large investments, especially mergers and acquisitions, will be value-enhancing, and equally rigorous in divesting underperforming activities. The choice between acquisitions and organic growth will need to be judged in terms of sustaining long-term growth in shareholder value. Thirdly, the board needs to use cash-flow to enhance shareholder value, which may be by returning funds to shareholders if investment opportunities are not judged to be sufficiently value-enhancing.

Measured against these three criteria directors' remuneration is only an issue if performance in creating shareholder value is inadequate. Outstanding directors are essential if outstanding performance is to be achieved. Incentives are important to high achievers, but poor performance or failure should be sanctioned not rewarded. The City misses the real point of making high rewards; where they are merited they send positive signals to the rest of the company and motivate employees to improve themselves and their performance. Higher pay in privatized utilities is not, in itself, a mistake. Changing those operations into effective businesses is a huge challenge, compounded by political pressures, and requires outstanding leaders. The higher pay should be given to talented people brought in to transform the companies where incumbent directors are inadequate.

Governance requires a clear set of values and openness. The Nolan principles are admirable, but should support and not confuse the drive for shareholder value. All companies need an effective system of checks and balances to maintain progress towards achieving shareholder value and avoid waste. It is encouraging that shareholders are becoming more active. LEX sees his role as facilitating the process by encouraging good practice and challenging actions likely to dilute shareholder value, such as adjustable value share options (currently a US phenomenon only). American shareholders are more dispersed than in the UK, so that concerted action is often harder to achieve. LEX believes that more chief executives have been removed through shareholder pressure in the UK than in the USA; this is another encouraging sign of increasing involvement by institutional shareholders.

This involvement is taking different forms. Sometimes there is direct intervention by a shareholder or group of shareholders with the board. More frequently shareholders will speak with their brokers for them to act as intermediaries. Companies are more active in briefing institutional shareholders. Where there is a major issue the chairman or chief executive will visit them individually to rally support, as Michael Grade has done recently.

LEX sees a 'free rider' hazard around corporate governance. Too many shareholders still hang back, letting others make the challenges which improve performance. The role of LEX is to rally a greater number of shareholders to demand improved value for their investment. This is having some effect, but other factors are now forcing investors to be active. In the past shares were easily sold if results were disappointing, but markets are now more sophisticated and large trades more visible. The adoption of indexing has locked investors into shares included in the index so that they now have to demand better performance where necessary.

LEX is very supportive of the appointment of strong non-executive directors. Chief executives may have to be fiery to be effective, but it is dangerous if they become autocratic. He dislikes combining the offices of chairman and chief executive, as this concentrates power and weakens debate. LEX recognizes the problem of appointing chief executives of other companies as non-executive directors, both in terms of being able to relate to the company's chief executive, objectively and in avoiding a ratcheting of salaries through benchmarking between different remuneration committees. For LEX totally independent non-executives are ideal but very hard to find. A university professor may be independent but will he have the character to face down a strong chief executive? On balance LEX sees the need for a mix of non-executive directors, some executive directors in other companies and some with relevant skills and contacts, but independent.

LEX believes that paying non-executive directors partly in shares is healthy. This helps to bridge the agent/principal gap with the shareholders. Non-executive directors should not be allowed to sell their shares in the short-term, perhaps within three years. The non-executive shareholders of Glaxo and SmithKline Beecham have small shareholdings – might there have been more glue to hold the merger together if their shareholding had been larger?

The pathway beyond the Hampel Report will be challenging. LEX is adamant that the 'Supercode' should be the last code of corporate governance. Time is now needed for the dynamic forces driving better governance to work through and establish better practice. Shareholders need to become more active and more effective. Non-executives need to be of a higher quality and more committed to their role. The short-termist debate needs to be brought to a conclusion, and the short-term bias of reporting and rewards readjusted to reflect the real importance of long-term growth of shareholder value.

Communication will be a crucial issue in achieving a sustained growth in shareholder value. Both companies and institutional investors need to take the initiative in creating a proper dialogue. Investors need to clarify what they really want. At present they focus on relative performance – do they not really require absolute performance? Investors need to spell out how they will judge performance both in the short- and long-terms. The process of creating shareholder value needs to be clarified between companies and investors and better models than EVA or current equivalents will need to be developed. The balanced scorecard approach will need to be brought into the model. Targets will need to be few, clear and audited. Targets are needed for nett annual cashflow, for value created within the company and for the value created in each SBU. At present the value created lies somewhere between the nett asset value in the balance sheet and the current stock market valuation of equity. Managements need to clarify where the gain lies and how it has been achieved.

Governance will also be driven by the increasing accountability of fund managers. At present their performance is only beginning to come under close scrutiny. The first takeovers of underperforming investment trusts seem to herald a concerted move to force greater accountability. In the field of pensions the shift towards defined contribution schemes away from defined benefit arrangements may begin to enfranchise beneficiaries. Despite the Goode Report governance of defined benefit schemes remains under the control of companies in most cases, and little has been achieved towards allowing beneficiaries to appoint a majority of scheme trustees, nor have funds, and potential surpluses, been liberated from company control. It is to be hoped that new pension schemes will push for models in tune with the Goode Report.

LEX is concerned also about the influence of private shareholders. The increasing intervention by institutional shareholders is creating a risk of sidelining small shareholders. He sees the possibility of consolidating proxy votes in order to strengthen their collective influence, possibly through agencies running 'proxy banks'. This would also allow PEPs holders to vote their shareholdings and different agencies might represent special interests – green shareholders, shareholder value buffs, etc.

LEX is not in favour of compulsory voting by shareholders. He sees such a move as likely to favour the board's line on the issues concerned and to exacerbate the 'free riding' problem. He is critical of the average calibre of pension fund trustees who often see no reason to disagree with company views on pensions matters. As the importance of pensions performance will increase, due to state withdrawal and greater longevity, it is important to incentivize pensions trustees on their performance on behalf of beneficiaries and contributors. Many companies still see the pension fund as their asset, not as the property of beneficiaries.

Media are not seen by LEX as stakeholders of the companies with which they interact. He sees his role as that of an agent for his readers with a mandate to try to influence events and behaviour on their behalf where they are shareholders. The LEX column is focused on facilitating fair play in corporate governance and on encouraging the spread of best practice. LEX is a coach, not a Cassandra.

4.2

REGULATION BY RESEARCH –
THE ROLE OF PIRC

❖

Pensions and Investment Research Consultants (PIRC) has its roots in the early 1980s when a consortium of public sector pension funds sought an alternative umbrella organization to the National Association of Pension Funds (NAPF). The consortium set up working parties on various issues (mergers, ethical investment, and so on) and found itself struggling to make sense of complexities which the City of London did not even recognize. In order to make real progress, the pension funds established PIRC in 1986 to carry out structured research and to provide independent and balanced investment advice. Alan McDougal, Manager of the GLC Superannuation Fund, took the helm and was joined by Anne Simpson, a professional marketter researcher, as Joint Managing Director. Non-executive directors are John Plender (author), Bryn Davies (actuary), Davie Pitt-Watson (consultant) and David Harker (CA Bureau). Advisers include Sue Ward (pensions expert), Jonathan Clarkham (ex ProNED), Michael Bratt (*Investors Chronicle*) and Victoria Younghusband (lawyer).

Anne Simpson recounted how PIRC has been built on the back of a series of challenges. After early successes PIRC had masterminded a winning proxy battle against Hanson in 1993, largely by mobilizing US shareholder proxies against proposed changes to the articles of association which would have reduced accountability. PIRC had led a challenge to British Gas on the issue of directors' pay in 1996 which failed for lack of institutional support, but represented a moral victory. As a result the institutions began to take the Greenbury Report more seriously, and PIRC built up its reputation and clientele. PIRC now has some 70 clients, including 8 out of 10 top investment funds, managing assets of £150 billion, with local government funds managing £30 billion of assets and corporate investors responsible for £50 billion of funds. Anne Simpson had battled the previous day to dissuade

Gerry Robinson from awarding himself and four other executive directors nearly £375 000 compensation for reducing their contractual notice periods. Robinson had stood his ground against a tide of shareholder fury at the AGM and had won a Pyrric victory at the expense of his reputation.

PIRC's growing standing as the leading champion of corporate governance in the public eye has been developed on the basis of sustained and painstaking research. Its corporate governance service to clients comprises a monthly newsletter, detailed briefings before major company meetings, shareholder voting guidelines and in-depth research reports on major issues, such as corporate governance policies, the independence of non-executive directors, Greenbury compliance, proxy voting trends and so on. Research is supplemented by conferences and by regular individual briefing of clients. Over time this process has made institutional investors more active on issues of corporate governance, although regular scandals and high profile AGM battles are needed in order to stimulate activity from the institutions.

Anne Simpson saw the corporate governance issue as having been driven by scandal and media reaction to corporate excesses. The Cadbury Report came from BCCI, Maxwell and other scandals, but was still an intellectual *tour de force*. The Greenbury Report was a short-term political fix following the outcry about huge pay increases for directors of privatized industries. The Hampel Report had originally been conceived as 'Cadbury II', but had ended as an exercise in consolidation. Hampel had been driven by the views of company directors and lacked shareholder, employee or any other stakeholder input. The intellectual argument had not been advanced by the Hampel Report; it had moved elsewhere to the Centre for Tomorrow's Company and authors like John Plender.

The issue of regulation versus self-regulation remained in contention. The new Financial Services Authority had tidied up the earlier confused pattern of regulation following the Financial Services Act, but the role of the DTI remained unclear. It would seem that the Government was trying to create a clearer framework within which self-regulation would continue. Calls for a SEC style regulation remained muted, although the record of self-regulation continued to be unsatisfactory. Shareholders had legal rights but no clear responsibilities. No organization at present coordinated action by institutional investors; the Council of Institutional Investors was not doing this and the NAPF and the Association of British Insurers (ABI) were at loggerheads. Pension funds had grown faster than insurance funds in recent years and the ABI was hostile to change. The NAPF had been supportive of PIRC but was not leading from the front.

Anne Simpson recognized the relative disadvantage of smaller shareholders in the realm of corporate governance. Not only were their votes fragmented, but their power was weakened by inadequate arrangements for nominee accounts. Where employees held shares through trusts, they rarely had any say on how the trustees voted. Unit trusts were unable to split votes to represent different opinions among unit holders. It was, however, encouraging to find that poll cards to accommodate split votes from fund managers had been issued at the recent Shell AGM. It was to be hoped that individual shareholders would find a more powerful voice in future – might it be through creating shareholder clubs to merge and vote individual proxies? Something similar had worked when challenging Hanson.

PIRC is not in favour of votes by a show of hands. It may appeal to the few shareholders who attend an AGM, but does not reflect the balanced weight of voting found in a poll. With institutions failing to attend most AGMs, the shareholder questions and voting from the floor are usually shadows of the real content of shareholder concern. At the Granada AGM there were 700 shareholders present. Two hundred institutions have Granada shares, but few had representatives at the meeting and none spoke.

This unwillingness of institutions to be seen to be active in support of corporate governance is worrying. The PIRC survey in August 1997 of institutional shareholder policies on corporate governance showed that 95 per cent of respondents claimed to have a corporate governance policy, but 88 per cent were unwilling to make them publicly available. Most of these policies dated from the time when controversy over pay had led to the Greenbury Report. The institutions seem to prefer private dialogue with investor companies and were largely aware of the responsibilities of shareholders in ensuring that effective corporate governance and sustainable profitability were achieved. Their unwillingness to 'name and shame' where necessary leaves the initiative with directors and allows accountability to be avoided.

The Cadbury Committee saw the presence of independent non-executive directors as crucial to underpin effective corporate governance. PIRC has developed specific criteria for assessing the independence of non-executive directors, recognizing that some non-independent directors can perform a valuable advisory role on the board, but seeking to ensure that there are at least three fully independent directors at any time. The criteria developed by PIRC to question the independence of each director are:

1 if they held an executive position within the company within the past ten years.
2 if they are a director or employee of a professional adviser to the company.
3 if they are a director or employee of another enterprise which has a notifiable holding in the company.
4 if they are a director or employee of another company in which the company has a notifiable holding.
5 if they have a contract or share options, receive remuneration other than fees or are eligible for pension or bonus payments.

6 if they are, or have been recently, a director or employee of a significant customer of or supplier to the company.
7 if they have been a director for more than ten years.
8 if they share common directorships or positions of authority with other
directors.
9 if they are related to other directors or advisers to the company.
10 if they hold a senior position at a political or charitable body to which
the company makes donations.
11 if there is not a formal and transparent nominations process.
12 if directors of investment trusts have connections with the trust's managers either as employees or ex-employees or as directors of other
trusts managed by the same group.

There remains the issue of shareholding by non-executive directors. While
many articles of association prescribe a minimum shareholding, it may not
be compatible with pure independence for a non-executive director to hold
any shares or to have any remuneration other than the fees reported in the
accounts. The Hampel Committee recommends the payment of non-executive directors in company shares – have its members never heard of the
Truck Acts?

The battle to bring effective corporate governance to British companies
has only just begun in earnest. After years of relative failure British business
seems to have seen the American model of unharnessed corporate aggression as the road to competitive survival. Boardrooms have attracted a new
generation of 'hard men', many of whom are forcing their own agenda on to
the companies whose servants they should be. It is for shareholders to take
responsibility for the effective governance of their companies in order to
preserve their investment for the long-term.

5.1

THE 'TOMORROW'S COMPANY' APPROACH TO CORPORATE GOVERNANCE

One of the key factors shaping the debate about corporate governance is the RSA inquiry 'Tomorrow's Company' launched in 1993. The inquiry arose through a challenge from Professor Charles Handy for the implications, for companies, of his own research into the changing world of work to be explored. The inquiry was chaired by Sir Anthony Cleaver and spent over two years on its investigation, culminating in a final report issued in June 1995.

The findings of the enquiry are challenging. It accuses British business of complacency and ignorance of world standards, of over-reliance on financial measures of performance and of reflecting the British adversarial culture. It sets out the vision of an inclusive approach to business relationships, involving the many stakeholders who influence the performance of the company, and enabling it to find a route to sustainable success. Such success needs to be based on a firm and shared belief in the purpose of the company, with shared values and objectives. Business leaders are called upon to open up and develop their relationships with customers, suppliers, employees and the wider community in which they operate, rather than see themselves as purely the agents of their shareholders. The report emphasizes that the centre of gravity in business success is moving from the exploitation of physical assets towards the competitive development and use of human skills. Learning will be an investment not a cost. Through external relationships companies will be able to supplement the skills of their employees and strengthen their competitiveness.

The inquiry produced an Agenda for Action, aimed at directors, managers, the investment community and learners/educators. This was intended to ensure that readers used the findings of the inquiry as a source of inspiration for change. To support this Agenda for Action the Centre for Tomorrow's Company was established and has continued the process of research started by the inquiry, has campaigned widely to increase awareness of and adoption of the principles emerging from the inquiry, and has established a Tomorrow's Company Forum to widen the debate and learning around the inclusive approach to company management. It has also motivated companies to join together on Pathfinder projects whereby they learn from each other on the journey towards a more inclusive approach.

The inclusive approach to management, in which a company identifies various stakeholders and defines its relationship with them, is much more than Tony Blair's vision of a stakeholder economy. The inclusive approach is not altruism, but a rigorous analysis of potential relationships and of their likely contribution to the company's long-term strategic success. When the analysis is done, it is then crucial to determine how the relationships can be developed and how the benefits can be assessed and rewards allocated. Too often strategies are expected to produce 'win-lose' outcomes; the inclusive approach favours 'win-win' outcomes, even with competitors. Today's competitor may be tomorrow's alliance partner – even competitors can be stakeholders!

Nick Obolensky, the Development Director of the Centre for Tomorrow's Company, expresses concern that conventional wisdom regarding competitive advantage is based on outmoded concepts. The theories of strategy have been developed out of the art of warfare in which one side seeks to defeat the other. War is a zero sum game, and business strategy has adopted the metaphors of war and the idea that one party must lose. Destroying the competition can too often become the focus of business endeavours, rather than concentration on customer satisfaction. Nick Obolensky sees competition as a source of learning in order to do better the prime task of serving customers. Competition is needed as a spur towards improvement and evolution. The analogy with sport may be more meaningful in that for any event there can only be one winner on the day. Sports people are competing fundamentally against themselves; they may not win the race but, if they are rational, they will have learned from the winner and have improved their own performance.

Competitive advantage is also an elusive idea for Nick Obolensky. Often competitive advantage is a spoiling game as in the battle for local supremacy between supermarket chains. Tesco picked off Gateway stores one by one; Gateway changed the game by opening Food Giant discount stores ahead of the opening of Tesco's new branches. In the event the real winner probably was the local populace who had access to cheaper and better food. However, if the two had fought on relentlessly, both would have suffered locally and the population would have ended up with two closed stores.

Nick Obolensky favours the 'win-win' formula, called by Andy Grove of Intel 'coopetition'. In an increasingly complex marketplace, killer competition can be unnecessarily destructive. In a world of fast change and high investment costs cooperation is often essential in order to make technical improvements viable. The main manufacturers of memory chips can only keep up with their equivalent of the working of 'Moore's Law' (that capacity doubles every two years) by taking turns to invest in each generation of product.

Nick Obolensky saw the concept of 'winning' in business to be slippery. Too often a large market share was seen as a victory, but it often acted as a bait for attackers. Few of the top 100 in the Dow Jones Index of 1900 survived today. Sustainability was crucial in deciding strategy; companies needed to understand and protect their long-term interests, so that survival could be achieved. Long-lived businesses often changed their market focus several times – Grace had begun as a shipping company and evolved into chemicals. Where companies did not renew themselves, natural law seemed to grant them limited life. The average life of American companies was 42 years. The fear of business failure was a good spur towards excellence, but in business people did not get killed (unlike in war) and could start again.

Attitudes and values drive behaviour, in the view of Nick Obolensky. Values are more sustainable than individuals and can underpin the long-term success of companies. Mike Jackson drove values into the deepest recesses of Birmingham Midshires in order to galvanize its ability to perform. At Dutton Engineering employees are involved in the making of strategic decisions. Baxi has also built its success on total employee involvement. Such open management processes depend fundamentally on sponsoring learning among employees so that their contribution is effective. Nick Obolensky quoted Springfield Marine Corporation of Pittsburgh where the 2000 employees were involved with Jack Stack in rescuing the company from potential failure and are now participating in all business decisions. Where companies can project clear and consistent values, they can create enormous trust among those dealing with them: Marks and Spencer has been able to do this, and survived a child labour scandal which would have severely damaged a lesser company.

Governance can no longer be solely shareholder-focused. Creating wealth is more than just making money – if money is the sole object, why not rob a bank? Wealth now involves self-fulfilment (John Spedan Lewis called it 'happiness') which can be measured more in what people have learned and have achieved than exclusively in money. In financial terms an employee might compare their salary on joining and on leaving a company, seeing the difference as value added, but the real value added is in personal development and contribution made to the company's success.

Nick Obolensky saw the economy as a means of sustaining and strengthening civilization. Most of the economy now belonged to people through their pension funds, so that the dichotomy between capital and labour now had much less relevance. The concentration of economic power in a diminishing number of powerful institutional funds was, however, a cause for wariness.

Who might be the opponents of the Tomorrow's Company model? Nick Obolensky did not see the institutional investors as a real enemy, although many remained sceptical. Kleinwort Benson had established a Tomorrow's Company Unit Trust which was performing successfully. The main opponents at present were sceptically conservative institutions. For example, smaller pension fund trustees may see the potential benefits of shareholder value, but are often suspicious of the risk of watering down profits through policies of stakeholder inclusion. They are often victims of 'triangular thinking' – a process in which stakeholders are placed in a pyramid and logic tries to force a ranking from top to bottom. Nick Obolensky prefers to treat stakeholders as spokes of a wheel – all are needed to move forward and each takes the load in turn. Corporate governance is an exercise in balance, like the wheel and, as with a wheel, inbalance leads to friction. Where companies operate ethically and with clear values, shareholder value is created. Operating through value systems is only possible if the company's stakeholders are included – values do not exist in a vacuum and must be shared to be effective. Both the IOD and CBI are interested in the Tomorrow's Company model, which they seem to see as a new lens for observing the working of corporate governance. The real enemies of the model are the 'zero-sum' mentality, and 'triangular thinking'.

5.2

STEWARDSHIP MANAGEMENT IN ZENECA AGROCHEMICALS

It is a requirement for companies quoted on the Stock Exchange to make a report to shareholders on corporate governance, in particular with respect to compliance with the recommendations of the Cadbury Committee. Companies are also expected to report compliance with the Safety, Health and Welfare Act 1989; such reporting is increasingly focused on 'safety, health and the environment' (SHE).

In recent years the action of pressure groups, the development of International Standards and the demands of consumers have led some companies to develop management concepts which go beyond the traditional boundaries of the management of SHE risks. Within ZENECA the Agrochemicals Business has, over the last five years, developed this kind of thinking and embraces it in the concept of stewardship which it defines as 'The ethical and responsible management of all activities from invention to ultimate use and beyond.'

The management of stewardship in Agrochemicals is integrated with the ZENECA Group Policy through the CEO and by the manager of the Stewardship Department, who maintains close contact with his peers from the other ZENECA Businesses. This ensures a two-way flow of reporting, and that best practice is shared through the Group. The SHE Management System in ZENECA may be seen as a 'virtuous circle', with a number of logical and recycling steps. These are policy, standards, guidelines, local procedures, auditing, letter of assurance and review. The whole system is contained in the ZENECA SHE manual and operates at three levels: policy (set by the Board and subject to management audit); standards (of which there are presently 19); and guidelines. The system has been compared with ISO 14000 and meets most of its requirements. The ZENECA system is not subject to continuous external appraisal, which may be an issue for the future, although an exernal audit was done by Aspinwall two years ago and another audit by Arthur D. Little was conducted in 1Q 1998. The possibility of creating an Advisory Committee on Stewardship issues, involving experienced external specialists (as done by a number of water and waste companies) is under consideration.

ZENECA's policy states:

> In pursuit of its business objectives, it is ZENECA's policy to manage its activities to give benefit to society ensuring that:
>
> O they meet all relevant laws, regulations and international agreements;
> O they are conducted safely, protecting the health of all employees and all persons who may be affected;
> O they are acceptable to the community at large;
> O their environmental impact is reduced to a practicable minimum at an acceptable cost to ZENECA and society.
>
> The SHE Standards established by ZENECA are:
>
> 1 Safety, Health and Environment (SHE) Commitment
> 2 Management and resources
> 3 Communication and consultation
> 4 Training
> 5 Material hazards
> 6 Acquisitions and divestments
> 7 New plant, equipment and process design
> 8 Modifications and changes
> 9 SHE assurance
> 10 Systems of work
> 11 Emergency plans
> 12 Contractors and suppliers
> 13 Environmental impact assessment
> 14 Resource conservation
> 15 Waste management
> 16 Soil and ground water protection
> 17 Product stewardship
> 18 SHE performance and reporting
> 19 Auditing.

Each Standard is set out in principle and each Operating Unit is expected to report performance in detail and to relate to specific targets. For example, Product Stewardship states: 'There shall be arrangements to ensure that safety, health and environmental considerations are taken into account prior to the launch of new products and the development of new processes. The safety, health and environmental factors associated with any product from conception through to ultimate use and disposal shall be managed responsibly and ethically.' This Standard imposes a holistic approach on product management which ensures that all potential risks are identified and thought through before a product is launched. Stewardship is essentially about risk-management in all its aspects, but can also be focused on creating new opportunities.

In Agrochemicals great care has to be taken to develop detailed guidelines on Stewardship so that managers can respond intelligently and creatively to the Standards. The focus is on creating a 'responsible and caring company' which 'can remain an accepted and respected member of the society within which we operate'. Use of the Guidelines ensures that stewardship activity is concentrated on the issues which really matter for the success of its business.

Procedures based on the Stewardship Guidelines are developed at local level, both to ensure that all local regulations and customs are observed but also to obtain local commitment.

Audit is a critical part of the Stewardship management process and is essential to test and prove the health of the system. Audit operates at three levels – management audit focuses on implementing Standards and is carried out by persons independent of the site being audited; specialist audit focuses on a specific issue – for example, environmental containment, and is carried out by experienced professionals who are independent of site management, and operational audit focuses on the implementation of procedures and instructions, and is done by local staff.

The Annual Letter of Assurance provides a key link between the Stewardship Management System and the annual business cycle. Each strategic Business Unit is required to produce a Letter of Assurance every year which outlines:

O   Strategic Stewardship issues impacting on its business
O   Compliance with legislation and the ZENECA Standards
O   Stewardship Performance over the past year
O   Key elements of the Business Improvement Plan.

The Letters of Assurance are consolidated level by level up to the top of each ZENECA Business. These Business-level documents are then reviewed by the ZENECA Executive Council and consolidated into an overall ZENECA document which is presented to the ZENECA Board. Following the review and in support of the Groups' strategy the ZENECA Executive will set high-level Objectives which are cascaded back down the levels through each Business.

The Agrochemicals Business, through its Stewardship Department, reviews both the process and the technical content of the individual responses made by the sites and Business Units. The outcomes of this review are both fed back to the respondents and utilized in the planning of the support activities and resource deployment of the Stewardship expertise. Because the Annual Letter of Assurance mechanism consciously reviews the external pressures on the Business, ZENECA Agrochemicals is in the position to respond promptly to external shifts.

The Stewardship Department has an increasingly influential role at a strategic level in the Agrochemical Business and its visibility continues to evolve. It is part of the Business Support function which also includes Human Relations, Public Affairs and Business Planning. This combination is powerful and allows the interaction between those activities to be optimized. Through a recently established project the Department is quantifying the risk and liability profile of the Agrochemicals Business so that it can ensure that the real risks are being managed in the most efficient and cost-effective manner and that it, as a service function, adds the maximum benefit to the Business. In line with this profiling, the Stewardship concept and the need to service its internal customers in the most effective way, the Department continually examines its operational mode. Increasingly the need and response is to move from the traditional approach of functional lines based on Safety, Health and Environment into activity teams which supply expertise and services, such as the setting of Standards, giving advice, training and audit.

The holistic approach of managing Stewardship's impact and opportunities across the activity chain from invention through to the end of use of the product and its disposal is a model which is increasingly becoming a prerequisite for many industries.

The Stewardship concept has been key to Agrochemicals in managing the sensitive issues around the invention, manufacture, distribution, use and disposal of crop protection products. In research Stewardship means that Agrochemicals continually asks 'can our products deliver positive, cost-effective benefits to our customers?'. The policy of putting expertise and resource into training programmes which cascade through the distribution network to the end users has been instrumental in gaining entry to the Chinese market and is a significant generator of goodwill and business for the Company wherever it operates. Additionally, the belief is that close working relations in Stewardship and the transfer of related best practice to suppliers and contractors is essential and that the Stewardship approach in Agrochemicals is a key in minimizing liabilities and ensuring the long-term reputation of the Business.

As public concern about the impact of industry and its products grows, there will be increasing competitive advantage for companies which can anticipate and deliver higher standards of Stewardship while producing innovative and useful products and services. ZENECA Agrochemicals sees Stewardship leadership as essential to the maintenance of its licence to operate and sell, as well as in maximizing the business opportunities created by the developments in the external commercial and regulatory environments.

5.3

GOVERNANCE AND KNOWLEDGE

One of the key roles of the board of directors is to be custodian of the company's assets. Historically this has largely involved physical assets – factories, machine tools, inventory and other requisites of a manufacturing business. Now that the service sector is preponderant in most developed economies, the physical assets on most company balance sheets are a dwindling proportion of total assets: companies have identified and valued their intangible assets (patents, brands, copyright, and so on) and have needed to capitalize premiums paid for acquisitions as goodwill. For most companies there remains a gap between their nett asset value (on the balance sheet) and the total value of equity on the stockmarket, or on an earnings basis for sale to an interested acquirer. This area may be thought of as 'virtual assets', not seen or identified but justifying payment as a source of future earnings.

Part of the 'virtual assets' of any business are its employees. Each employee brings a range of skills, competences and personality traits to bear on the needs of the company's business. Another 'virtual asset' is the data which flows through the company rather like ore extracted from a mine. In mining the real value lies not in the ore but in a progressively refined bullion or metal. In business the value of data is enhanced by synthesizing it into information and then into knowledge.

One of the pioneers of 'knowledge management' in the UK is ICL, whose Programme Director, Knowledge Management, is Elizabeth Lank. Moving from being a hardware company to focusing on software, ICL has restructured its business and is reorientating its thinking to meet the challenges of competing in the emerging 'information society'. Elizabeth has identified and driven the issue of marshalling ICL's information base in order to enhance its competitiveness. She sees this as the first step towards developing a strategic knowledge capability. Knowledge is seen to have four elements – know what, know why, know who and know how. The basic element is information (know what), which leads to seeking interchange (know who) and leads towards knowledge (know why and know how). The process of distilling knowledge also involves its transfer from individuals into a shared pool of knowledge. This process is delicate, as knowledge is power and some individuals are reluctant to share power. Unless knowledge is pooled, however, the company cannot own it but can only rent it on a haphazard basis. Elizabeth is committed to succeed in the process of knowledge capture and this undertaking has not been a major issue at ICL because of its open culture and the care taken to maintain mutual trust with employees. The computer services industry has grown towards shared architecture, systems and programmes so that sharing knowledge is natural in a context of serving customers.

A key driver of success in the computer services industry is continuous learning. The pace of obsolescence is fast and quickening, so that progress feeds on mistakes as well as successes and mistakes are openly acknowledged. Bill Gates did not appreciate the implications of the Internet until almost too late, but was able to admit his error and galvanize a rapid change of direction.

Elizabeth Lank had some difficulty initially in engaging the interest of top management in the strategic value of knowledge. The positive arguments, such as better understanding of customer needs, more effective teamworking and personal learning, were lost in the chaos of initiative overload at ICL. Support was galvanized by recognition of the problems caused by knowledge deficiencies, which include:

O   duplication of effort
O   repeated learning curves
O   wasted time
O   higher risk
O   slower rate of innovation
O   less speed and quality of service
O   reduced business value.

It is too early to quantify the potential savings from using knowledge management to tackle the inefficiencies of, for instance, a typical business project. Elizabeth sees the long-term potential as being of the order of 30 per cent of project cost, with initial savings targets of 10 per cent to fund the cost of placing real resources behind knowledge management.

The value of the knowledge management process is beginning to be recognized. ICL was instrumental in establishing a consortium involving Ciba-Geigy, ICI, ICL, Monsanto, Neste, Statoil and Unilever, under the chairmanship of Keith Todd, ICL's Chief Executive. This has support in depth and has carried out intensive research, including a study tour to USA and Japan, leading to the development of management frameworks, tools and measures for running knowledge-based businesses. In parallel with this work a committee, chaired by Dr Robert Hawley, Chief Executive of Nuclear Electric, and sponsored by KPMG, has been examining the issue of managing information as a company asset. Its report produces useful recommendations on the collection, control and use of information and sets an agenda for the board to provide leadership for the process. This agenda is as follows:

The Board should satisfy itself that its own business is conducted so that:

1 The information it uses is necessary and sufficient for its purpose
2 It is aware of and properly advised on the information aspects of all the subjects on its agenda
3 Its use of information, collectively and individually, complies with applicable laws, regulations and recognized ethical standards.

The Board should determine the organization's policy for information assets and identify how compliance with that policy will be measured and reviewed, including:

4 The identification of information assets and the classification into those of value and importance that merit special attention and those that do not.
5 The quality and quantity of information for effective operation, ensuring that, at every level, the information provided is necessary and sufficient, timely, reliable and convenient.
6 The proper use of information in accordance with applicable legal, regulatory, operational and ethical standards, and the roles and responsibilities for the creation, safekeeping, access, change and destruction of information.
7 The capability, suitability and training of people to safeguard and enhance information assets.
8 The protection of information from theft, loss, unauthorised access, abuse and misuse, including information which is the property of others.
9 The harnessing of information assets and their proper use for the maximum benefit of the organization including legally protecting, licensing, re-using, combining, representing, publishing and destroying.
10 The strategy for information systems, including those using computers and electronic communications, and the implementation of that strategy with particular reference to the cost, benefits and risks arising.

Elizabeth Lank also sees information management as a major issue of corporate governance. The board of a company needs to provide the leadership to establish an effective management process, both to concretize the information as an asset through proper inventory and to direct its profitable exploitation. The valuation of company information and knowledge can only realistically be done by using it in the marketplace. Tools exist to value intellectual property and Interbrand has means of valuing brands which are recognized by the accountancy profession. Valuing knowledge as capital is as yet an imperfect science, but Skandia attempts to do so in its annual report and a British company, Celemi, has developed an 'intangible assets monitor' to analyse and explain the impact of knowledge on its business.

The model which ICL is following in developing knowledge management is driven by leadership, sustained by a culture of teamwork and trust, enabling a knowledge infrastructure to be built. By sharing knowledge ICL staff are able to create new knowledge, feeding new products and services and improved customer service. As human capital is replicated into company structural capital, new roles are created to reflect the new structure – chief knowledge officer, webmaster, information service provider, knowledge sponsor (board level custodian), knowledge owner (the individual) and knowledge facilitator (to facilitate knowledge capture). As the inventory of knowledge grows, users and others search for gaps and decisions are taken on how to fill gaps which are important for the company's business. This process of 'gap analysis' is strategic in intent and takes knowledge management into the strategy process of the company, to which it should make a growing contribution.

Elizabeth Lank likens the process of knowledge management to that of equipping a factory. No factory manager can be effective without the right tools and drawings needed to produce the required output. In a service business there are no machine tools or drawings, but employees need a clear definition of what to achieve and the means of doing so. Knowledge is one of the virtual tools needed to deliver results.

The process of building knowledge can be helped by auditing past projects. Price Waterhouse has developed a 'harvesting programme' in which consulting projects are reviewed, often with the client involved. The US Army has a 'lessons learned' process which is similar. Hewlett Packard has 'knowledge facilitators' who capture learning from completed projects. Elizabeth Lank sees the role of 'knowledge facilitator' as an ideal source of learning for young people.

The effect of disinformation is felt largely in situations involving competitors. Elizabeth Lank's process does not focus on competitive intelligence, as this has to be carefully filtered to remove untrustworthy material. This is perhaps a dimension of information management which needs further consideration.

Ownership of knowledge is a significant consideration. At one extreme some intellectual property can be owned and protected. Some US companies have tried to force employees to write down what they know in order to register copyright. ICL sees the transfer of knowledge as a multiplier, empowering a growing number of users without loss to the initiator. Nor does ICL fret about the knowledge in the head of ex-employees; computer services knowledge is rapidly obsolete and ICL methodology is difficult to replicate on a small scale. Elizabeth Lank challenged me to say how a knowledge product could be reverse engineered! Some countries have national knowledge strategies to leverage knowledge across all sectors of business. Holland is setting up knowledge centres to feed local companies; Finland and Singapore manage knowledge nationally.

The board of directors in every company is custodian of its virtual assets as well as of its balance sheet assets. It needs to have a governance process which enables knowledge to be turned from human to structural capital and then leveraged to obtain both competitive advantage and increased share-holder value. It needs to find ways of evaluating virtual assets, whether or not they can be included in the balance sheet, and of measuring the costs of managing them and the revenues which they produce. Directors need to take this responsibility as a board and also act individually as sponsors to support different parts of the process. The board is required by the Stock Exchange to report on its corporate governance in respect of the Cadbury and Greenbury codes. A growing number of companies report on other aspects of governance – for example, environment, health and safety and work with local communities. It would seem logical for companies to report on the stewardship of their virtual assets as they do in respect of their physical assets, particularly as for most companies profits are today mainly lever-aged on knowledge and relationships.

REFERENCES

Cadbury, A. (1990) *The Company Chairman,* London, Director Books.

Cadbury, A. (1998) 'The Future of Governance: The Rules of the Game', Gresham Lecture.

Cadbury Report.

Campbell, A. and Alexander, M. (1997) 'What's Wrong with Strategy?', *Harvard Business Review*, Nov/Dec.

Case, J. (1997) 'Opening the Books', *Harvard Business Review*, March/April.

Cox, A. (1997) *Business Success: A way of thinking about business strategy, critical supply chain assets and operational best practice*, Boston, Lincs, Earlsgate Press.

D'Aveni, R. and Hamel, G. (1997) 'Most famous artists went to art school', *Financial Times*, 1 September.

Davies, A. (1991) *Strategic Leadership*, Cambridge, Woodhead-Faulkner.

Davies, A. (1995) *Strategic Marketing*, London, McGraw Hill.

Demb, A. and Neubauer, F. (1992) *The Corporate Board*, New York, Oxford University Press.

Drucker, P. (1992) *Managing for the Future*, Oxford, Butterworth Heinemann.

Ford Partnership (1997) *Under Pressure: Trends in the Governance of large charities for the 21st Century*, Leicester, Ford Partnership.

Ford Partnership (1997) *Twenty-one trends for the twenty-first century*, Leicester, Ford Partnership.

Fortune (1998) 'Fortune's Hundred Best Companies', *Fortune*, 12 Jan.

Galbraith, J.K. (1975) *Money*, Harmondsworth, Middx, Penguin.

Garrett, B. (1994) *The Learning Organisation*, London, Harper Collins.

Garrett, B. (1996) *The Fish Rots from the Head*, London, Harper Collins.

Geus de, A. (1998) *The Living Company*, Harvard Business School Press.

Greenbury Report.

Greenleaf, R. (1977) *Servant Leadership*, New York, Paulist Press.

Gregor, N. (1998) *Daimler Benz in the Third Reich*, Yale University Press.

Gouillart, F. and Kelly, J. (1995) *Transforming the Organization*, New York, McGraw Hill.

Hamel, G. and Pralahad, C.K. (1994) *Competing for the Future*, Boston: Harvard Business School Press.

Hampel Report.

Handy, C. (1997) *The Hungry Spirit*, London, Hutchinson.

Harvey-Jones, J. Sir (1989) *Making it Happen*, London, Fontana.

Hutton, W. (1995) *The State We're In*, London, Vintage.

Hutton, W. (1997) *The State To Come*, London, Vintage.

IoD (1991) *Guidance for Directors*, London, Institute of Directors.

IoD (1995) *Good Practice for Directors*, London, Institute of Directors.

Jacobs, J. (1994) *Systems of Survival: a Dialogue on the Moral Foundations of Commerce and Politics*, London, Vintage.

Jonquieres de, Guy (1998), 'Rules for the Regulators', *Financial Times*, 2 March.

Kaplan, R. and Norton, D. (1996) *The Balanced Scorecard*, Boston, Harvard Business School Press.

Kendall, N. and A. (1998) *Real-World Corporate Governance*, London, Pitman Publishing.

Knight, R. (1998) 'Mastering Global Business', survey in *Financial Times*, 20 March.

Lloyd, B. Dr (1996) 'Corridors of Responsibility Lead to Long-term Success', *Professional Manager*, March.

Magretta, J. (1998) 'Governing the family-owned enterprise: An interview with Finland's Krister Ahlström', *Harvard Business Review*, Jan/Feb.

McKiernan, P. and Urquhart, J. (1999) 'Corporate Governance: a psychological perspective', *British Journal of Management*, Jan.

Millstein, I.M. (1995) 'The Professional Board', *The Business Lawyer*, Nov.

Mintzberg, H. Prof. (1987) 'Crafting Strategy', *Harvard Business Review*, July/Aug.

Mulgan, G. (1997) *Connexity*, London, Chatto & Windus.

Müller, R.K. (1981) *The Incomplete Board – the unfolding of Corporate Governance*, Lexington, Mass., Heath & Co.

NVCO (1997) *Towards Voluntary Sector Code of Practice*, London, Joseph Rowntree Foundation.

Nolan Report.

Pinnington, A. and Morris, T. (1996) 'Power and Control in Professional Partnerships', *Long Range Planning*, Dec.

Plender, J. (1997) *A Stake in the Future*, London, Nicholas Brealey.

Porter, M. (1991) *Competitive Advantage*, New York, Free Press.

Puttnam, R. (1993) *Making Democracy Work*, Princeton, UP.

RSA (1995) *Tomorrow's Company*, London, Gower.

Servan-Schreiber, J-J. (1968) *The American Challenge*, London, Hamish Hamilton.

Simons, R. (1995) 'Control in an Age of Empowerment', *Harvard Business Review*, March/April.

Smith, T. (1992) *Accounting for Growth*, London, Century Business.

Vickers, G. Sir (1972) *Freedom in a Rocking Boat*, Harmondsworth, Middx, Penguin.

Watson, G. (1993) *Strategic Benchmarking*, New York, Wiley.

Wirthlia Worldwide (1998) 'Furthering the Global Dialogue on Corporate Governance', *International Survey of Institutional Investors*, London, Russell Reynolds Associates.

Zohar, D. (1997) *Rewiring the Corporate Brain*, New York, Berrett-Koehler.

INDEX